JOURNEY FROM OBSCURITY

I. CHILDHOOD

Wilfred, Harold, Mary, Colin

1902–1903

William HAROLD OWEN

Journey from Obscurity

Wilfred Owen 1893-1918

MEMOIRS OF THE OWEN FAMILY

I. CHILDHOOD

London

OXFORD UNIVERSITY PRESS

NEW YORK   TORONTO

1963

Oxford University Press, Amen House, London, E.C.4

GLASGOW NEW YORK TORONTO MELBOURNE WELLINGTON
BOMBAY CALCUTTA MADRAS KARACHI LAHORE DACCA
CAPE TOWN SALISBURY NAIROBI IBADAN ACCRA
KUALA LUMPUR HONG KONG

© Oxford University Press 1963

*Printed in Great Britain
by The Chapel River Press,
Andover, Hants.*

FOR PHYLLIS

CONTENTS

	Prologue	xiii
1	LEAVING PLAS WILMOT 1897	1
2	THE DOCKS	17
3	BIRKENHEAD	49
4	IRELAND	73
5	BROXTON	92
6	SHREWSBURY 1907	122
7	UFFINGTON	144
8	'BLESSED WITH GOLD'	174
9	TORQUAY	189
10	ART SCHOOL	202
11	KELSO	228
12	WILFRED	246
13	SUMMER 1911	260

ILLUSTRATIONS

Wilfred, Harold, Mary, Colin. *1902-1903*   *Frontispiece*

1   Mother and Wilfred. *Plas Wilmot*   *facing page* 82

2   Father, Mother, and Wilfred. *Plas Wilmot*   83

3   (*a*) Wilfred with his sword   98
     (*b*) Wilfred as a soldier, *Plas Wilmot*. The Hussar's tunic and tent were made by Mother

4   (*a*) Wilfred with the yacht built for him by Father, now   99
     in my possession. *Photo: C. H. Deakin, Shrewsbury*
     (*b*) Mother and Mary

5   Mother and the four of us. *1902-1903*   178

6   The canal, Uffington village. A water-colour I painted   179
     in the early summer of 1909. *Photo: Bushell, Henley-on-Thames*

7   (*a*) The whole family at Scarborough, on a visit to Cousin   194
     May Susan. *About 1906*
     (*b*) On holiday at Kelso. *L. to r.: An unidentified guest, Walter Forrest, Harold, Bill Bulman, Blanche Bulman, Mrs. Bulman, John Bulman, Colin, Mother, Mary, Father*

8   (*a*) Father in Bombay as a young man. *Photo: P. Vuccino*   195
     & Co., Bombay
     (*b*) Wilfred as a young student. *Photo: Arcade Studio, Reading*

APPRECIATIONS

To Mrs. May Skinner my especial tribute and acknowledgement of her secretarial work in deciphering difficult manu-
script and for her unsparing exactitude in the final typing of
this book; to Miss Hope de Pass who helped me by acting as
honorary amanuensis and typist, my gratitude; and to Patric
and Sheila Dickinson my particular thanks.

THE OWEN CHILDREN

WILFRED EDWARD SALTER   b.   18 March 1893
   d.   4 November 1918

MARY MILLARD   b.   30 May 1895
   d.   27 November 1956

WILLIAM HAROLD   b.   5 September 1897

COLIN SHAW   b.   24 July 1900

PROLOGUE

I N Plas Wilmot, a house a few miles on the English side
of the Welsh border, Wilfred Edward Salter Owen was
born on 18 March 1893. On 4 November 1918 he was
killed in action on the banks of the Sambre Canal.

It is his story, and that of his immediate family, that I
wish to tell.

Chapter One

LEAVING PLAS WILMOT 1897

PLAS WILMOT, on the outskirts of Oswestry, was the house of my
mother's family: it was here that she herself had been born; it was
from this house that she went to be married to my father. It was
back to this house that she returned as the bride of my father. . . . It was
in this house that Wilfred their first-born, a few minutes after his
advent, screamed out his first defiant protest. . . . It was in this pleasant
house of Plas Wilmot two years after the birth of Wilfred that Mary,
the only girl child of the family, was born; it was here in the same
pleasant bedroom that she too, one warm silver evening in May 1895,
spluttered out her first tiny choke. Two more boy children were to
follow, but not in this house. . . . It was to this house, four years after
the birth of Wilfred, that my father and mother had to say goodbye
and leave all its warm pleasantness, its gardens, fields, and coach-houses,
and the gracious way of living that had seemed to them, although their
own lives were not at all affluent, to wrap about them, not only a warm
happiness, but a sense of security.

The break was final, and sudden, and occurred with the death of my
grandfather.

Never again were they ever to live in quite such surroundings, or
perhaps find such peaceful happiness, and bitterest of all, never again to
the end of their lives were they or their children once again to have any
feeling of real security. It was here in Plas Wilmot that Wilfred for his
first four years could be, and was, so carefully nurtured. It was here
that Wilfred by the sweetness of his infant years brought so much pride
and delight to his ageing grandfather. Here it was that my father and
mother not only had time but peace of mind as well, so that love and
gentleness flowed over Wilfred and, later, his young sister. It was here,
in one of the old coach-houses, that the S.S. *Susan*, a perfect replica of
a sea-going ship—three feet in length, later to become renowned as a
family possession—was built and fashioned by my father especially for

I

Wilfred, most exquisitely wrought throughout with superb craftsmanship. The steering system was exact and could be set to steer a course;
the steering wheel itself, carved in one piece from the lid of a cigar box,
was masterly in execution; the lifeboats were gems in themselves, complete with minute—but removable—canvas covers, and could be correctly lowered to the water-line by working davits. It was properly
equipped with regulation navigation lights, binnacle and real compass;
so delicately carved was everything about it that even the skylights
were glazed with real glass. Fitted into the ship were real boilers with
furnaces fired by methylated spirit and cotton-wool for fuel, which
drove the engine geared to the propeller shaft. The fog-horn fitted to
the foremast funnel was operated from the bridge by lanyard. It was
here that the small Wilfred, hand in hand with my mother and father,
would watch with ecstasy the manœuvres of the miniature ship as it
steamed around and across their lake. One of his earliest and most
treasured memories was of the day when the little ship caught fire in
mid-lake, and of my father plunging into the water fully clothed and
swimming out to submerge it. The beautiful little craft survived all the
vicissitudes of our family, and is sailing to this day.

Upon all this, with their two small children, Tom and Susan Owen
had to turn their backs and with little more than my father's meagre
salary, which did not amount to one hundred pounds a year, find a
house or rooms and set about the difficult and uncertain task of rearing
a family. This transition must—although carrying more responsibility
and anxiety—have been easier for my father than it was for my mother.
While he had not yet faced real poverty, a lack of the finer niceties in
life was not new to him: for my mother it was new—something which,
until now, she had never experienced. But their love story was a beautiful one, and they loved one another very deeply, with absolute loyalty,
and his quiet courage and generous nature helped her as nothing else
could have done in the difficult times of those early and bitter years.

My father sprang from good and very sound stock, his immediate
forebears coming from Cheshire and Shropshire, but there is no doubt
his ancestry traces back over the border and into Wales. For the most
part latterly it seems to have been of some yeoman stock, with here and
there a flurry of more exalted station, and here and there again an out-
cropping of adventurous seamen. In his more nostalgic moments he
claimed, quite seriously, descent from Baron Lewis Owen who, during
the reign of Henry VIII, was Sheriff of Merionethshire. This supposi-

tion can never be established with absolute certainty, but it was a family belief and the legend, it is known, has been passed down orally from father to eldest son for many generations. My father in his turn passed it on to Wilfred.

The one thing that is certain about my father's family is that his fore-bears—down the generations—consistently lessened their foothold in the world, diminishing with each generation their material acquisitions. There was, and is, a noticeable inability in the males of this line to make money or acquire possessions; the females, however, without exception seem to have been able to spring away from this shortcoming, and through marriage to found offshoot families of some importance. My father's father had some connection with the wool trade and mills, but made no more than a competence, not always that, and died leaving no money and no property—but, in justice to him, no debts.

It was into this financial uncertainty that my father was born in the year 1862, the only brother to three older sisters. There seems to have been little money for anything except casual education, but true to tradition the girl children, when the time came, married well, two of them to the same man. This came about through May, the eldest sister, marrying Edward Quale, a wealthy broker in tin-plate and steel: she bore him one son and shortly afterwards died. After a suitable interval Edward Quale paid suit to Emily, whom he later married. To do this they had to go to the Channel Islands as the law of England did not, at that time, permit marriage with a deceased wife's sister. She bore him one son and one daughter.

The third sister, Anne, married a widower, John Taylor, who from his first marriage had two sons, Harry and Frederick. Harry from the beginning was marked out for big things in business; eventually he went out to India and quickly climbed from success to success, early becoming a powerful man of affairs in Calcutta—jute, I think it was. The younger son Frederick went to sea—in sailing ships—at an early age; later he commanded liners. During the 1914–1918 War he served with distinction as a Naval Lieutenant-Commander and commanded a 'Q' mystery ship. He was a powerful red-headed man and widely re-puted to be a fine seaman. Anne's marriage to John Taylor produced one daughter, Edith. As a child she was remarkable for a thick mane of hair, of the finest texture and pure gold in colour, which reached far below her knees. As a young girl in the nineteen-twenties she went out to India to stay with her half-brother Harry and his wife Louise, and while out there she met and married a young Regular Indian Army Captain, Bryan Dymott. They remained in India until he eventually retired from the command of his Regiment.

Although my father, among his immediate family circle, seems—in these early years—to have been the least fortunate in opportunities, nevertheless, out of all the difficulties he managed somehow, mostly by his assiduous reading and some attendance at local schools, to obtain for himself a considerable education. In these circumstances it could not, of course, in any sense be an academic one, but he continued his serious reading, and his thirst for learning continually drove him on. The classics he had to seek out for himself as he went along. It was a proud claim of his—it amounted almost to a boast—that his first educational years had been spent in attendance at a Dame-school, and he would entertain us when we were children with stories—some of them, to us, excruciatingly funny, others more lurid—of the fierce old hag who owned and ran the school, of her savage witch-like demeanour, and of her violent physical attacks upon the little boys. But with undeviating loyalty he always maintained that the grounding which was driven into him here with such iron discipline was of incalculable value to him, and that without it he would have had no stepping-stone whatsoever from which to reach out, and so find for himself more learning.

At an early age it was indicated to him, quite heartlessly, that he would have to fend for himself. At the age of fifteen he applied for a post as junior clerk with the railways; he got through the interview and passed the examination sufficiently well to be appointed at once. This was no mean feat in those far-off days of keen competition, and railway posts were much sought after by young men and boys of little means as an avenue to higher executive positions. He was immediately posted away from his home in Cheshire to Oswestry, where he found himself a room of sorts, and from then on steered his own course, with only a few shillings a week and without any help from anywhere.

He was, I think, a boy of pleasing presence, and he possessed a lovely voice; his singing attracted attention so that he found friends, and some pleasant social atmosphere. His cricket too, rather surprisingly, was good and he became a member of a cricket club. Either through this or else socially he met Edward Shaw, the somewhat profligate brother of my mother. Later, through his friendship with Edward, he met my mother. They were spontaneously attracted to each other, and immediately loved each other deeply. He was accepted and so much liked in my mother's home that his suit was permitted although there were, I think, designs for her elsewhere. But the situation was not without its complications, for his prospects were not really at all good, especially as a suitor for the hand of the beautiful Susan Shaw; my mother and her two sisters were renowned in the county for their looks, and were usually referred to as the three Shaw beauties.

My father realized his lack of prospects and made up his mind to get out of England in the hope of finding better advancement; and as this also fitted in with his ambition to travel, especially in the East, and to get about the world, he set himself to find some post abroad. Entirely through his own efforts he succeeded in doing this and, while still a minor, was offered a post with the Indian Peninsular Railway in Bombay. The post stipulated payment of his own passage out. My father of course had not this considerable sum, and knew nobody at all from whom he might borrow it. Nevertheless he accepted the job, hied himself to Liverpool, and hunted the docks, day and night, until he could find a ship's captain who would sign him on as a deck-hand for the single voyage.

At first his quest was hopeless; but just as despair was gripping him he found a small ship, with a more friendly captain, which was short-handed and due to sail for India. He just had time to rush back, see his beloved Susan Shaw, and with her ardent promises ringing in his ears get back to Liverpool and join the ship.

One September morning in the eighteen-eighties he signed on as an Ordinary Seaman in the ship *Benalder*, 1,330 tons, Captain Buchanan. After an adventurous voyage of considerable hardship he reached India, took his discharge certificate from the ship, and before Christmas took up his new appointment in Bombay.

This seaman's 'Certificate of discharge' he was to treasure all his life: it was, I know, one of his most prized possessions. During the dullness of his later life it became emblematic of early adventure, and a signal mark to him of real manhood . . . he had at least once been a sailor before the mast. It became as well one of the earliest bonds between him and me. I so well remember as a very small boy when, one day finding ourselves alone together in the house, he, having with enormous solemnity first of all bound me to secrecy, showed me this certificate and told me the story of his voyage, exaggerating the terrible storms, near shipwreck, and the barefoot work about the decks and up aloft, painting all the time a gruesome picture of the dark fo'c'sle, the decomposing food, and the strangely dangerous sailors who were his companions. In my imagination it became a tingling mixture of nightmare terror and breath-holding enchantment.

The atmosphere of conspiracy which he created about all this held me enthralled. The getting out of this certificate became a ritual between us, so that all the rites had to be observed: we must be alone in the house, the key must be produced with drama, the removal of papers must be done with mystery, and the fumble to find the 'secret' drawer in his desk had to be carried out with stealth and a pretence of guilt. While this was going on I was allowed to look—tremendous concession—but never to peer. This taking out of the certificate became one of my greatest excitements; we never got tired of looking at it, and each time the story was a little more embellished. On very special occasions I was allowed to hold it. The secrecy was genuine, my father was reserved and often shy with his family, and I think he felt my mother might look askance at this reminder of his sea-fever.

When I was older and had myself been to sea, my father in unguarded moments, when bitterness hit him, would sometimes say to me how he wished he had forfeited the Bombay post and never left the *Benalder*, and with anger glinting in his eyes and a sardonic twist about his mouth, aver that had that happened, he might now be commanding a fine ship. . . .

After his death I found among his papers the certificate, sere now and in places indecipherable. I keep it as a memory of those times and as a reminder of his youthful difficulties.

The real story of Wilfred Owen and his family must begin before he was born, at the time my father returned home from India to England four years after he had said goodbye to Susan Shaw. He did well during these four years in Bombay, and had established himself so securely that his prospects for a career that might have been spectacular, and anyway would have been of real importance, with work that he liked, were very bright indeed. The lure of a foreign land and, especially to him, the glamour of the East, did much to reconcile him for his disappointment in not being embarked upon a seagoing career.

6

Altogether he loved the life out there; he had joined the Indian Militia Volunteers and a sailing club, and enjoyed them both immensely. At this time he undoubtedly had visions of Susan Shaw coming out to him and of their being married out there, and thenceforward founding their family and living their early lives in India. During those four years they both wrote to each other twice or three times a week, and their love for each other intensified.

About this time events both in India and in England took a wholly adverse turn for both of them. In India my father had become dangerously ill: he had developed some tropical fever or disease and was in hospital for months. When he was finally discharged from the hospital, a very sick young man indeed, he was recommended for leave in England. This he did not want to take, fearing, I think, that he might never get back, and accepted local sick-leave instead. However, a letter from Susan Shaw arriving at this juncture made him change his mind. This letter was a distressing one and from it he knew that his Susan's mother was dying, and that her brother Edward Shaw was, through his wildness and uncontrollable drinking bouts, causing her terrible anxiety. As well as this she told him of her real worry about her father's financial affairs and things generally at Plas Wilmot. My father without further hesitation decided to return to England immediately.

He arrived home to find, much as he had expected, that things at Plas Wilmot were indeed altogether in a far from happy state. My grandmother had died, and this had left my grandfather aged and decrepit; and most disturbing of all he found his Susan dreadfully distressed over the disappearance of her brother. Before this happened she had become tired and almost exhausted from the constant anxiety of the long vigils—waiting for Edward's nightly returns—and the ministrations which his intoxicated homecoming from these wild spells brought upon her. The general finances of the household, too, seemed to be obscurely unsatisfactory, due to some extent to the extravagances and the unthinking spending of the young Edward. This brother, Edward, who down the years has become something of a legend and a rather romantic family skeleton, was indeed a delightful and likable boy, but irresponsible and much given to wild drinking parties and, I suspect, much attracted to the more light-hearted ladies. Anyhow, he managed to invest himself with a reputation for gaiety and wild drinking. In his bouts he was liable to extraordinary attacks of outrageous

7

behaviour and was much given to firing off shotguns in the precincts of the house in the early hours of the morning, so that in his alcoholic disregard for safety he was liable to set both himself and his father's house on fire. This resulted in the family having to detail guards to await his fantastic arrivals and shepherd him to his bed and remain with him until unconsciousness overcame him. Much of this duty fell to my mother, his favourite sister. This wild uncontrollability was undoubtedly brought about by the excessively morbid religious atmosphere and the rigid Calvinistic doctrine instilled by his parents and their unbending and wilfully blind attitude to life. His affection towards his parents was very real and at times even demonstrative, but none of this could survive the puritanical condemnation with which they so constantly repudiated him, and which inevitably brought them bitter retribution. The culmination came about when Edward, embarking upon a period of carousals of more than usual wildness and abandon, brought upon himself violent recriminations and scriptural upbraidings. When he recovered from this final spell, driven by remorse and his innate niceness, he sought forgiveness from his parents, only to be met with yet more rhetorical reproaches and admonitory Calvinism.

One night he failed to return home at all. At first it was thought that he had only temporarily disappeared, perhaps on another carousal. However it was soon established—through his closest drinking companion—that he had not so much disappeared as run away. With this friend he had left an explicit message for his parents to tell them he was alive and well but with no information of his whereabouts, except that he was making for America, and stating his intention that he would never return home. He never did. For a year or more his disappearance was complete. He was next heard of—traced in a roundabout way—as having arrived in America. In the year 1893 it was established with certainty that he was in Denver, Colorado. He must have moved on quickly: letters never reached him, or if they did, were never answered. From that time, nothing has ever been heard of him. His tale I think would be an interesting one.

This tragedy of Edward running away, and all the other difficulties, my father found waiting for him upon his return from India to Plas Wilmot; my grandfather he found far from well, and depressed over the illness and death of my grandmother. The dissolute behaviour and now the final loss of Edward caused my grandfather disappointment

8

and bitter sorrow, which in his ageing grief he found difficult to support. In his frailty, he welcomed the youthful strength of my father; his one wish and hope now seemed to be that his favourite daughter, Susan, should marry Tom Owen as soon as possible, and that they should set up house with him in Plas Wilmot. If this happened he felt that happiness might return to him for his few remaining years, and that my father would help somehow to straighten out the financial difficulties. My father decided that in all these circumstances a return to India was quite impossible, and that the only thing to do was to marry his Susan and reconcile himself to employment in England. To secure this end, he hid his disappointment and, abandoning all hope of an adventurous career in the East, obtained for himself a post with an English railway; and with a salary of only seventy-five pounds a year, married my mother.

They were married in the village church, my mother being dressed in deep mourning for her mother, who had died so recently. I suppose the convention of the period demanded this, but it has always appeared to me as rather terrible and overshadowing for both of them. After a short honeymoon my father and his bride returned to her father's house, hoping to bring about a more sensible economy which would place the family finances in a sounder condition. However, my grandfather became querulous and extremely difficult, and insisted, with the obstinacy of old age and failing health, in not only holding on to this largeish country house, which was sensible, but in continuing to maintain it with its large gardens, orchards, and paddocks, with the consequent eating into capital. Actually, as it transpired later, this had been happening for years.

My father had come into the Shaw family too late to alter things in a permanent way; the tapestry of living in Plas Wilmot was too closely woven for him to bring about any lasting benefit. Nevertheless under his guidance the household did become temporarily more stable. In spite of my grandfather's querulousness some retrenchments were made, so that it became feasible to continue the ménage in a moderate but comfortable manner. This ensured tranquillity for my grandfather during his last years. The presence of my mother and father brought to him a quiet happiness, and later the infancy and early childhood of the little boy Wilfred wrapped about him grandfatherly love and great joy, which did much to lessen his bitter grief over the deliberate absence of his only son.

9

My grandparents, revered as they were by my mother and her two sisters, were rigidly Calvinistic in upbringing and conviction. It seems that they must have been unduly bigoted and puritanical, even morbidly so.

The effect of this environment not only produced no rebellion at all in the three daughters, Edward's sisters, but instead a ready acceptance of this Calvinism, so that they became indoctrinated. So powerful was this indoctrination that in varying degrees it not only permeated their own lives but caused them to instil it, after marriage, into their own families and the upbringing of their children—not of course in every case successfully. One of the notable exceptions was May, the middle daughter, whose marriage completely changed her outlook.

Emma, the eldest daughter, married a successful London business-man, John Gunston, brother of a Cambridge Wrangler. They settled down in the Spencer Hill district of London, and shortly after bought a house and moved to Wimbledon. In about 1910 John Gunston retired from business while still a youngish man, bought some land in Berkshire, and built a house for himself and his family. Wilfred was to see something of this aunt and uncle and his cousins during the time they lived there. They had two sons and two daughters. This aunt retained her puritanical fervour for the whole of her life and influenced her husband in this direction to the detriment of his wider interests, which were numerous.

The other sister, May, married an idealistic doctor who had a practice —mostly without profit—in the East End of London. Here she promptly discarded the effects of her religious upbringing, threw herself whole-heartedly into practical partnership with her husband, and both of them devoted their entire lives to the relief of misery and suffering in the docklands and the tenements of the East End. They wore them-selves out by living a life of unbelievable austerity, and died within a few weeks of each other at a very early age.

My mother Susan and her two sisters, Emma and May, were, as was usual at that time, educated at home, so that from earliest infancy they shared resident governesses for general instruction and regular visiting mistresses for painting and music; at one period they had another one for needlework as well. My mother when quite a little girl became engrossed in the technical art of painting, and at an early age became an extremely skilful painter in oils, producing many hundreds of reason-ably well executed paintings, none of which however showed any indi-

cation of important ability as an artist, not even latent promise, and no
hint whatsoever of originality of thought or any imaginative conception. It was merely the accident of having a painting mistress whom, at
the time, she adored, and a natural skill of brush control, which produced these works. Painting was simply an accomplishment and never
the serious effort of a would-be painter. This skill which she applied to
the most prosaic needlework produced precisely the same effect as her
painting. Her music, which she took much less seriously, I have often
thought—that is when, many years later, I came to think about it at all
—would have repaid her more fully than her painting ever did. Her
piano playing, which never went beyond the average for her age and
era, was just the result of teaching, and never became anything more.
One of her music mistresses introduced her to the harp; the success of
this was instantaneous: perhaps some Welsh blood responded. Anyhow, when quite a small child, she quickly mastered the technique and
almost immediately was playing with softness and great feeling. Her
father was inordinately proud of this skill and at once bought her a
beautiful instrument, which must have been about twice her own size
at that time. The small child and the huge harp intrigued her parents'
friends enormously. In later years when she was beautifully accomplished, she was much called upon for chamber music, both in her
father's house to entertain his friends, and in the houses of these friends.
Her rendering was moving and very beautiful. Many years later I was
to be most profoundly affected by the spirituality of her playing.

Throughout the changes of circumstances which were to be come to us
my mother's piano, her harp, and all her painting materials, were always
somehow retained and cared for, though in the immediate times of
struggle that marked our early years as a family, the harp and the
paints—except for sporadic patches—went into desuetude.

It was not until the death of my grandfather and the final disposal of
Plas Wilmot that my mother—except for these intermittent spells—
gave up her painting and harp playing. The piano, her least achievement, she used only very occasionally and then only to amuse and entertain us children. The instrument itself remained with us until the death
of Wilfred. Down the years it was used by every member of the family
except myself—Wilfred, Mary, and Colin all at one time or another
had music lessons. At that time I was very much looked upon as the
family Philistine; it was thought—and said—that any attempt to teach
me to play would not only be a waste of time and money but the

height of ridiculousness as well.

My father remained always passionately devoted to his own un-tutored playing. Later Wilfred was rather to monopolize the piano. Indeed, not the use of the instrument but the manner and time in which it was played often caused some discord between my father and Wilfred; musically, they could never agree.

In 1911 or thereabouts, when things were easier for us, my mother, under pressure from Wilfred, resumed her painting; under pressure from me, she revived her harp music. The war, when it came in 1914, once again stunned both these revivals, and when in 1918 it was over, neither of these graceful acquirements of hers, I found, had survived. They had died with Wilfred.

These, then, are something of the happenings and circumstances be-fore Wilfred was born and during the first four years of his life, and the first two years of the life of Mary, his only sister: a time pre-natal to myself, the next born, and of course to Colin, the last born child of my parents.

In the fabric of Wilfred's life, and the lives of his family, some of these people will reappear; the consequences of these happenings will appear in the effect they had upon Wilfred, and especially the influence of this early environment during these first four years. This influence was, I think, and Wilfred himself always maintained, formative in a wholly advantageous way. In after years he was to think of them with pleasure and gratitude and as something benedictory. So sharply defined was the division between those first years and the times that were to follow after leaving Plas Wilmot, that this short era became —as such things will in families—a legend, much talked of amongst ourselves, and most likely, as legends do, gaining enhancement with the years. Wilfred built up, by questioning my mother and father, a romantic picture of these early years, which became an actual part of his experience. As a family we all in our different ways tried to hold on to the imagery of these more generous times, as something which was a part of ourselves and to which we belonged. Our inclination to do this sprang, I am sure, from a protective instinct and a desire for more illustrious surroundings and doing this, it seemed to us, in some way made up for the privations which beset us all.

I myself very nearly succeeded in being born in Plas Wilmot, but I must have mis-timed myself, or more accurately, death—not choosing to wait for my arrival—came to my grandfather just too soon for this to come about. Instead, I was deposited in a tiny back bedroom of a small, rather shabby little house in a long street of other mean little houses—all exactly the same except that in the tiny impoverished patch of ground in front of ours, a laburnum tree had somehow rooted itself and, clinging to life in the sour soil, brought forth its gold. I still like to remember this even now. This street was an outlying one on the fringe of the market town of Shrewsbury. I have always been very sorry that I did not come into the world in Plas Wilmot: I should have liked very much to have been born into all the pleasantness of it. I have always been slightly jealous of Wilfred and Mary for their good fortune but even so I was more fortunate than Colin. It became his fate to greet the world from another, even smaller back bedroom, this time in the smelly July heat of a slum area of the vast seaport of Birkenhead—some three years after my own birth.

My father at this age was young and ambitious, but in spite of his four years in India was still suffering acutely from his sea-fever, which had redoubled through his disappointment about his English post and the poverty of prospect it entailed. His professional future must indeed have looked very dreary to him. In appearance my father was a pleasant-looking—even, it has been said, a good-looking—young man. He was a small man, lean and well proportioned with broad shoulders, but in spite of his smallness of build there was a robustness about him that gave him great solidity, and lent to him an impression of powerful physical strength. His eyes were good, really grey in colour but variable to his moods: they could be green, or a frightening icy blue. He had straight lightish brown hair and wore a rather long moustache, which drooped pleasantly down to and away from the sides of his mouth.

An early photograph which shows him dressed in a white cricketing jersey and flannels, holding the infant Wilfred in his arms, bears a very striking resemblance to Robert Louis Stevenson. He was full of zest and a love for life, and greater love for his young wife and two small children, but all the time aware that the tentacles of need, and the heavy commitments of the very poor, were already feeling out for him, and soon would entangle him—inexorably. This, then, was my father at that time—a young man of unchallenged integrity whole-heartedly de-voted to his even younger wife but consumed with anxiety for the future, and gnawed and fretted with the fearful knowledge that he was now irrevocably embarked upon a career which he not only disliked intensely but knew that he would go on detesting more and more as the years went on. He told me later—and this I thought so terribly tragic—that even then he was in his thoughts dreaming of his life from the time when he would be sixty and have the freedom which his professional pension would then give him. Although bitterness was gripping him, it was only a bitterness about his own career; for his young family there was no bitterness—only bitter apprehension for them; but he was resilient and would not, in these early years, give way to despair. Instead he brought gaiety and often light-hearted frivolity to his young family, so that he made them happy—already in the little Wilfred he was imagining to himself how, somehow, this child should live out the life which he now knew would be for ever denied to him. Already in his mind he was planning for Wilfred, his only son at that time, a life at sea (hence the S.S. *Susan*), or at least a life active and adventurous. What seeds of near-tragedy he was sowing here he was not yet to know, but in this dark-haired grave little boy that was Wilfred all his passionate hopes of fulfilment that he had once held for himself were now dangerously, and as it was to turn out, hopelessly centred.

My mother at this time was acknowledged widely as a beautiful young woman. Although somewhere in her father's blood line there seems to have been a dash of Scottish blood, all her characteristics, both physical and in temperament, were certainly Celtic with strong emphasis towards the Welsh, which showed itself in her dark hair, too blue, where it caught the light, to be called black, and in the oval face and the fine-quality skin, so clear and astonishingly white. Her eyes were very dark blue, widely and finely set. Perhaps one of the most marked of her physical attributes was the extreme beauty of her feet.

She was never, either at this time or later, to be assailed to the same extent with the anxieties and doubts that haunted my father. She seems to have embarked upon marriage and the contemplation of a largeish family with complete equanimity; this was no doubt largely brought about through having lived all her life in absolute security. She was reared, as young girls were in those days, in an atmosphere of assurance which allowed no room for thought about the ways and means of living—so sheltered was her life in her own home that the possibility of penury or even need never crossed her thoughts at all. Neither my mother nor her sisters were brought up with any idea that it might ever be necessary for them to be responsible in any way for their own livelihood, and of course a career for any of them was never mentioned, much less contemplated.

Another factor which added to the innocent tranquillity of her outlook was the bondage of her over-emphasized religious training; so much so that 'God will provide for everything' became not only a comforting way of dismissing any doubts which might vaguely trouble her, but a tenet in itself. This was to cling to her for the rest of her life, sometimes to make difficulties, and always to be a serious contribution towards her real lack of practical ambition for her children. At this age, when she married my father, my mother was light-hearted enough, and physically slightly plump in a very warm and rather jolly sort of way. In spite of the all-pervading puritanism of her home, the taint of smugness had not overlaid her natural brightness.

Thus it was that in the year 1896 Tom and Susan Owen were still living in Plas Wilmot with their two children: Wilfred, a grave healthy little boy, now with a shock of very dark and straight, but unruly, hair (in colouring he was to remain the darkest of all of us children; even his eyes, although they were grey, always gave the impression of darkness), and Mary, the only girl child, who came into the world with such a tenuous hold upon life that from her first moments fear for her survival was always with my parents. But they fought hard and by constant care and devotion nursed the fugitive spark of life—the fear, though, was to remain with them for many years; indeed it was only by using the small capital that came to my mother from the sale of Plas Wilmot that the fluttering little life was eventually persuaded to occupy the tiny body at all. Mary was to remain frail and structurally very small for the whole of her life, but the spark once fostered to a flame burned brightly and steadily, and never at any time admitted the limitations of the perfectly proportioned, but diminutive, shell that contained it. To Wilfred and to me, this extreme fragility and her smallness, combined with the perfection of proportion, was always something which brought us joy and delight, and aroused tremendous admiration.

So far this is only the story of Tom and Susan and Wilfred and Mary, before they set up house for themselves and commenced their own independent life as a family and without other ties, or the responsibility of my grandfather and Plas Wilmot.

In the year 1897 my mother's father died. Plas Wilmot was immediately sold; a sale was arranged which disposed of outdoor effects and some of the larger indoor furniture; everything else, the silver, linen, and smaller furniture was divided up between my mother and her two sisters. By arrangement my mother's portion consisted mostly of the silver and linen, and the china and glass.

So it was that Tom and Susan Owen, houseless now, and with little else except this large quantity of linen and silver, set about the task of facing their difficulties and rearing their family, an increase to which— me—was even then on the way.

As had long been suspected, my grandfather's estate, when realized, left no more than some few hundreds of pounds to each of his daughters; it did not I think come to one thousand pounds each.

My father applied for a transfer from the Oswestry district and was appointed to Birkenhead, but they had difficulty in finding a house here, and my mother's health, which since the birth of Mary had been causing some anxiety, worsened in the miserable rooms they had had to take so my father applied for another transfer. These repeated applications did not help his professional prospects but he was temporarily sent to Shrewsbury. Here it was that he rented the shabby little house with the struggling soot-poisoned laburnum tree, the house where I was born. Not long after this he was re-appointed back to Birkenhead. I have, of course, no recollection of this short time in Shrewsbury so that it is from Birkenhead that my first memories spring. This move was a permanent one: we were to remain in Birkenhead some nine or ten years, but during these years we moved, from time to time, to different houses. It was I think the real starting point of our life as a stabilized family; it was in this town that Wilfred spent his boyhood, and I spent my childhood. It is from here that I can recount happenings that emanate from my own memory of experience.

Chapter Two

THE DOCKS

WHEN we made this move to Birkenhead my mother and father had still not only the courage (this they kept always) but the hopefulness of youth, and the conviction—quite unwarranted—that somehow things would come right for them.

It is important, I feel, to establish what they were like at this time—their youthful vigour, their high hopes for themselves, and above all their ambitions for the family they had started. They did not believe at that time that their immediate difficulties would not dissolve themselves, or foresee these as anything except temporary problems. My father was disappointed about India and my mother was finding it difficult to run the house in our straitened circumstances, but these things in themselves could at this time do no more than mist the brightness of their young hopes and could not alter their view that goodness, practised in their own lives, would ultimately prevail and in itself solve their difficulties, which were wholly a question of means. There is, looking back, a naïvety about this which is hard to believe, but at the time it was true. My father could still look at his little son Wilfred and his miniature daughter Mary and dream dreams for them; my mother, much less inclined to dream, was still able to think about her two children with complacent feelings and happy reflections about their future, and both of them could and did look forward to the next child, which was so soon to come.

These two people, Tom and Susan Owen, were still young and fresh and eager; all they lacked was money—and in their eagerness even this lack had not yet really troubled them, much less cramped their inborn niceness. I emphasize this because in the story I have to tell, which really starts with the beginning of this Birkenhead period and the commencement of my own first infantile recollections, there is the danger, when describing these nerve-fretting times, that I might give a wrong impression of them by insisting upon isolating Wilfred, which the difference in our ages helped to stress, and give an unpleasing picture of him. This would not be true.

It was in this period that the acute lack of money began to exert its insidious influence upon our home, and as a consequence the corrosion of disillusion began to blunt my parents' ambitions. It became a time for us when existence, food and housing and keeping free from debt, was in itself the immediate and only problem, and so dominant was this preoccupation that the future for us children had to be something which must look after itself. If what I paint is stark, which I intend it to be, and the colours appear crude, which I do not intend at all, it will only serve to underline the truth that while the hardships of this time, 1898 to 1907, had their effect upon Tom, Susan, and Wilfred Owen, in a way that may appear to make them less likable, this would be wrong and is not true. The constant contending with a lack of means did have a blurring, even perhaps sometimes a tarnishing effect, but the results were only correlative to the events. In all of us, but especially in the triangle of these three, an overlay of pettish triviality may appear, and sometimes what may well look like a hardness of feeling. The important truth is that, while all this could and did have an effect upon them which remained crippling for all of us, it was the result of poverty—and poverty only— and not any fundamental change in any of these three people. Their simplicity and integrity remained a part of them . . . the niceness of them, as people, could not be destroyed.

I was very young indeed when I first became conscious of being alive and when my memory began to function, so that I have vaguely retained impressions, some of them full of allurement and others of hazy fearfulness and terror.

My earliest conscious remembrance is of being swung about in a swaying room that refused to keep still. This room was dimly lit with yellow, smoky lanterns, and I remember the terrifying dreams that persisted even during the frequent spells of wakefulness that interspersed themselves in my troubled sleep. I remember very vividly that the people, and there seem to be a continuous stream of them lurching and reeling through this sickeningly revolving room, appeared to my fevered imagination to be enormous, hairy, ape-like beings, and when these frightening creatures commenced whirling, first high overhead and the next moment diving far down below me, I became petrified and wet with icy terror. The culmination of my horror came upon me when one of these creatures detached itself from the violently spinning stream, bent over me and enveloped me in hot breath and fiery whiskers. It was the scream that tore itself from my small body that brought both oblivion and my mother to me at the same time. I was to learn long afterwards that I was being brought back to England from Ireland where my family had been staying during a transitionary period between leaving Shrewsbury and settling in Birkenhead, and that during the sea-passage I had developed a violent temperature with accute tonsillitis, which subsequently turned to measles, and that the hairy beast was a bearded, kindly passenger who was much concerned over the obvious illness of the little child.

My next moments of consciousness came to me as I was being unloaded from a dark and dripping cab on to a black wet pavement in a dank and evil-smelling street outside one of a long line of small, squalid, and near-slum dwellings. Our cab driver, who was terribly drunk, threw off our boxes and bags, somehow regained his seat and drove away, cursing and singing very loudly. When we had groped our way into the house, and my father had made a light, the floor and walls of the passage and the small room leading from it appeared to surge and lift as if covered with a simmering treacle. We had been welcomed to our new home by armies of black beetles. The disgusting crunching as our feet pressed down on these horrible insects, the loathsome smell of the air in the house, following as it did the nightmarish crossing from Ireland, with the wet cold blackness of my arrival in the slummy street, was more than my small body could withstand. I was immediately and very violently sick, and the last impression I had before consciousness once again drifted away from me, was of Wilfred's protective rush towards me, the feel of his arms around me, and the fearful sight of the racing heaving black mass of beetles converging upon what I had thrown up.

It was, I am certain, during these last few seconds in the evil-smelling passage that I became aware of an entity all my own. These were the moments of time when I realized I was a person, and henceforth I was myself and would remain individual for ever more. I had emerged from helpless infancy, I had begun to live. Perhaps it was Wilfred's protective rush to me, and the warm gathering up of me by my mother, and the dim looming figure of my father which threw a long black shadow, so terrifying in the horrible darkness of this frightening house; perhaps the spur of terror lent acuteness to my consciousness;

3   19

whatever it was, I am sure that it was in that moment of time that transition took place in me, so that I changed from infant dormancy to intellection. It was in this instant, surrounded by this black evil-smelling ugliness, that the awareness of the existence of the other members of my family established itself in my infant mind.

These years in Birkenhead were bad ones for all of us. In the year 1900 Colin was born. Although the birth of Mary in 1895 had caused my mother some serious illness, this had in no way seemed to be a permanent indisposition; but after the birth of Colin her health deteriorated rather seriously. This was perhaps due more to the transition from one mode of life to another, the sordidness of our social surroundings, and of course to the work entailed in bringing up unaided a family of small children under such conditions; perhaps, too, to the delayed shock of realization that this life upon which she and my father had embarked so gaily was going to be hard and very difficult; the realism of it all was hitting her hard. It was this, perhaps, rather than any physical defect which accounted for her enervation, for while no specific disease could be diagnosed, she seemed somehow unable to regain any vitality and lapsed into a condition of semi-invalidism, a state of negative good health which was to remain with her, in varying degrees of severity, for most of the rest of her life, and not only made the running of our home much more difficult but added greatly to my father's anxieties and too often increased his moods of discouragement. Looking back, I can see what a bleakness of outlook, especially during the first three or four years in Birkenhead, faced them both. The extreme fragility of Mary, my mother's invalidism, the very young baby which had developed some bone weakness, all these required expensive medical attention, and this cruelly reduced my father's resources—at that time he was not earning more than ninety pounds a year. Caused by the burden of this inadequate income, insidious domestic debts had founded themselves and were increasing with amazing fertility—in the way so bitterly well known to everyone who has endured real poverty. All this, of course, reflected back upon our mode of living, and while it is absolutely certain that neither in this troubled period, nor yet at any time in the future, were any of us to be actually hungry—and this I think must be stressed in order to emphasize the ingenuity and improvisation which my parents had to bring to bear in order that this should never come about—nevertheless these circumstances did have effect upon the diet of our house. Filling foods, bread, cheap jams and syrups had to be used in large quantities to take the place of higher quality and essentially nourishing foods. All the usual additions to children's diet were unknown to us, as of course they were to the hundreds of other children living around us who somehow survived in the dirty little houses and smelly streets, and like them we all of us developed a pinched and rickety look.

We were, though, in this respect in a rather worse plight than these others in the neighbourhood, as, unlike them, we were not indigenous to it and were never allowed to become a part of the district. My mother and father held themselves aloof from their neighbours, and refused to admit that their circumstances had really altered. Instead they persisted in presenting to the world a veneer of outward well-being, which showed itself mostly in themselves always being well turned out and insisting that us children, should always be dressed with care and suitability although most inexpensively so. This was in a sense to them the flying of a flag whereby they refused to admit by outward appearance the bitter truth of poverty, and was a further drain on their income, a direct result of which meant not less food in the house but most certainly food of less nourishing quality.

This determination of my parents not to be submerged by adverse conditions was actuated by a genuine wish to do the best for us children, but these were the years when the insidious process of the dulling of sensitivity really began—later this was fought against, and serenity regained. This process gradually caused all real long-sighted ambition for our material success in life to drain away. In its place had arrived a subjugation to expediency with the dire result that the earlier bright hopes were ground away, until only a dull and enervating respectability remained, so that the immediate need to retain this respectability became much more important and vivid to them than any real plans or arrangements for our future. The perpetual struggle against poverty and threat of debt gradually wore them down until they seemed powerless to prevent this expediency taking the place of design.

The early refusal to recognize in any way the locality and its inhabitants caused us to be regarded by them as wishing to hold ourselves apart, which we did, and of thinking of ourselves as superior to them, which we did not. The immediate effect was that every emergence by us children from the house held a hunted and nightmarish quality, as of course we were the natural prey of the stevedores' and dock labourers' children, who lay in wait for us and with jeers and screams of laughter set upon us, egged on with ribald encouragement by the slatternly women who seemed perpetually to fill the dark doorways. Another consequence was that we had to go far afield, and get right away from our own neighbourhood, before we could feel safe to start playing. A small dingy sort of park was found, which never seemed to be used, and beyond it some empty waste-land, dotted with scrofulous-looking trees and bushes, which gave the whole place an indescribable atmosphere of melancholy unwholesomeness. Wilfred was trained to take us there and look after us, but walking there was tiring so that when we did arrive it was without much energy left to amuse ourselves. The place was drear and frightening, Wilfred did little to dispel this atmosphere, and his natural instinct to dramatize the surroundings and make them a backcloth for the imaginative stories he was then absorbing with such avidity, led him to exaggerate the latent eeriness of the place.

The nearby waste-land ran up to a piece of dark and mangy wood, and sometimes if it suited the particular story that Wilfred was trying to bring to real life, he would persuade us to penetrate into these forbidding depths. Any entry into this wood was always full of misery and foreboding for me, especially if Wilfred insisted upon secreting us separately, which he sometimes did, without thought of harm: he was not very old himself. It was on one of these occasions, when I was hiding in this horrible wood, that a man slouched by. He was filthily bearded and clothed in rags. I remember that patches of the yellow skin of his dirty body showed through in many places. Suddenly catching sight of me, he whirled and sprang on me and lifted me up in a loathsome embrace, pushing his hairy face into mine. Such a shaft of burning fear tore through my small body that it must have actuated it to frenzy. I remember biting and screaming and kicking and tearing with all my four limbs in an ecstasy of desire to hurt. This must have been effective for he dropped me in a few seconds and himself fell to the ground doubled up. I expect one of my little flailing boots had caught him, with a perfection of splendid accident, full in the testicles.

I rushed out of the wood, found Wilfred, and released my remaining fear and fury on him, but Wilfred, perhaps sensing danger, or maybe he too caught sight of the tramp, seized hold of me with one hand and Mary with the other and ran and ran, until we could run no more, and fell down with exhaustion hammering in our chests and in our temples.

This, I think frightened Wilfred. In any case, from that time on Wilfred lost his full control over me and I would only participate in his schemes if I chose my own part and place, and no amount of persuasion ever succeeded in making me enter the wood again. We continued using the waste-land for our only playground. As we were already weary when we arrived, we were always dreadfully tired by the long dragging walk home again.

The incidents of my childhood and boyhood are not in themselves of any importance, except for the effect and reflection they had upon Wilfred, and to provide a means of describing the varying environments in which us four children spent the years until 1911. It was not until this year that any separation in the family occurred; until this time the six of us remained as a complete family unit, always living together under the same roof. None of us ever went away to boarding school, so that except for short holidays, we were never apart. In this way anything which affected one of us affected all of us in a greater or less degree. In these early years the gap in age between Wilfred and us other three was very noticeable, being accentuated by Mary's extreme smallness of stature and her delicacy which always made her appear younger than I, so that the four years and a half between Wilfred and me came to be accepted as the demarcation between Wilfred as the eldest and responsible child, and us three others as the small children, always in need of care. This demarcation was to remain in lessening degree until Wilfred left home; in a sense it was a recognizable division in the family, my father and mother and Wilfred on the parental side, and me, Mary, and Colin on the small children side. Owing to my mother's delicacy and my father's very long hours of work away from home this very often threw undue responsibility—for so young a boy—upon Wilfred, and did account in great measure for his early gravity, and made him mature far beyond his years. My mother encouraged this, indeed with her indifferent health she had little choice, which meant that in the beginning Wilfred was very often in sole charge of us three. This established an early bond between her and Wilfred, and had the tendency to separate Wilfred further from us three. It was also, I think, the beginning of a fixed feeling in Wilfred's own mind that he really belonged to and shared the responsibility of the parental side. In this way I always think Wilfred was denied, if not his boyhood, at least his boyishness. In later years, as he became more and more preoccupied with his reading, this characteristic became even more pronounced, so that his quiet gravity was very noticeable even outside the family.

Another consequence was the way in which Wilfred's maturity not only showed up but most markedly betrayed my own immaturity and natural boyishness. One effect of this was the ready acceptance of me as the rather commonplace child of the family, a relegation which was to hang over me for a great many years. It was something which often not only made me childishly angry but set up a harmless sort of hostility between Wilfred and me, the effect of which was to make me exaggerate my own Philistinism and thereby to accentuate Wilfred's disbelief in me so that on the whole I came to think that this position in the family fitted me very well, and I came to see myself that I was not really a very satisfactory sort of child. Indeed it was extraordinary, but in these early times nothing did seem to go right for me, my timing with the rest of the family seemed to be all wrong; if one of us was to be ill at some crucial moment or if some childish accidental damage happened in the house, it always seemed that it was I who was responsible for these happenings—this did not subdue me, instead it increased my pugnacity far beyond my wish or natural inclination. Wilfred and I were different in this way, for while these infant tribulations aroused in me this assumed bravado, they made him quiet and moody and sometimes depressed, and for release he would rely much more upon invective and the sardonic reply than upon a normal exhibition of boyish temper. Perhaps it was because of this that my mother, while freely scolding us others, rarely disagreed with Wilfred and never reprimanded him. My father, when any of us displeased him, was more inclined to personal crossness than any considered scolding. Unlike me, Wilfred only rarely displeased my father in minor matters; the difference in their outlook—Wilfred's determination for a scholastic career, and my father's hopes that he would undertake a practical and adventurous one—made their incompatability at that time a deeper and more serious disparity than any youthful misdemeanours would have brought about.

We went on using the waste-land but since the tramp scare the place had never been the same for us; even before this had happened I had always had a dread feeling about this haunt, and afterwards I found myself waking up in the mornings hoping for rainy days. If I saw it was raining really hard, a welling-up of happiness would surge through me at the thought that we should not have to go there but instead would stay at home and play in the dingy little kitchen and the six-feet-square backyard, for here, at least, seemed warmth and protection.

Memory of these early times brings nothing but a grey dreariness, and remembered through the brightness of the happier years that were to follow I always have the feeling that to see them properly I have to look back through a murky curtain that stains these memories with a monochrome of shadowed greyness. Indeed there is such division here that behind this veiling of unhappiness only isolated incidents show through with any real clarity—in these Wilfred always looms dominantly, more so I think than my mother or father, perhaps because we were so much in his charge. It must have been about now—Wilfred would be nine or ten and the infant Colin two or two and a half—when he, Colin, was stricken with scarlet fever. This was a disastrous calamity for our small home, and but for the resourcefulness of Wilfred would most likely have ended very seriously for some of us. When the disease was diagnosed, either the isolation hospitals were all full, which is extremely likely, as the disease was raging, or, and this is almost certain, my mother refused to let him go; in any case she decided to nurse him at home. This of course meant some method of isolation, and a sheet was soaked in carbolic, draped over a bedroom door, and kept wet for six weeks. My mother and Colin were kept confined there. No contact was allowed between the rest of the house and them, leaving my father, Wilfred, and Mary—who could have been only about six—and myself to look after ourselves as best we could. There was no help available from neighbours. For one thing my mother did not know any of them, and then of course the risk of infection was too great to expect any offer of help.

My father I expect did something to help with housework during the evenings, although he was never very good at this, but between seven-thirty in the morning and six-thirty or seven at night, Mary and I were entirely the responsibility of Wilfred. It was necessary, too, to keep us out of doors and as far as possible away from the house. My overwhelming recollection of all this is of even greater tiredness than usual caused by the long walks that Wilfred had to enforce upon us. He must, I think, have taken his instructions to keep us far away too seriously. One of his walks was to a green hill a long way out of Birkenhead and far too great a distance for Mary's and my own short legs.

I suppose to amuse us—it could not have been for safety as we did not always use them—he made some reins out of thin clothes-lines, and at the beginning of the day would make great play for us by driving us tandem or abreast, and would invent situations and destinations for us to bring reality and entertainment into the games. In the evenings he used them to help to drag us through the last streets on our journey home, for sometimes Mary and I were so exhausted that he could only get us home by dragging us with the lines and by endless coaxing and persuasion.

One day these reins were to cause Wilfred the biggest fright and up-set that he had so far experienced. It happened one pouring wet morn-ing when we were out on the green hill. Wilfred had harnessed me up, and by some fluky mischance had unknowingly tied the rein on one of my arms with what must have been a self-tightening knot. Very soon this began to tighten on my arm most painfully and I called out in distress to Wilfred who struggled to release the tightening band, but the wet was shrinking and stiffening the cord. It became too strong for his small fingers and the more he struggled the tighter it became. I re-member Wilfred calling out frantically for help but there was no one in sight, so he trotted us down to some nearby roads and houses and as soon as he saw a woman he called out to her. She ran up to us, but in trying to release my arm only made it still tighter. My arm was now swelling painfully and growing cold, but she must have been sensible for she hastened away and soon came back with a rough-looking man who managed to cut the cord with his pocket knife. Wilfred was almost frantic with anxiety and remorse. No sooner had the man done this than he turned on the small Wilfred in a most threatening and abusive manner, accusing him of deliberate cruelty to his small brother and threatening to thrash him there and then. This frightened us all badly. Mary and I closed up with Wilfred and piped up in shrill defence of him. The man made a grab at Wilfred, but the woman intervened and the man turned revilingly upon her. Wilfred, gathering us both by the hand, ran us safely out of sight. I expect the man was drunk. The un-pleasantness together with his acute concern about having damaged his charge had upset and unnerved Wilfred and he took us home as fast as he could. My arm was not very painful now, but was flapping about in a cold, dead sort of way which made me feel a bit frightened.

When we got home Wilfred rushed upstairs, breaking the quarantine to unburden himself to my mother, after which I was taken up and my arm only was put through the carbolic sheet for examination. I suppose instructions were given to Wilfred, and I remember immersions and swabbings with hot water which, in spite of all his care and gentle tenderness, hurt very much. When my father came home he bandaged my arm and afterwards, to distract me, played wounded soldiers with us.

It must have been when Colin was about three years old that it was thought necessary to send me to a preparatory school. Wilfred was already installed in the Birkenhead Institute. This curiously named school had an excellent reputation, and I now suppose it to have been somewhat similar in character to one of the grammar schools. Anyhow he was firmly established in the lower half of the Senior School as a very favourite pupil indeed, so much so that it was openly discussed in front of me whether or not, if I was sent to the school, I should jeopardize his chances in any way.

It must be admitted that even at this early age my parents had made up their minds that I was a child not only of little promise but of some stupidity with a tendency to untruthfulness. This last impression was undoubtedly given them by my not always being able to distinguish between imagination and fact; it was to dog me through my school days. On the whole I was not considered an infant upon whom it would be wise to spend much money or time, far less that any risk should be taken of my being allowed to dim, by unworthy connection, the brilliance of Wilfred. This curious attitude towards Wilfred and me was to persist for many years. It was never, as far as my mother was concerned, to be entirely extinguished. All this caused me to assume a derisive pugnacity which I did not really feel. My physical appearance helped to foster this alienation, for compared with the others I was sturdily built and I think generally gave the impression of a greater tendency to aggressiveness than they did. My mother was quite undivided in her opinion that from the point of view of a prospective student, I compared very unfavourably with Wilfred, whose apparent studious and somewhat diffident nature seemed to claim a right to be thought of as naturally scholarly, and the more his suitability for preferential educational treatment was thrust at me, the more belligerent and defiant I became.

Curiously enough Wilfred himself was not guiltless of this attitude and even abetted it, albeit unconsciously, for this scholarly seriousness of his came not from any selfish attitude or any desire to seek greater opportunities for himself at our expense. It was something else, something so vitally inherent in him that it was altogether outside his own

27

control. Even at this age he was so obsessed—there is no other word—
with the necessity to equip himself scholastically that he was utterly
unaware of any unfairness. . . . This is, I think, extremely interesting,
showing, as it so clearly does, that even at this early age he was possessed
by the urgency—perhaps inseparable from creative artists—to develop,
at any cost, his dormant powers of creation, as yet only instinctively
realized. There is a danger in recounting these things about Wilfred of
giving an entirely wrong impression of him, unless it is remembered
that he was completely magnetized—so that he could not deviate even
had he wished to do so—by this almost panic-stricken necessity to prepare himself, so that he would be able to release a power which he so
urgently sensed. Separated from this creative singleness, he could be
made to appear as ordinarily selfish, self-centred and, for his age, unnaturally absorbed with maturity and his own future, and in this way
might appear to be really priggish, which he never was. But to represent Wilfred as an average-type schoolboy, who later on developed a
literary bent, would convey a greater falsity. The truth lies in the certainty that even when acting as nursemaid to us younger ones in the
waste-land and scarlet-fever days he was already irretrievably dedicated
to letters and above all to poetry. This coloured all his thoughts and
actions and emphasized his mature feelings towards us younger ones,
always so pleasingly that this must never be taken for self-righteous-
ness. And if upon occasion there was a suggestion of superiority in his
bearing this was often merited by our disregard for his deeper purpose;
more truthfully it could always be traced to his own genuine humility,
and was really something thrown up both as a barricade against viola-
tion and a buttress to stiffen and support his own determination not to
be weakened in his pursuit of knowledge and achievement. He had as
well, like so many people harassed by the wish to create—and again
almost unknowingly—a powerful urge to experiment, as if by so doing
he could find some of the answers he so desperately sought . . . we made
good guinea-pigs for him.

Of course we, being more ordinary in our outlook, countered much
of this with healthy hostility, and often enough defended ourselves
naughtily with a great show—never really felt—of outspoken belittlement of his cherished aspirations. While all this was normal and wholesome enough, just the same it did have the effect of alarmingly over-
emphasizing the division between us; so much so that we began to
believe it ourselves and appeared less interested in all to do with schools

and learning than perhaps we were.

Another result was the division of plans for us which came about through a lack of agreement between my father and mother concerning us, and made them inclined to foster individual opinions and to express them to one another in a way wholly divorced from what they each in their own mind knew to be the truth; the result being that my father, who possessed much more literary bent than my mother, tended, quite contrary to his own conviction, to discourage Wilfred's intense reading—really and truly just because my mother was too intent upon his doing so.

My father was always unhappy about this situation and, being a very proud man, tended to entrench himself behind a façade of indifference, with outbreaks of petulance, and sometimes open hostility to my mother's preoccupation with Wilfred's too serious outlook. My mother, almost unknowingly, quite certainly allied herself to Wilfred, not without some hurt to my father who, being so obviously excluded, swung into a position of non-active opposition, cultivating a wholly assumed appearance of indifference. An unspoken and perhaps hardly recognized state now existed whereby my mother and Wilfred made up one side, and my father and I the other. This pull from two sides, although it could not destroy the happiness of our family life—it dissipated itself into insignificance later on—did in the first years have a troubling effect upon us all. Wilfred became rather more morose than his age and general environment warranted. He and my father were inclined to hold themselves aloof from each other, which was a loss to them both. I myself resorted to my protective fence of pretended disregard for all that Wilfred held most close, so that I too became remote from him and felt baffled anger that he could not or would not see how much I really cared.

This division must, of course, have existed for some time and was manifested mostly by a show of irritation by my father towards my mother over her concentration upon Wilfred, and by his annoyance with Wilfred for not showing more eagerness and vitality for normal boyish pursuits. But my mother's influence was strong and overcame the suggestions and efforts he made to get Wilfred out of doors more often. I think as well that even in these early days an inertia and despondency were settling upon him. The years of struggle and, what must have been much worse, the constant sense of insecurity were doing their dreadful work on him only too well so that I feel that at this time his only preoccupation was to keep his family free from starvation until such time as we children at the earliest possible age could go out and earn our own livings, in no matter what capacity and entirely without direction. Always nagging like a cancer in his brain was the knowledge of his own inability to make money, and the harping doubt about even retaining his present post. This last was of course exaggerated in his own mind, brought about by his worried state, but the fear remained. He knew only too well that all the salaried posts in the railway companies at that time were extremely precarious, competition for promotion amongst his colleagues and contemporaries was desperately keen and not always scrupulous, and of course apart from this hazard, there was always with him the knowledge that even a slight error of judgement, not necessarily by himself but by one of his subordinates, could mean dismissal, and this without avenue for appeal. At this time he could not have weathered three months unemployment; he knew this, and the knowledge was a perpetual and dangerous anxiety to him and dis-coloured what should have been his naturally sympathetic and loving attitude towards us all.

My mother's ambitions for her children were blurred for altogether different reasons and were brought about by her Calvinistic upbringing which she seemed unable to throw off. This was sometimes rather hard on my father, and I suspect increased his testiness very considerably. Indeed this attitude of my mother's of relying so much upon God, not only to know what was best for us all but by some miracle to provide us all with careers—or if He didn't do this then arguing that this must be all to the good and that we were not meant to have them—must have been most difficult and dispiriting for my father, a young man struggling to support a family. So muddled must her thinking have been at this time, that while she was so evangelically content to leave our futures solely in God's hands, any immediate problem she insisted upon dealing with herself, and as a consequence we always lived at the limit of our means in order to keep up all possible appearances. This bothered my father quite a lot; his inclination was to live just below his income. He found it, I think, very difficult to believe that God would pay the grocer's bills and the school fees. Nevertheless, although this insistence upon keeping up appearances might seem misguided and hypocritical, in the sense that it absorbed the small pittance that was keeping the family together, leaving nothing to put by for our future education, yet it did go deeper, for I am certain that the real compulsion was a determined resolve not to allow these material circumstances to force us all down to a level.

I think that always with them was an instinctive fear that if they once let go, even if it meant an immediate material advantage, we would be irrevocably overwhelmed. It really amounted to deciding between an environment for us during childhood after which we would have to rely on our own resources, or a lessening of the momentary advantage and saving of finances for a later education. In the end circumstances denied us much of the first and, with the exception of Wilfred, excluded us entirely from the second.

It is curious and I think interesting to see how these divergent outlooks of my mother and father, while causing fretfulness in the early years, combined together, as we matured as a family, to bring about an effect which was entirely good. It will be seen later how immensely valuable this slow welding together became to us all, especially to us children. It not only left us free to think for ourselves, but actually forced us to do so. This I am sure is particularly marked in the early and healthy rivalry that existed between Wilfred and me. This sounds and is contradictory, for while a closer and perhaps softer relationship between us would have brought about immediate results, I am certain that the slower process of fusion proved in the end to be of immeasurable value to us both in our separate ways. We were all of us in our outlooks divergent, our actions were often unpredictable, and we must appear as a contradictious family.

Something of all this may have been floating about in my father's mind when one day, putting my coat on me, he took me by the hand, an unusual action for him, telling me that he was taking me to see Wilfred's school, the Birkenhead Institute. As we walked along he discussed with me the possibility that, provided I would show a little more aptitude and work very hard, and provided I was careful not in any way to disgrace Wilfred, I might one day be allowed to enter this great school. By this time we had reached the building itself, and one look at the gaunt and, as it appeared to me then, prison-like building with its cold-looking stone and the bare asphalt playground that surrounded it so filled my childish mind with horror and fright that I there and then decided that never, if I could help it, would I become part of it, and that Wilfred could keep entirely any advantages it might contain for himself.

My father probably sensed something of what I was feeling, and quickly told me that he had decided to send me not to this building but to a preparatory school sometimes used for entry to the Birkenhead Institute, a very different place.

It was while walking down the hill that ran alongside the main building that my father, still holding me by the hand, commenced to deliver his peroration. It was a curious trait of my father's that although he was a moderately good and mostly an interesting conversationalist provided it in no way concerned a considered opinion of his own, yet all his life he was bothered with an inherent shyness, so that if he was voicing an idea or view that was his own, he was only able to do so by projecting what to most people would be ordinary statements into this sort of set speech. I was to learn many years later that this diffident shyness was so great a handicap that when he had occasion to talk seriously, it was only by previously rehearsing what he wished to say over and over again that he was able to express anything at all, and then, of course, it came out with the pre-thought-out effect of a speech. It was in this stilted way that he delivered his ideas to me while we were walking around the school, the main theme being the difficulty of affording the fees which sending me to school would entail, and that to do so he and my mother, if they decided to give me this start in life—I was only six or seven years old—would have to make large sacrifices. The impact of this word on my small mind caused it to fill with an imagination of Isaac stretched out and bound to a slab on the mountain-side, with his father standing over him all ready to plunge a long and gleaming knife into him. My father, continuing his peroration, told me that of course I must do my best to emulate the brilliance of Wilfred. However, he seemed to entertain but the faintest hopes of this happening, although even his slight hopes must have been stouter than my own, for I had none.

I gathered from all this that though I was composed of the most un-promising material and that the outlook for my future was pretty hope-less, he nevertheless felt that I ought to be given some chance, and that he himself had insisted, almost against my mother's wishes, that I should later join Wilfred at the Birkenhead Institute and that everything now depended upon my own efforts. If these were insufficient, then I might embarrass if not disgrace Wilfred and the rest of the family. Should this happen, I would be placed in the Free Board School and after the allotted period there I would be put out into the world and left to devise my own existence. This horrifying picture froze my small heart, and the horrid word sacrifice my father still kept using kept alive the vision of Isaac lying bound below the dazzling knife; but this was now being replaced by another one of myself standing alone in an unfriendly world with nothing to eat and nowhere to go. This grim prospect made my inward parts screw themselves into a hard knot. However, by this time we had reached the proposed preparatory school itself. It was a sombre, dark-looking converted private house, fronted by a small square of soot-corroded shrubs. The building was in one of the residential parts of Birkenhead and appeared to me to be such a vast improvement on the prison-like Birkenhead Institute itself that my small spirits rose a little.

My father and I gazed at this uninspiring place for some time. I can remember that my gazing made me feel rather sick. I became restive and my father, quite silent now, took me home.

I suppose it was at the beginning of the next term that I entered this school. Wilfred was detailed to take me there on my first day and to show me the way. The school was a considerable distance from where we lived, and the route was tortuous. My apprehension became acute when Wilfred instructed me to take good notice of all the turns and crossings, as although he would fetch me on this first day, after that I would have to find my own way to and from school. Wilfred was very solemn and rather discouraging, and in truth did nothing to make me feel happy about my first day. On the contrary, he was unsympathetic and coloured the picture with as much grey and black as he could. I think there is little doubt that he disliked the idea of my eventually joining him in his school. He inherited and shared with my mother a sort of distrust of the ability or intelligence of any immediate member of the family, but in an infuriating way—or so it seemed to me—was more than willing not only to seek for but to recognize it anywhere outside the family. Wilfred's perception gradually overcame this propensity and he lost it entirely towards the end of his life. Full of these misgivings and what were probably jealous irritations, he gravely escorted me on my first day finally handing me over to the care of Miss Foster,[1] a mistress of this preparatory school. Having done so he washed his hands of me as much as he could, still feeling I think in his serious and preoccupied way that any later entry of mine into his school could only be a menace to his own progress.

[1] Fictitious name.

My entrance to the school was, however, something of a success. Miss Foster took an immediate liking to me, although she embarrassed me very much by proclaiming before the whole class that my knees were quite the best of any child's there. Miss Foster was a lady who took a great interest in small boys' knees and limbs and seemed to be always studying and comparing them as they protruded underneath the narrow desks. Mine must have given great satisfaction. She was much given to favourites, and I was quite soon established as one. This office entailed being a general sort of run-about, with many rewarding kisses for chores well done, and also the ritual of preparing her 11-o'clock break coffee. This was effected with the aid of a gas-ring and a bottle of Camp coffee and meant, of course, losing one's own break and being confined alone with Miss Foster in the classroom. But it also meant some coffee for me, and as I was always a hungry little boy, it suited me very well.

This pleasant state was not, however, to last very long. It was Miss Foster's rather unusual custom to invite pupils from time to time, especially the favoured ones, to spend a week-end with her, entailing two nights' stay. She lived quite alone in a small neat little house some distance from the school. Whether her idea was domestic help in the house, of which she was very proud, or merely a means to enliven her monotonous and lonely existence I do not know. In either case the chosen boys were put to work dusting and sweeping and running errands. I was quite soon honoured in this way and looked forward to it very much and was very proud of the invitation, and in due course one Friday afternoon Miss Foster took me home with her.

The preparation of tea and various household tasks intrigued and entertained me, and it seemed the visit would be an enormous success until bedtime came round when Miss Foster, with the air of conferring the greatest possible treat and favour to a very small boy, told me that I was to sleep with her. I rebelled at once against this suggestion. To a child she must have appeared rather gross, she was certainly large and fat. I made a terrible scene and no cajolery, threats, or promises would shake my determination not to suffer this. It was only after I had exhorted a solemn promise that I should sleep by myself that I allowed her to put me to bed.

I woke in the morning with Miss Foster's heavy arm across me and with my small body pressed against her flabbiness. Another scene ensued and the upshot was that I refused to stay with her and was taken home in disgrace. Here it was immediately assumed that I had been

34

rude and ill-behaved. Not being asked, I did not proffer any explanation but contented myself with a simple statement that I no longer liked Miss Foster. This, of course, added fuel to the fire and I was temporarily outcast, except by my father who always disliked Miss Foster, but even he was persuaded that my behaviour had been offensive.

I was throughout my school days much given to making these quite simple statements which nearly always led me into trouble although they were engendered by a child's uncomplicated vision and never said with any wish to be disagreeable or rude. Expediency and effect did not occur to me; but, for some reason, the more truthfully I expressed myself, the greater was the effect upon adults of prevarication or downright lying. As I no longer liked Miss Foster, I could not see why there was any possible harm in saying so.

Wilfred was displeased over this incident, and showed his displeasure by an aloofness to me after he had made it quite clear that he thought the fault was entirely mine . . . other infants had enjoyed these visits to Miss Foster's house so why must I be troublesome about it. He made it clear, too, that any more of this behaviour would soon make me unfitted to enter the Birkenhead Institute, and, being only young himself, he did not keep out of his reprimanding voice his hopefulness of this happening, and the quicker the better.

His prophecy was to come true very shortly, as quite soon this small school was closed down and my father sent me to the Junior School of the Birkenhead Institute. This, of course, brought me into closer contact with Wilfred, for although he was in the Senior School we now used the same playground.

An incident occurred during my first term in the main school which was probably the deciding factor in causing my parents not to keep me on there. I had made great friends while at this other little school with a boy a little older than myself named Matheson; he too at the closing down had been sent, like me, to the Junior School of the Birkenhead Institute. During a break one afternoon I was walking across the playground and, noticing an unusual crowd of boys in a cluster, I ran up to investigate and found Matheson being set upon by a bunch of senior boys. It was without any sense of heroics and, in fact, without any trepidation of possible hurt to myself, that I immediately joined in the scuffle and very soon with Matheson was getting very much the worst of it. A stinging blow from one of the seniors so hurt me and infuriated me that I lost my temper completely: all fear of being hurt left me and I lashed out with such good effect and with such—to the senior boys—obviously bad-tempered dangerousness that what had started as probably only unpleasantly rough horseplay had now developed into a vicious and rather dangerous mêlée. Fortunately, a master came along and with some difficulty broke up the fight. We were all bruised and bloody. The master reported the happening to the Head, and even before I could clear myself of mud and blood I was taken before him and, to use his own words, was asked for an explanation of my unprovoked assault on half the school. As I had no idea of the meaning of the word 'assault'—I could only think of table salt—I was rather nonplussed and remained silent. After a penetrating stare at me, his eyes twinkling pleasantly, he delivered some sort of homily, telling me I was to remember that the Institute was not a training ground for prize fighters, and closed the matter by pushing me through his door in a friendly way.

It was perhaps unfortunate that Wilfred gave a different version to them at home. An explanation of my condition, for I was quite badly knocked about, was necessary, and Wilfred was very angry with me, and was convinced I had again seriously disgraced him. Undoubtedly, the episode set my parents wondering if it was worth expending the fees on me in order to keep me at this school. In reality, of course, it was the difficulty of finding the money that decided them, but I think they found it easier to take me away after I had myself supplied this other black mark. However it was, at the end of that term I was taken away from the school, but not before I had earned the nickname of 'The Birkenhead Bullfighter', a nickname which was to follow me around all my various schools and, by a curious coincidence, even to the schools in another county.

It was now decided that I should attend a Free Church School of some sort in Birkenhead, and I well remember my father taking me out one dark and rainy evening, this time not so much to see the school but more to be interviewed and approved by the master conducting it. We arrived wet and I was shivering with cold. After climbing a flight of outside steps which were vaguely lighted by a distant street lamp, my father pulled a jangling bell and we were admitted by a mouldy draggled-looking individual who proved to be the master. We had entered by a door immediately into the classroom. This was a horrible room, long and narrow and lighted by a single bare gas jet which forked up spasmodically to a dim light, dying between the forks to almost nothing. The room, of course, contained the usual school desks with yellow wooden tops and cast iron legs. These in the flickering light appeared to me to be jumping about in a most eerie way, and the whole atmosphere was pervaded with a cold sour smell so strong that it seemed almost visible to me, and I felt that if I opened my hand and then closed it again I would be able to imprison it. I did not, of course, know at the time that it was fetid stale perspiration of dirty unwashed children's clothes and the smell of sour urine coming from the improperly kept school lavatory.

The dirty unkempt individual kept up a desultory conversation with my father, occasionally asking me some educational question and taking not the least notice of my answers. The feeble conversation soon died away to a lethargic silence, and my father took his leave. They must somehow have arranged for me to go to the school, for after we had stumbled down the steps and regained the street my father told me that I would be starting there on the following Monday, after which we relapsed into a mutual damp dismay and misery, and with our hands in our pockets trudged silently home.

My recollection of this school is rather blurred and vague, probably because it was marked with little incident. Wilfred was again given the task of delivering me for my first day, and this time unbent and tried to cheer me up. We approached the miserable square of set-in bricks— it was really a backyard but served now as a playground—and walked in. He had his arm protectively round my shoulder and giving me a gentle squeeze walked away and left me to the stares of the urchins who had by now surrounded me. Young as the two of us were, I am sure this was the moment of time when we both realized our affection for each other and were made dimly aware of something yet to come that would be a bond between us. This moment was fugitive, and other such moments were to remain elusive and buried deep beneath the healthy bickering and competitive relations which formed our everyday life. It was the sight of his small sad figure as he turned away to leave me, as it seemed reluctantly, that poured over me a flash of illumination which was heightened when he reached a corner, stopped, and looking back gave me the little dark half-smile I was to know so well in later years, at the same time raising his small hand in encouragement as he turned out of sight. I think he was sorry at that moment for the forlorn little creature that was me, with my hands and face blue with cold, and standing so alone in the pools of scummy rain-water. His consternation at leaving me like this was not without remorse for his previous frigidity and discouragement.

Apart from the usual curiosity about a new boy, I had little trouble from the other children, and as it soon became known that I was the Birkenhead Bullfighter from the Institute I was looked upon, even by the bigger boys, with some awe. This suited me very well as I was not even at this age gregarious. The other pupils, coming as they did from some of the poorest homes in Birkenhead, were ragged and dirty, always with running noses and often with running sores. I disliked them all intensely and was never able to mix with them, but this did not matter and never seemed to be noticed. In this place nothing mattered. We were marshalled into the schoolroom for regulation hours, piped some miserable hymn or the Lord's Prayer, and after chanting a multiplication table (I cannot recall any other instruction we were given) we children would sit at our desks in apathetic trances of varying degree. The master in charge sat at his desk, scanning a piece of newspaper in an even more dejected and disinterested manner. I can only suppose that his utter indifference to what we did was so genuine that it made no fun for us to be unruly, so that apart from wandering around the classroom, which we all did freely, I can remember no disorder at all. We were all cold and hungry and I suspect the general physical condition of the school was so low that energy was easily absorbed by merely sitting and vacantly staring. The only vivid memory of this place is the sick torment I endured on the occasions when I really had to look at the master. The sight of his drooping moustache matted with old mucus and continually overlaid with fresh, which was permanently running from his nose, so revolted me that I was nauseated to the point of illness. On the dreadful occasions when he caught up a descending piece with his mouth, I was sick where I sat. I did not remain here very long. Something of the conditions of this place must have got through to my father and I was whisked away from it very suddenly. It was decided after this that I should remain at home, so for a time no other school was sought out for me.

My mother now whenever possible gave me some instruction, and a time was set aside each morning for this, but we were never able to make very much progress. The cares of the house and cooking and seeing Wilfred away to school left little time, and from commencing with set times the instruction became more and more intermittent and gradually ceased altogether.

At about this time, a slight general improvement in our financial position came about. My father must have been promoted again and we moved to our third and to what was to be our last home in Birkenhead. The house my father was able to rent was situated in a very much better neighbourhood, and although it was very small and dark we were once and for all out of the slum and tenement area. It was one of many hundreds of houses which made up the long and still very dreary roads, but the class of people who lived in them were altogether different and were mainly drawn from the lower middle classes. We settled down rather comfortably here. The house itself was semi-detached and stood a little back from the road. This allowed for some ground in front of it which was enclosed by neat iron railings and intersected by a tidy gravel path which led around to the side of the house to a patch of barren garden at the back. The house that was attached to ours was occupied by a quiet elderly woman, the widow of a sea-captain. She lived alone but had two sons, also captains of merchant ships, who used to stay with her between voyages. This house and district were really beyond my father's means and he would have preferred to remain in the poorer house and keep his extra salary as a margin of safety. My mother, however, was insistent upon going to a better-class locality. They were always to pull different ways over this question. My father's instinctive plan was always to remain socially stationary and to save all the money he gained by professional advancement to use for us children later. My mother's wish was to advance us all socially at whatever future cost to us. They were probably both right, but I know my father realized very bitterly that his prospects in his occupation were so poor that he would never be able to project himself far enough in the social direction to be much advantage to us. They found it difficult to agree upon major or minor points of any sort, and the consequent arguments and fundamental discord, although not apparent yet, were tiring and wearing to them both and brought about a lack of companionship and unified effort that eventually was to make everything during this temporary period difficult for all of us.

One sequel to this inability to view any problem or project from the same angle was the development in them both of a self-protective tendency immediately to take opposing views. The result was always a biased and untrue view of things for them both. It was this more than anything else that was to bring about the fretfulness that existed between them over Wilfred. My mother from the beginning was jealous that my father should exert any strong influence over us children and most especially over Wilfred and she undoubtedly gained supremacy over Wilfred and to a less extent over the rest of us. As this supremacy increased in power, so my father tended to become indifferent and even antagonistic to any scheme or arrangement concerning Wilfred, and although the good of us all was always in his heart, the absolute determination of my mother to create a bond between herself and us children, especially Wilfred, was so marked that it led my father into an untrue position and made him cloak himself with a false bravado that was wholly alien to him and damaging to Wilfred.

However, the move from the poorer part of Birkenhead to the more respectable Milton Road was eventually effected, and I am sure it was made easier for my father to give way and agree to move when he learned that the adjoining house was occupied by a sea-captain's widow. At this time my father's mania for the sea and all to do with it was so great that the remotest connection was an attraction to him, even the proximity of a sea-captain's relict. Anyhow, our move brought about more social activity. My father was persuaded to attend church and was soon to become a churchwarden and honorary secretary and treasurer of various charitable juvenile clubs and activities in connection with church affairs. All this in itself was unimportant to him, but it pleased my mother and did open to him a source of interest away from his work and helped a bit to satisfy a genuine wish to be of some social use.

Possession of a beautiful tenor voice made him welcome any excuse to sing, and by this time he had taught himself an almost endless range of songs which included nearly all the Gilbert and Sullivan works and many excerpts from serious opera. His passion for music was second only to, if not equal to, his love of the sea. Not unnaturally, he was in great demand for the many concerts taking place for various charities. Although nothing would persuade him to join a church choir and only occasionally would he consent to sing a solo in a church, I do remember being taken to hear him sing on one of these rare occasions. I found it difficult to associate the beauty of the glorious voice which floated and resounded through the church with my father who was so often irritable and sometimes morose.

It was after he had sung at one of these charity concerts that he was approached by some secretary of a Seamen's Mission and asked to go and sing to the sailors in some dockland hall in Liverpool. Some of his enthusiasm must have got across to the hard-bitten crowd and he was an enormous success. He was at once asked by the Missionary Society to help as a voluntary worker with the Mission. He seized on this opportunity, not because he was at all evangelically minded but he saw what a chance it presented to him to make contacts with ships and sailors. With this end in sight, he accepted the onerous work of distributing tracts to the ships in dock or in the river. This meant authorized access to ships, and very often trips by launch up the Mersey to vessels at anchor.

I was now at an age when I could be taken about, and my father after much priming as to the treats in store for me, and having made a few trial trips, told me one day—with a flatteringly conspiratorial air— that from now on I was always to go with him on these adventures. I was overwhelmed with joy, for already something of the romance of it all was beginning to prickle in me.

To begin with, these outings were not quite the success we had hoped for. At first I was rather overawed. The immense ships looming up above me so threateningly, the ceaseless clang of steel on empty steel from the riveters' hammers, the enormous gantries rearing upwards like one-armed giants, the ships' derricks loading and unloading and swinging out their huge slings of cargo—aiming them as it seemed to me straight for us—the constant avoidance of falling over the great steel and hemp hawsers that stretched like snakes and iron bars from ship to quay-side, the throngs of dock labourers and roaring stevedores, and the seamen themselves, these the gentlest and quietest of all—of so many different colours from coal black through the browns and yellows to the whites—all this was perhaps overwhelming for so small a boy, but I soon came to enjoy it all. What really did frighten me was having to walk with my father along the narrow quay-sides which surrounded the docks. He persisted in walking as near as possible to the edge, which always gave me the feeling that sooner or later against my own volition these hungry-looking dock basins would, with some dark power they seemed to exert, suck me down into their depths. This horrible feeling was especially strong when we stood on the bare unguarded lip of the deep graving docks to watch the shipyard workers crawling about like ants underneath the ships. My father delighted in doing this and always forced me to do the same. He would seek out all the narrowest gangways and unrailed planks from ship-side to quay and make me walk or stand with him. I was able to become accustomed to this, but the feeling was always strong enough to spoil what otherwise would have been perfection. I was never quite able to lose this curious floating, almost lightheaded, feeling when walking along a narrow gangway, even after I had been at sea for years, so that walking along a dockside remained something of an ordeal. My father's favourite place to stand was on the narrow two-foot sluice gates, for choice when the rope life-lines had been removed just prior to flooding so that we had cold, angry-looking water a few feet below us on one side and twenty feet or more of yawning stone depths of emptiness on the other.

Once on board a ship, I lost all this unpleasant feeling and would climb up and down ladders and balance on guard rails and bulwarks with a dangerous facility, and as we spent most of our time actually in the ships I was often able to forget it.

For our routine for these trips, we would leave home very early on Sunday mornings—except in the summer months when we could go out in the evenings. They had to take place on Sunday as this was the only free time my father had. We would call at the Mission first of all to collect the tracts, and with these stuffed well out of sight in his pockets and mine we would set out for the docks. My father would select the ship he liked the look of best and board her. At this point, it was necessary to produce the tract as a reason for our visit. He would pull out a bundle, wave them about rather vaguely and, with a splendid assumption of disownership, would either put them down on a con-venient locker for the wind to scatter, or stuff them back in his pocket. After the first few times he never again made the mistake of expecting a captain, one of his officers, quartermasters, or seamen who happened to be on the gangway to take them from him. He was quick to realize that accepting and holding the silly things made them feel uncomfort-able and foolish.

My father must have shown great adroitness over these difficult en-trées and never more so than when boarding a ship in the anchorage, for the approach of our launch wearing the Mission pennant would quickly be sighted and word would go around the ship's company that the Bible-punchers from the Mission were coming aboard; but my father's tech-nique rarely failed and a few minutes were usually enough to make us welcome. He would talk away by the hour with the officers and men, with never a breath of missionizing. Hospitality was always offered, cups of black syrupy tea, gritty cocoa, or weak coffee for me, and after much delving about in lockers and under bunk mattresses, fascinating-looking bottles were produced for my father. He would never accept a drink from any of them. He told me years after that he would never do this as by so denying himself he could salve the soreness of his conscience for the hypocrisy and farce he used about the tracts and his total lack of missionary spirit.

There is one ship I remember very vividly. She was a smallish, three-masted barque with a crew who could hardly speak any English. She was, I think, Norwegian or Swedish. She was laid up for months, probably for re-rigging or just lack of cargo, and occupied a berth in what to my childish mind appeared to be the countryside. Anyway, there were fields near. She was probably in some riverside creek. It used to be a long and tiring business getting to her but it was well worth it, and although communication, owing to the language difficulties, should have been impossible, it never proved so.

With smiles, nods and gestures and great bursts of roaring laughter and occasional English words we seemed to understand one another perfectly and, to complete the fairy-tale picture in my mind, this ship carried as cook a huge kindly negro who made special pastries for me. The captain, a large, yellow-haired man, took his wife with him on all his voyages, as was not unusual in that type of vessel. She, too, was fair-haired and handsomely built. They appeared quite old to me, but were probably very young. Anyhow, between them with their chief and second mate, the tea parties they made for us in the cuddy were very happy and gay. I was always grateful to this woman, as she took so much care to minister to my physical needs, and always seemed to sense the moment when I needed to disappear, and to make the necessary arrangements for me to do this without an embarrassing fuss so that I could always approach her parties with the comfortable feeling that I could drink as much milk or tea as I liked, without fear, knowing that provision for getting rid of it would be forthcoming at the right moment. My father was extremely bad about this essential attention to his small child, and would be very cross if I did not perform when he gave me the opportunity; but he never offered the chance at the right time with the result that my small bladder often caused me great pain through over-distension.

Wilfred was never taken with us to this special ship but my father had made him come along to the general docks several times very much against my mother's wish, which angered my father rather a lot; but these visits were not a success. Wilfred at that time was old enough to know that there was discord about his going. It may have been this consciousness of being pulled from two sides, or that he just did not like coming, but whichever it was, he always looked very miserable, hated going on board the ships and was petulant to my father and irritable and cross with me. Another factor which made him disinclined to come with us was his preoccupation at this time, much encouraged by my mother, with constructing an altar in the sitting-room at home. As this always took place on Sundays, it may have accounted for his disinclination, but I do not think it was only this. My father did not insist, and it became a recognized thing that he should be left at home with my mother.

My father in the beginning made great efforts to persuade my mother to come with us on suitable occasions on our dockland jaunts, and was especially anxious that she should come to the barque, but my mother was not good at sharing in or following my father's pursuits, especially seafaring ones. Of course, domestic conditions made it impossible for her to leave the house frequently, but occasionally it could have been managed and would have done much to add to my father's happiness. However, he never succeeded in persuading her to come with us; even a warm and pressing invitation from the captain and his wife to visit their ship did not avail.

These visits of ours to the ships and docks were not to continue regularly for very long. After the hospitality we had received on board the barque my father was anxious to do something in return, and as he could not persuade my mother to go with him to the ship, he invited the captain and his wife to spend a day with us in our home. A visit was arranged to which they obviously looked forward very much. My father went to their ship to collect them early one Sunday morning and brought them along. My mother, as was usual with her, had prepared especially nice food for the visit, and my father was hoping for a really happy and successful day. Especially as they were so eager to meet my father's family in his own home it should have turned out well, but from the very arrival of my father with them, the atmosphere seemed to go wrong, and in spite of all my father's efforts and theirs refused to right itself. I think my mother was antagonistic to my father's absorption in the sea and sailors; they became sensitive to this and although they did their best to overcome it, the day prolonged itself into complete failure. The broken English which had never before been an obstruction to us, was difficult for my mother and rapidly became an impassable barrier, and the situation deteriorated to a painful strain. An early departure was made and, of course, my father was not able to ask them again. This marked the beginning of the complete cessation of our visits to the barque and was the forerunner of the gradual diminishing of our Sundays in the ships until they became spasmodic and finally ceased.

For a long time after this we did not go to the barque but went around the steamers in the main docks, until one wintry Sunday morning my father told me we were to go to the barque for the last time and that we were going only to say goodbye. We had tea in the saloon as usual, and although our old intimacy and understanding was still there, the gay spontaneity had somehow gone. When we got up to say goodbye the great yellow captain picked me up until my face was level with his, looked long and hard into my eyes and, putting me down again, turned to my father, placing his huge hands one on each of my father's shoulders, and gripped him with affection. The woman hugged me to her, kissed my father gently on both cheeks and sped us out of the cabin. We stumbled over the deck and down the gangway into the cold gloom of the November evening. We walked along the quay-side until we were almost out of sight when my father turned and stared long and steadily at the beautiful ship. Something of his sombreness must have permeated into my small being, for I was suddenly overwhelmed with the beauty and sadness of the gaunt delicacy of her towering masts and yards. Her rigging, black in the half-light, looked beautiful with lace-like fragility. The combination of the yellowing nightfall with the flat loneliness of the setting, a bare bleak stretch of country all around and, in the very far distance, lights glinting out . . . she seemed in that level stretch of waste land to be a ship dying for want of water.

It was almost dark now and the topmasts had disappeared in the descending curtain of night. But the lower hamper and the reflection of the still water underneath her counter threw off a ghostly glow on the poop. Leaning over the rails two motionless figures were just visible to us. It was not until they and the ship were one with the darkness that my father, shivering now, moved away and we started our tiring journey home.

It was perhaps this experience which gave to me my first strong emotions and my first realization of sadness. As we plodded on through the sordid back streets and foul alleyways of the dock area childish depression closed in around me, and my head throbbed and banged in unison with the clanging and sparking tram-cars that we climbed on and off so many times, until at last one put us down within a long walk of our own house. I somehow managed to keep trotting along beside my father, who seemed now to be remote and distant, until he opened our own door. It was then that my tired misery overcame me. My father for the first time since leaving the ship now noticed my extreme exhaustion, and in some remorse prepared me some supper, which I refused to eat, and afterwards put me to bed. For some days after, I was running a high childish temperature.

It was weeks before my father went down to the docks again and when we did start going it never seemed the same. My father avoided the sailing ships of the outlying docks and merely visited the cargo steamers in the nearer basins, but he was never able quite to revive the intense interest and seemed to have lost the magnetism that had before made all his contacts with seamen so delightful and successful. He seemed now to be more interested in the ships than in the sailors, and spent most of the time in the shipbuilding yards. Here he would take me along and make me go with him down the almost perpendicular slippery stone steps to the very bottom of the slipways so that we could walk right underneath the ship itself; at other times we could clamber about and explore the half-finished interior of the vessel.

My father was to make one more effort to bring an atmosphere of the sea into his own home. This was the never-forgotten occasion when he insisted upon inviting four Lascar seamen whom he had met through befriending them when they had somehow missed their ship. They were just ordinary seamen from some steamer in the India trade. It was a heaven-sent opportunity for him to practise his Hindustani—all his life he maintained his fluency in this.

An evening was arranged and my mother was duly instructed to prepare a special curry, the recipe of which he had brought home from Bombay. The evening when he did bring these Indians home created something of a stir in the road we lived in. For some reason, not one of them would walk abreast with my father but insisted on shuffling along behind him, in single file with their flimsy slippers clipping and slapping on the pavement as they moved along. Following closely behind them came the young street rabble, shouting and calling out rude insults. The Indians like my father remained stoical and impassive. Ceremonial was gone through before entering our home, slippers were carefully removed and the beautifully ornamented round silk caps retained on their heads. They were perfect guests, appreciative and complimentary and delightfully courteous. They enjoyed the food immensely and ate entirely with their fingers. Knowing from my father their national weakness for sweetmeats, my mother had placed four or five pounds of home-made treacle toffee on the table. The sight of this seemed to have a mesmeric effect on them in a most extraordinary way; at the expense of the other carefully prepared dishes, they could not stop eating it, and although they did this with restraint and dignity, they finished every bit.

Perhaps their nicest touch of all was the trouble they had taken previously to find out from my father how many children he had; all of the four Indians had prepared a separate little gift for each of us, carefully wrapped in Indian tissue paper and tied with tinsel thread. My mother was presented with glass trinkets and my father with a bundle of cheroots. All were tendered in the most graceful manner with low bows and spoken benedictions. Altogether the evening was a success, although my mother did not give the proceedings quite her full approval. We children were completely fascinated with these brown seamen, especially their dark skins and to us curious garb, and most of all by the eight bare feet so carefully arranged underneath the table. This was very much Wilfred's evening, as he was old enough now to be a small person in his own right in a different way from the rest of us who could still be lumped together as children.

He had begged my father to teach him a few polite phrases of Hindustani, and had taken great pains to become word perfect. He did not do this with any special desire to please my father or the Indian seamen, but more because this was, as it appeared to him in his serious small way, an opportunity for gaining knowledge and, best of all, a knowledge that if he was able to acquire at all he would be able to test out immediately. This characteristic of wishing to prove to himself the actuality of his knowledge presented itself very early in his life and was, I think, brought about by a perpetual doubt about his own ability for true scholarship. It was as if the knowledge and impetus of power was always with him as something without any doubt at all, but the uncertainty as to the ability to arm himself sufficiently to express and use this power fretted and tormented him. It was this early realization of unsureness which even as a small child drove him to such self-discipline and almost frantic effort to glean and store up knowledge. He seemed always to have to prove himself to himself. However, although the reason was not what my father thought, it pleased him immensely, and might have lit a spark between him and Wilfred which would have burned on. But it did not do so, and many years of misunderstanding and mild antagonism were to pass before even a remote appreciation of their separate aptitudes could come about. However, it helped the evening along. The Indians were intrigued to be addressed with such serious intent by the small English boy in their own language, but when the visit was over Wilfred's interest in Hindustani died almost immediately.

It must have been about this time that my father decided that, at whatever cost, my mother must now have some help in the house. An advertisement was put in a newspaper and in consequence permanent help arrived in our home. This took the form of a supposed widow who came in answer to our advertisement. From the first she was mysterious and without credentials, but a long story of hardship and difficulties overcame to some extent my mother's uneasiness concerning her. She was installed as a sort of housekeeper and she immediately showed real efficiency in running the house. She consolidated her position by making a great fuss of Wilfred. This devotion to Wilfred dispelled any lingering doubts my mother may have had. From time to time unexplained happenings and curious episodes took place, but her efficiency and plausible explanations were so extremely clever and her complete unselfish devotion to Wilfred was so great, that strange occurrences were overlooked until, going out on one of her many mysterious evening errands, she failed to return. She was held in so much regard by us all that, fearing some accident had befallen her, the police were informed. They soon identified her as being notorious to them, and acting upon their advice we soon discovered that every bit of linen and all the silver, in fact everything in the house except what was in current use, had been systematically removed. Most of this my mother had brought from her home and it was being kept as a form of insurance against financial emergency. This was a blow to my parents and undermined their security seriously. Some of the silver was retrieved by the police from pawnshops over a wide area but the woman herself was never caught, and in spite of her criminal behaviour we were all relieved and glad, for she had forged a genuine affection between herself and us. Her devotion to Wilfred was undoubtedly very real, although it was probably born out of an adroit and clever reading of my mother.

I was still not at school, and one of her self-appointed tasks had been to give me regular lessons. This she did very pleasantly for me and succeeded in teaching me more than anyone else had so far been able to do. I had great affection for Mrs. Moore, the alias by which she was known to us.

Chapter Three

BIRKENHEAD

WILFRED by now had developed a strong sense of drama and a desire to bring about situations in which he would play the leading and controlling part. His age and my mother's indulgence of all his whims encouraged him, and was the cause of much childish fright and alarm to us younger children. Again, it was as if he must test out his own power of make-believe, and satisfy himself in a juvenile way with the effects he was able to bring about. These always took the form of bringing us into a state of fear, and sometimes to a state of unnatural religious fervour; this last, of course, was directly influenced by my mother. It was in no sense a desire for domination over us, nor yet any wish to make us unhappy. It was as if we were to him something upon which he could experiment, and it was only in this sense, that we were convenient to his purpose, and not for what we were ourselves that he acted or rather used us in this way. This was proved without any doubt by his protective behaviour towards us. He was always ready and prompt, if we were threatened by any form of outside danger or inside accidents, to shield us without thought for himself. Nevertheless, this excessive bringing about of dramatic situations, nearly always of a deep melancholy and often adult eeriness, evoking as he did in play spirits and ghosts from other worlds, was very hard indeed upon us little ones. One of his favourite forms of experimentation was to place us in dark rooms or cupboards and then give us ghostly visitations, he playing the part of the ghost. For these purposes of inspiring us with fright he would drape himself in sheet and cowl and with shaded candles and mumbling incantations approach us with terrifying solemnity, and, especially to my own infant mind, with a dreadful and blood-chilling unreality. All this horrible paraphernalia of dread and terror would be accompanied by suitable bangings, or worse still to me, quiet and imperceptible closing of doors. My mother seemed unaware of what was happening, and that what had started as a sort of game was deteriorating into a dangerous hysteria.

I was the first to rebel, but even I did not do this until after an experience which left me cold with horror and drained of vitality, and with a realization of presences not of this world. This dreadful experience did not take place under the spell of one of Wilfred's games, and for this reason was more frightening. We were playing away at some childish amusement in our tiny living-room on a dark winter afternoon when the darkness seemed to close down suddenly. Too late I realized I was badly pressed to make water. By now of course Wilfred had instilled in me a fear not of the dark but of dark places, and I knew that unaccompanied I must make the nightmare journey up the stairs and along the horrible passageway into the lavatory. I held on downstairs as long as I could until I reached the point when I knew if I did not nerve myself to make the journey I should wet my knickers, and the certain knowledge of my mother's anger and her physical chastisement of me drove me to make the dreaded journey. My ascent of the stairs was uneventful, although by this time painful; I reached the lavatory just in time and aiming carefully so that the noise of the falling water would be company for me, released myself happily. I turned to bolt back to light and safety and it was when I was half-way along the tiny passage that I became petrified, standing where I was with one foot off the ground. An unseen thing was there, something so menacing, so utterly unphysical and unheard of and, with my awareness of the uncanny, so terribly, terribly dangerous, that I felt with clear and absolute knowledge that here was something far beyond any nonsense of Wilfred's, something terribly unknown but realized with a clarity and a vision brought to me by a new sense I had not before possessed. It was as if I had plunged out of this world and I literally saw my own little body poised with one foot off the landing; then suddenly came the inexpressible relief of pure sublime panic. At that instant, my body was galvanized into action and I found myself floating from the landing at the top of the stairs to the hall below without touching one of the stairs. I landed on all fours physically unshaken and unhurt—the flying through the air had seemed without danger—but possessed with a knowledge not to be thought of.

I walked into the living room. I had now fully recovered control of myself but my appearance was evidently alarming for my mother flew to me, probably in fear of my whiteness, and stormily accused me of being a naughty, ill-behaved little boy who had been greedy at tea-time. My mother never did concern herself with anything except my physical condition; any emotional distress or upset was always classed as misbehaviour. After this upbraiding I became mute and stubborn. I was exhorted to give some reason for my unwellness, but of course explanation was now impossible and I refused to admit or divulge anything. As a consequence I was sent to bed without supper and in disgrace, feeling a thoroughly bad little boy. Here I lay and bit through my sheets in a torment of fear; what this fear was I did not know. This sheet-biting had become habitual since Wilfred's wretched activities and was the only means I knew that would prevent me calling out, but it was always attributed to positive malicious self-will and stubborn ill-behaviour on my part. This experience of levitation was not to occur again until years afterwards and then in the region of Latitude 51° south.

I must have bitten myself to exhausted sleep, for the next thing I remember was being awakened by something padding around the room with moans and groans and incantations. This was Wilfred in another of his efforts to make me leap with fright, but somehow after the deadly reality of the earlier vision in the dark passage this did not now seem anything but what it was—make-believe; and now anger and fury with Wilfred came to my aid, so that I was propelled out of bed and into violent attack upon him, and this time I really meant to hurt. The complete surprise and ferocity of my attack unnerved Wilfred himself, so that he was incapable of retaliation or even defence. It was my father who rushed up and separated us, with a strength that surprised me, and with a gentleness that was something new to me tucked me back into bed. My mother was both angry and hurt over the incident, took pains to point out Wilfred's restraint in not retaliating against my unprovoked attack, and gave me a great scolding for behaving so roughly and stupidly. While this left me sullen and angry, I also knew it to be untrue and in the few moments of my attack upon Wilfred I had tasted power and knew it for what it was. It was during these moments of combat that Wilfred received a first glimpse—born out of my determined action—of real danger.

After an interval, through my mother's influence, Wilfred was again allowed to practise his dramatic effects upon us, but to me they had now become unreal and not anything more than mildly frightening, and not very often even that. It was as if the feeling that I had experienced on the landing had given me, through this frightful vision, an immunity, as well as an obscure awareness, that could not be broken through. It was probably this serenity of mine that spoiled the games for Wilfred, and as his efforts proved powerless to provoke anything except childish irritation in me, he soon gave them up.

All this had convinced my mother more than ever what an unsatisfactory little boy I was, and it was very soon after this that I was again placed in another free board school in Birkenhead. This was a much larger school and there must have been hundreds of boys; otherwise the conditions were much the same. The same red and blue bricks and the same wet pools all over the playground. The thought of school again made me miserable and I hated it all, so much so that I went through the necessary routine of walking to and from the horrible place with a lethargic depression which prevented my taking any vestige of interest in the school itself while I was there. My only interest was a hope—a dim one—that I should not have to remain there for long. Nobody seemed to care if I was there or not; and it was only by looking forward to the hour of release each day and continuously going over in my mind all sorts of nice and exciting things that might happen to me on the way home that I managed somehow to sit through the succession of lessons without bringing any undue attention on myself from the numberless and strange adults who controlled our movements for the necessary hours each day.

My revolt against Wilfred and his attempted authority over me had given me a subconscious sense of power and a propensity for violent action to dispel any undesired domination; and it had, I think, imbued me with a feeling of confidence that I was now able to look after myself with sufficient strength to repel any attacks which might be made upon me. Something of this may have shown itself in my bearing, for I did not encounter the molesting meted out to other new infants. Something of my infant reserve impressed the teachers, and I was left very much alone. It was not until later in other schools and in other towns that I was to encounter the hatreds and dislikes of teachers and fellow schoolboys.

At this time I found my real happiness on my journeys home, which were as usual unaccompanied. This gave me a freedom of action and thought which was denied me at home or at school. I would wander around the poor and shabby streets and garbage-strewn alleyways which abounded in the district, peer and stare into the windows of all the fusty little shops and corner stores I could find, and would wander over adventurous-looking pieces of waste ground and empty building sites. This exploring of mine caused consternation at home, and it was Wilfred who was driven out to find me. This angered him for it disturbed him from his own pursuits, so that immediately he found me, and this usually happened when I was walking happily about somewhere quite off the right way home, he would vent his irritation on me, lecturing me on my stupidity and hectoring me for my lack of brains in losing my way. This was untrue as my deviation was always calculated and I was never by now at a loss to find my way back through the confusing streets and always did so successfully on the occasions when Wilfred missed me. He would sometimes report unfavourably about my conduct to my mother and when I was questioned I came out with one of my simple statements and told them that I liked walking about in strange places before I came home. This was too much altogether and I was plainly told that I was not telling the truth and doing so in order to cover up the real truth—that I was unable to get home without losing my way. This was accompanied by much cajolery from Wilfred and my mother to force me to admit it, but I could see no reason for admitting something that I knew only too well was not true. Had I complied and satisfied them with an admission of inability all would have been well and gentleness would have been offered me and arrangements made to bring me home. However, I resolutely refused and my reputation for stupidity and waywardness increased. Also, I had no intention of completely giving up my small explorations and became exceedingly clever at timing them so that I was just home before alarm or annoyance set in. This worked well and apparently suited everybody. This characteristic of mine of offering simple and perfectly truthful statements when explanations of my conduct were demanded was to get me into serious trouble and difficulties in the years to come, and the simpler and more straightforward they were—from my point of view—the more they infuriated the people to whom I offered them, so that my excuses were classed as prevarication or downright lying with unpleasant consequences for me.

The family as it grew up tended towards some curious divisions of loyalty. My father's love for his first-born was extremely real and a lovely thing, but the passionate determination of my mother that all of Wilfred should be hers alone embittered my father's love for him and explained the cold and antagonistic attitude he took, not so much towards Wilfred, but more towards his future ambitions and endeavours.

I think my mother was, without realizing it, unscrupulous here and it was only an inbred dignity of conduct in my father which prevented open strife between my parents.

Even this in later years could not prevent undisguised irritations, and some show of hostility regarding anything connected with us children. This was always most noticeable over Wilfred. I think the experience my father gained over Wilfred, his first child, had brought to him some vague awareness of what was happening, and he took pains to combat it over me his second son, and in this way to secure more of me for himself and thus lessen conflict. The only daughter, Mary, most likely because her life was despaired of so often, was not to be engulfed so deeply as Wilfred and I were, and they seemed absolutely happy to share her. Colin, the baby, too, seemed more immune, although the ceaseless petting and fussing that my mother lavished on this infant always annoyed my father intensely and very often brought angry but controlled rebuke from him. But I do not think it went a great deal deeper than this, for I am sure that by now my father, feeling that he had been thwarted of his share of Wilfred's affection, was striving to gain what he had lost in him through me. He had, I know, most scrupulously avoided favouritism as long as he was possibly able to do so, but my mother's stubborn and unbreakable determination to exclude from him all that mattered in Wilfred forced him into it. Although this more or less petty hostility between himself and Wilfred was to remain always between them, it was not even thought of by either of them as an open rift. It never was one, and it was only the drag of different loyalties which prevented complete understanding between them. Even in spite of this, they were to approach so closely at times that only the narrowest space separated them. This applied in a less marked degree to us other three, always with the difference that we seemed able to find common ground in which to narrow the gap more frequently. In spite of all this pettiness, affection remained constant, perhaps because realization of each other's difficulties was never far away; instead, the perpetual shortage of money was always with us and bonded us together. Downright poverty and total lack of security continued to eat into my father's vitality and initiative, so that to him it seemed that all his life he must for ever improvise and never plan, and it was the immediate monthly balancing of salary against outgoing which became almost the only cause for concern and consternation. He fought this losing battle, and his own perception of what was happening, most fiercely; but he was, I think, too intelligent to deceive himself, and the optimistic and cheerful display that he cultivated was quite the most deceiving thing about him and deluded many people, especially my mother and Wilfred, and blinded them—to their perpetual loss—to the deep melancholy and emotional awareness which was his most closely guarded secret.

My father was to show considerable stubbornness over small ideas which became fixed in his mind and to exhibit a determination and pride which seemed to us out of all proportion to the importance of the matter. These rather curious conceptions were to unfold themselves as time went on, and one of the first of them to affect me was his wish that all his children should be first-class swimmers. The rule was made that we should all be able to swim the breadth of a swimming bath at six years old and the length before reaching eight years. He was himself a really fine swimmer and could do anything in the water, and so as a few visits to the swimming baths were a very cheap recreation, he was able to indulge in this amusement. Wilfred had been put through this routine and came through it extremely well, showing a lithe aptitude for the water; this gave my father enormous pride and pleasure. This was not however shared by my mother, who could never quite reconcile herself to this swimming business, and most particularly to the ritual that my father insisted upon taking place some time midway between achieving the swimming of the width of the baths, and before we were able to swim the length. This meant that a future and definite date was fixed, and on the appointed evening the victim would be taken to the baths, led up to the deep end, picked up bodily by my father and thrown in from the middle diving board. My father would then plunge in and proceed with the rescue. The date for this test of courage was always fixed well in advance so that he could give us full instruction as to our conduct upon hitting the water. This he would do at great length and with full details of action. In this way he built up a sort of family event and painted the picture so well for us—he was always rather good at this—that he had each of us in turn quivering with excitement, not of course unmixed with a delicious sort of fear of the whole affair. My mother was very much against this throw in and rescue and did her best to persuade my father from carrying it out on Wilfred, but he was firm and the affair went through well, Wilfred doing better by far than was expected, and it ended happily—especially for Wilfred as my father took great pains to magnify and enhance

Wilfred's share in it. He did this to all of us in turn so that it became important, and it imbued us with a fine sense of achievement about our babyish swimming.

My own introduction to swimming did not commence so happily and very nearly ended in tragedy. It was my father's habit when going swimming to bicycle to the baths; this was to offset the extravagance of the price of the bathing ticket by saving the tram fare. Accordingly, one evening he announced that he was taking me to the baths to teach me to swim and that I would ride on the back of his bicycle. I was delighted, but my mother was very angry and a real altercation took place between them before my father finally had his way. Altogether it was a very bad start. My father was in a dreadful temper, and clanged and banged the bicycle about, lifting it up and hitting its forewheel hard down on the ground. He eventually freed it and practically hurled it from the shed to the pavement. After striking half a box of matches, he managed somehow to get the lamp alight. The next business was to get both himself and me on the bicycle at the same time, and after many false starts we wobbled off into the dark street. He was always an atrociously dangerous cyclist. We swerved along the level and careered down the hills for some distance. By this time a cold drizzle was falling and I was getting numb and wet. To make it more difficult for me, the lamp now chose to throw back streamers of flame. To avoid having his face scorched, my father would suddenly throw himself backwards, nearly pushing me off the back. However, I managed somehow to compensate for this fresh hazard and clung on. We had negotiated the tram lines and traffic fairly successfully and had reached the quieter streets near the baths when the wretched smoking lamp, which was really on fire now, went out with a final spout of burning oil. My father somehow dismounted us both and grasped hold of the lamp which immediately retaliated by taking the skin off his fingers (it must have been nearly red hot), causing a fresh outburst of fury as he dragged it off and flung it with great force across the road where it hissed and sizzled in the gutter. My father now became calmer and we walked across to examine the damage to the lamp. After pushing it around with his foot to cool it, he picked it up and tried to relight it. After some attempts he finally gave this up, and debated silently as to how to proceed now, and I think it was typical of him that it would not occur to him to return home. Apart from giving up, which was alien to him, the unspoken triumph of my mother would have been too unbearable, so we remounted and staggered off again with the lamp out. By this time, I was shivering with cold and thoroughly wet and miserable. It may have been my numbed coldness, or having no light, or my father may have hit a pothole or the kerb: anyway, my heel was suddenly imprisoned in the spokes of the wheel, the bicycle went over with a splendid crash, and we found ourselves in a confused heap on the muddy road. My heel was still entangled in the wheel, so my father freed me, and moving out of the traffic to a safer position struck matches to examine our damage. A thin piece of skin was torn off my ankle and there seemed to be a lot of blood. He, too, was pretty badly grazed, but after cleaning ourselves up we went on, I limping along and my father wheeling the bicycle until we arrived at the baths. My father led me along the echoing corridors, so filled with the wet smell that is peculiar to swimming baths, our footsteps resounding rather frighteningly. However, the humid steamy warmth was pleasant after the cold outside. I was awed by the shimmering, greeny-yellow depths and the great expanse of the bath itself. My heel was hurting me a great deal, and I was by now wishing very much that I could be safely at home with my mother. After a few words with the attendant, to whom my father was well known, this individual took himself off leaving the bath to my father and me. There were no other swimmers and not likely to be on such a night. Inside a dark little cubicle my father donned his bathing costume which he had brought with him, helped me to undress and producing a tiny double triangle covering which he had brought for me, threaded it round my middle and tied it at the waist, and before I really knew it my father had me in the water. After the first gasp I enjoyed it, my father suspending me flat on the top of the water by a hand under my chest. After a few minutes of this, I was set down on the steps of the shallow end and my father told me to watch while he swam up to the end and back. All was well the first time up and back and he, I suppose, thinking I was quite safe, turned to swim up again. It was at this moment that I expect I felt that I should like to follow him. Anyhow I was tired and cold sitting on the steps and the water was warmer. I remember that what he was doing seemed so simple to me, and without any realization of danger I pushed myself off the steps and into the water and, of course, immediately sank to the bottom. Except for an astounded surprise and a green chokey feeling that drifted into blackness, I remember nothing till I woke up being held by my father upside down, suspended by my heels and water pouring out of my mouth.

My father had not missed me until he turned at the end of the bath, he then had to get back to the shallow end, find me and fish me out. He and the attendant, who had been frantically roared for by my father, must have done efficient work on me and I was soon able to be carried to the attendant's kitchen where I was wrapped in a blanket and toasted by the fire. The attendant's wife administered hot milk to me and menacing rebukes and threats to my father and her husband—two very frightened men.

After some time, during which I had fallen into a dazed half-sleep, the woman dressed me up again in my clothes and wrapped me up in a shawl, and we set off for home by tram-car. I am sure when we arrived home my father did his best to gloss over and make light of the incident, but he was quite the worst dissembler I have ever met and probably ended by recounting every detail. No more evening excursions to the baths were taken for some time, and I do not think that Wilfred was ever taken again by my father. My father had not at the time made me feel in any way to blame for what had happened, but this happy state did not last and later I was to be continuously reminded and rather nagged about the extreme stupidity of my conduct and, worse still, my father now seemed to take this view and as usual Wilfred was contributing his share of the scoldings. I think this really was a family conspiracy to try and instil into me some sense of self-preservation. It had not been so long ago that I had eaten a large quantity of poisonous red lead. It was only due to Wilfred's quick information to my mother and her prompt action in tickling my throat with a feather, that another disaster had not taken place. I think they were getting a little tired of my propensity for dangerous situations. But it made me feel rather forlorn and miserable and this was not helped by Wilfred's stern authority.

My mother was still in very indifferent health and often seemed not well enough to take full charge of the family. Added to this, the baby Colin was causing great anxiety for he developed a bone weakness in the legs which necessitated visits to specialists and treatment, and this ate up the last bit of my mother's slight inheritance. It also meant difficult journeys for my mother, carrying the little boy in her arms to Liverpool; eventually it was necessary to encase the rickety legs in heavy iron splints to try and straighten the present bowing of the leg bones and prevent further deterioration. All this caused much extra work for my mother and constant broken nights, as the infant Colin was fretful under the heavy iron and liable to damage himself in his sleep. In this way Wilfred was delegated more and more frequently to take her place and generally act as nursemaid to us younger ones. This constant responsibility for the care of three infants was really becoming too much and added—rather dangerously—to his already natural seriousness of outlook. It also led to the assumption of an authority which was altogether unnatural for his age. Assumption is quite the wrong word here, for he did not so much assume this authority as have it thrust upon him, by the force of our family circumstances. This assumption of adult authority which he so quickly absorbed pleased my mother and she encouraged it. It displeased my father and he did everything he could to discourage it, but my mother's influence over Wilfred was the stronger.

It was somewhere about this time that it was thought necessary for my mother to go away for a holiday, and to make this possible a slatternly woman was imported into the house to look after my father and us children. This was the first of a series of sluts who were to be inflicted on our home during the next ten years or so as helps for my mother. This holiday of my mother's was a disastrous and utterly miserable few weeks for me. Mary was too delicate to go for walks and Colin too young, so it was arranged that Wilfred should stay at home and look after them both. This meant that I must go for my walks with this slatternly female, and of course in this way I was completely at her mercy, which no doubt fitted in well with her certainly irresponsible and most likely unsavoury designs for her own entertainment. Every afternoon after an early mid-day meal, we would set off on a dreary journey to a locality unknown to me and at which we arrived only after long walks, short tram drives, and a final weary trudge through some low district until we came to a small park with broken-down seesaws and so on for children. Here the woman, having given me some cautionary ill-tempered shakes, and with instructions to await her return, abandoned me entirely and I was left to amuse myself as best I could. This I found impossible, most likely because I was overtired. I could only wander about kicking at the stones, tin cans, and rubbish that littered the small area of so-called grass. Sometimes I would just stare at the other children. But I was already too wise to make any overtures and in any case I disliked everything about them and only wanted to get as far away as possible from them. After a few hours this woman would collect me and we would start off on the dreadful journey home.

These outings were cloaked for me with a nightmarish quality that gave me a feeling of unreality, and an uncertainty that was hard to bear. When we arrived home I was too tired to eat or sleep and could only sit in moody silence which was interpreted as sulkiness. This was given credence by the woman's lying account of my continuous misbehaviour, but I was too unhappy even to deny this or care what any of them thought.

After about two weeks of being dragged about by this woman, nature came to my aid and developed in me real weakness and a violently sore throat. For some reason or another I was not put to bed, but laid each day dressed in my clothes on a sofa in our only living room. My throat very shortly became almost closed and was too weak to move. My father saw me for a few minutes each evening, and although illness must have been obvious he did not recall my mother or call in a doctor. He was always rather bad at owning up to illness in us children. I am sure that it really was a desperate sort of feeling on his part that if it was not recognized it would go away of its own accord and save the dreaded expense of doctors' fees. My mother, on the other hand, was inclined to fuss us, especially Wilfred, as it rather appealed to her to think of him as delicate. This concern was usually misplaced and little action was taken except to cry wolf to my father too often, with the result that it only made him swing the other way. Anyway, I was left on the sofa to pull through more or less as best I could. I remember the awful feeling of guilt I had and how wretched this made me. I expect the horrible woman gave me callous ministration of a sort, and Wilfred, who was only a small child himself, trotted back and forth with endless glasses of water and held me up while I fought between thirst and the pain of swallowing.

When my mother returned the woman was quickly sent packing and I began to make progress. As soon as this happened, my father, I expect because the worry of expected expense, which he could see no way of meeting, was diminishing, began to take notice of me and to try and entertain me in the early evenings. He would recount to me stories of India and his hunting expeditions, of which I never tired. He would read me children's stories too, and it must have been this that laid the foundation for his reading aloud. This was to become a feature of our family life which was to continue for many years. He developed a natural aptitude for these readings, enjoying them intensely himself. His voice when reading aloud was soft and low and quite different from his conversational one. The words flowed out smoothly and every sentence had meaning for us. The readings were not frequent and did not degenerate into a daily routine; they were kept as a special event and fixed for a few days ahead, which made my pleasure and excitement more acute, and I stored away the thought of the coming pleasure as something to be taken out and enjoyed beforehand. *Uncle Remus* was always my early favourite. He took us through most of the other children's classics, but Br'er Rabbit and Br'er Fox never lost their allure and reality for me. At the beginning, Wilfred was content to listen to my father, but he was soon reading for himself and gradually dissociated himself from the gathering and in time came to prefer my mother to read to him alone. After the readings were over, my father would ceremoniously prepare for us what he liked to call sailors' fo'c'sle food. This ritual was carried out with full seriousness, and only on these occasions. Bowls were produced, the kettle boiled, slices of bread diced into exact squares, a lump of dripping placed in the bowl underneath the bread and the whole covered with boiling water. After a few moments to brew, we would attack it with great gusto and we thought it was the finest food we ever had.

With the petering out of our Sunday visits to the docks and ships after my father and I had said goodbye to our lovely barque, my father found himself at a loose end on Sundays, and this probably made it easier for my mother to persuade him to undertake some Church work. Apart from his occasional solos, he was averse to this sort of thing. However, to please my mother, he commenced the undertaking and conducted the older boys' classes in the Sunday School. This, of course, meant that us children had to attend on Sunday afternoons, in the junior and infant classes. Wilfred and I abhorred this, and could only be dragged to them under protest. Wilfred, I think, disliked the teachers themselves; I was not old enough or actually interested enough to feel this, but the fusty smelly dreariness of the Church rooms formed my chief repulsion. This phase did not last very long. My father was not good at mixing with the other Church enthusiasts and disliked the whole atmosphere. He met with open disapproval from them through his habit of talking to his boys' classes about ships and sailors and foreign ports— instead of instilling the Gospel as he was supposed to do. As most of them were sons of sailors or stevedores, this was not unnatural, but he soon gave up the work. It was typical of him that he kept in touch with the boys themselves and visited them in their homes. Even after we left

Birkenhead he regularly corresponded with them until they were killed off, one by one, in the First World War.

My mother's object in trying to establish my father's interest in church affairs was partly religious and partly social. The social aspirations of my parents were curiously divergent, and this helped to build up a very fortunate oddity about the family which was to follow us into each district and social stratum in which we were to live, and was an immense and lasting benefit in preventing us as a family from getting caught up and eventually swamped in any small-town social clique with its inevitable provincial mannerisms and narrowness of outlook. Our peculiar circumstances, too, always disallowed us from fitting in properly. Either we were living in a slum area where we obviously should not have been, or else in a very nice sort of district that was just beyond our means, so that the only way of remaining there was to avoid entertaining in a social way. For this reason we very largely excluded ourselves, but not quite altogether, from the very people whose society we should all have not only enjoyed but benefited from as well, all of which caused some mystification to surround us as a family. It also left us wide open to accusations of the unforgivable sin of being different wherever we were placed, and this led to some avoidance of us by those who would have liked otherwise to draw us into their own circle. There is no doubt we did possess a baffling oddity as a family and that our peculiar circumstances succeeded in putting us out of our element. I can see now how socially classless we were as a family during this early Birkenhead era. It seemed that we really belonged nowhere, which left us lonely and somehow isolated in a most pronounced way so that we tended to hold aloof from our immediate neighbours, and our struggle for existence threw up another barrier between us and the other people with whom socially we should like to have mixed more freely and on equal terms. Later on in Shrewsbury, when a semblance of affluence came to us, we were able to some extent to counteract this, but in the Birkenhead days this was impossible and we lived a rather lonely and exclusive life, which of course left us very much dependent on one another in our family life and cemented us together very tightly. My father, even so, did make some efforts to build up if not friends at least acquaintances, and contacts which were interesting to him. However, these were drawn almost entirely from seafarers and as they ranged from stranded Lascars through boatswains, ships' officers and captains, to ship-owners, this again only emphasized our classlessness; but my mother could never bring herself to enter with my father this atmo-sphere of the sea or understand his passion for ships and sailors, so that these efforts of his were usually abortive.

There was a far more serious aspect to this lack of social companion-ship. My father in his official capacity was constantly in touch with his professional seniors, as well as other influential men, many of whom—especially the latter—were eager to help him, for in spite of his dis-interestedness in railways they recognized his integrity and ability; but his natural reserve of manner was accentuated by the realization of his inability to run the sort of household that the implementing of these contacts necessitated, so that these proffered friendships and influences, which could have brought about so much, were broken off short. If he could, instead, have cultivated these spheres, his career during this critical time might have advanced very swiftly instead of taking the laborious course which in the end it had to do.

In spite of all this he was, when still a young man, offered an appoint-ment as Director and General Manager at a high salary of a small rail-way company that had not yet been absorbed by the big companies but was still in hostile competition with them. To have accepted the ap-pointment would have severed him for ever from all the big companies, and although his position with these was tenuous, nevertheless it was the only small security he had. He was extremely tempted, but the risk of the wealth of the powerful companies overwhelming the small one was enormous. He debated the decision for some time, but in the end the invalidism of my mother and the responsibility of his young family decided him that he would not be justified in accepting the post. The danger of the small company collapsing was too great. If he could have been certain of even five years' tenure he would, I know, have taken the post.

He was by now a fairly senior official and head of his own depart-ment and therefore able to take Wilfred and me down to the railway whenever he liked and, after instructing some foreman or other to keep some sort of eye on us, he would leave us alone to wander about and amuse ourselves. Wilfred never liked this very much and, I think, thought of it as a waste of time. I myself found the great station rather grim and I disliked the resounding noisiness of the high vaulted roof-ings, so that it had none of the allure that the ships and docks held for me. Anyhow, my father did not encourage these visits very much and Wilfred soon stopped coming altogether, although he was sometimes deputed to take me to the station in the mornings until I was old enough to find my own way there. After he had delivered me to my father he would take himself home again, and I would stay in the station until my father was ready to take me back with him. It was a cold black and grey place practically on the banks of the river Mersey itself. In fact there was an unloading quay attached to the station, probably used to unload engine coal from barges. My father would often walk me along this quay and the menacing grey waters would come slapping up against the unprotected narrow stone side. The wind was always blowing and I did not like the place much. When I was older my father would detail me for childish duty, patrolling this quay to watch out for coal thieves. When this happened, I would dutifully walk up and down, always cold and often shivering, and try to overcome my fear of the powerfully sucking and seeking water—I never really succeeded—as it slapped and reared against the parapet in dirty grey waves, sometimes licking my face with greedy salute, to recede again with disappointed sucking moans.

My policing role was an entirely negative one, for the daylight thieves, anyway, were always children, tiny ones with ancient faces, wizened by constant hunger, sent by their parents to steal pieces of coal. These undersized little humans with matchstick legs and arms showed astounding cunning, and the eyes of them all—both boys and girls— had the brilliant wariness of rodents. I did not of course realize this at the time, but years later when I had ship's rats to deal with, I was always reminded of these Birkenhead child thieves. The similarity of tactics— the furtive peering from behind cover, the tightening of the eyes as they calculated chances, and then the perfectly co-ordinated unhurried speed as they moved into action—was disconcertingly the same.

Occasionally my father would catch one of these skeletal little creatures red-handed, but when he did the fire went out of him and except for a cursory order for the disgorgement of obvious lumps he took no action except to shoo them gruffly away—the lumps cleverly hidden between their tatters and their dirty little skins went with them. Upon some of these occasions my father would have business in Liverpool, and would take me with him; I would trot along by his side. To get to Liverpool we had to cross the Mersey by the great steam ferry boats which clawed their way across crab-fashion. The approaches to the ferry from the Birkenhead side always filled me with disquiet and often alarm. These were, I think, covered gangways on the pontoon principle. Whatever they were they seemed to me unstable and the constant surging motion of the water under my feet I found hateful. The noise of the huge paddles and the fumbling uncertainty with which the ugly boats came alongside gave me a forlorn feeling which I did not like. In mid-stream, my father would point out different ships to me, perhaps to cheer me up; but looking at the grey turbulence of the river with its wide stretch of cold, hungry-looking water increased my small depression, and even on sunny days the river only seemed to assume an artificial brightness. To me nothing could ever quite hide its starkness.

Not a great many years were to pass before I myself was helping to navigate cargo ships out of and into the river, but familiarity and even a seaman's interest never wholly overcame my intense dislike of this river. All the other rivers and estuaries from the great Hoogli in India, the Rio de la Plata of Uruguay and Argentina, the creeks of Guinea, and the Straits of Magellan, to enchanting London river itself, all of which I was to know so well, always had something to give me, but the Mersey was to remain for me morose and sombre and completely unromantic and always retained its power to fill me with uneasy apprehension. This I think is more remarkable because it was in one of the creeks of this river that the beautiful barque had lain, the ship that my father and I had visited with such joy—the sight of which had brought to me my first awareness of romance, and the parting from which had brought me my first knowledge of sadness. I was to find later that it was the actual river itself, and not its docks and warehouses and ships that caused my foreboding. Wilfred, I think shared my childish dislike of the station and the Birkenhead approaches to the Mersey, although of course we were too young to discuss it at the time, but even Woodside was to hold a red-letter day for both of us—one of the few of our early childhood days when we shared delight equally, and when our difference in age (which was rather noticeable at that period) was forgotten, and my shortcomings overlooked.

During public holidays when the travel rush on the railways was very great, my father had to station himself some distance down the line, probably to give himself better control, and for this purpose he used a lonely cabin abutting on the railway lines. On one of these occasions, he decided to take Wilfred and me with him. He awoke us very early and took us to the station on a workman's tram. At the station a light engine was waiting especially for us. We were hauled up on the slithery foot-plate, the engine gave friendly little tootings, and we puffed off.

Almost immediately we were into a long dark tunnel, and when we emerged into daylight again we were allowed to drive. The engine driver and his fireman must have been very nice friendly men, looking to our safety and going to pains to see that we enjoyed ourselves. Wilfred and I were loth to leave the engine, and would not do so until we were assured that this was only a first run and that many more were to follow. Inside the cabin was a roaring fire and a fine smell of boiling coffee and stacks of thick sandwiches. The various inspectors, signalmen, porters, and so on, who kept coming in and out of the hut kept plying us with these and saw to our constant entertainment in many other ways. On top of all this pleasantness, we were allowed to rake the fire and pile on as much coal as we liked, a most satisfying diversion in itself. Every hour or so either the light engine would come for us, or another passing train would be stopped and we would make the trip to the main station and back.

Word was now passing up and down the line about the two little boys who were travelling on the footplate. I think Wilfred's small dark gentleness and good manners rather intrigued and fascinated the burly gangers and men. Possibly, word got about too much for my father's peace of mind and later in the day we had to crouch down by the side of the cab shield and so keep out of sight when we entered the main station. We did not arrive home until well after dark; we were tired, and smothered in soot from the tunnel and oil and grease from the engine.

This excursion was not repeated, for I think my father had hoped to smuggle us about more or less unnoticed, instead of which we had made impressions everywhere and created quite a small stir. This did not fit in with my father's plans at all, and I think led to some awkward queries. However, it was smoothed over, but I think that he thought it was wise not to take us again. This was perhaps not such a disappointment as might be expected, either to my father, Wilfred, or me. This particular day had just been one of these accidental happenings when all the details had fitted happily to make a pleasant whole, and had no foundation in an attraction for Woodside Station or anything to do with railways; detestation for them remained in all three of us as strongly as ever.

I think it was more for the sake of my small companionship that my father would take me with him when he supervised the monthly loading of horses into railway vans. These always took place on Saturday afternoons and entailed a long journey on foot over networks of railway lines and through labyrinths of dirty railway buildings and dreary patches of waste land littered with refuse, in order to reach the depot where the loading took place. The loading itself could be an unnerving experience and my father did not enjoy it. We were sometimes trapped inside a corral arrangement and I was often very frightened indeed. The great beasts would come tearing in, rearing and plunging in crazed fear. The men handling them with inadequate halters were pulled about all over the yard. Quite often the horses would break loose and then excited fear would enter into me, pandemonium would reign and often near-panic when the infuriated animals lashed out in all directions, splintering woodwork and shivering iron railings. Men were often slightly injured and sometimes very seriously. I became accustomed to the sight of blood from both beast and man. My father would render first aid for minor gashes on the men and I would assist by holding the bandages for him.

My father was extremely agile and when danger threatened would whip me up like a little sack and flash me to safety. We must have had some narrow escapes but we were never hurt. When the loading was over, I always had a fine feeling that a whole month was in front of me before we had to do it again. This gave me a rather uppish elation and on reaching home I was inclined to boast and exaggerate my bravery in the ordeal. This braggadocio of mine seemed to annoy Wilfred, who would never come with us, and caused my mother alarmed exasperation over my father's foolhardiness, and I have no doubt it diverted my father who, unless my version became too fantastically coloured, did not give me away. Anyhow, he was in need of bolstering up himself and disliked maddened horses quite as much as I did.

During the time we lived in Birkenhead, which lasted until Wilfred was fourteen and I between nine and ten, we were able as a family to take some holidays in spite of the financial difficulties that beset us. I think my father must have budgeted very carefully for this and it was made easier by the actual cost of travelling never having to enter into the calculations. My father in his official capacity was entitled to free passes for the whole of his family once or twice a year, and greatly reduced fares at any time to any part of the United Kingdom. This gave us unlimited choice of district, and as it was possible in those days to get rooms for very small weekly sums, which included the cooking of the food which we would buy ourselves from the local shops, a holiday did not need to cost much. Doing it this way added very little extra expense to what would have been spent if we had remained at home. In spite of this, we must have been living so closely to our income that some years had to be missed. When this happened we children would be sent alone to relatives, or my mother would take one or two of us either to her own or one of my father's sisters. One of my earliest recollections is of being taken with Wilfred by my mother to spend such a holiday with her sister and brother-in-law in a residential district in London. I can vaguely recall the fuss of the journey and I distinctly remember Wilfred's sailor suit and wide-awake hat and the horse-buses. It was by changing from one to another of these that we reached our destination some distance from Paddington.

It was, though, the real family holidays which filled all of us with joy and happiness. My parents must have made real and unselfish efforts to make these weeks of holiday—there were only two of them each year —a really happy delight to us. They seemed able to radiate some power of freedom and enchantment that they never seemed able to do in the sunless streets of Birkenhead. My father's tired irritability which was so marked in our ordinary life was replaced by a boyish excitement which infected us all, and my mother's somewhat perverse and contradictory attitude to all my father's ideas and projects turned to a sweetness and compliance which was wholly delightful.

For one of these holidays my father took us all over to Ireland again, this time to Tramore, a small village near Waterford. They had secured rooms in a white-washed fisherman's cottage. It was perhaps the best of all our times. The fisherman and his wife were quite perfect hosts, and the accommodation though tiny was pleasant. As a family, we were happily divided in pursuits. The mornings would be spent bathing. My father and Wilfred, who was now good in the water, swimming; we smaller ones submerging ourselves in the surf with occasional swimming lessons. There was a hut on the sand that we used for undressing. In this my mother, who never bathed with us, made coffee and provided biscuits. In the afternoons we would separate, my mother and Wilfred going on short walks, or more likely reading together; the baby Colin would be put on the bed to sleep with Mary in charge of him. My father and I would put out to sea in a small boat for the fishing. The evenings would be spent all together in a pleasant languor.

Several rather dramatic happenings marked these particular two weeks which, in retrospect, made the period seem much longer than it was and provided us as a family with much comment and recapitulation for years to come.

The first drama took place during a morning bathing time. The wind and sea were very rough, and although begged by my mother not to swim and advised in the same way by the few fishermen about, my father refused to be deterred and all of us had to enter the water, Wilfred being made to accompany my father the ten yards or so into deep water which was his recognized limit. Wilfred was very soon in trouble, and it was only by courageous struggling on his part, encouraged by my father, that he was able to get back into shallow water, and from there be carried to safety by one of the men who had waded out to meet them.

My father, instead of being at all alarmed over this, was exhilarated and triumphant, flinging himself about all over the beach, blowing sea water through his moustache with roaring noises of expelled breath and between gasps he would break out into song, and with much chest-beating would persuade us all that this—battling with rough seas—was the only life worth living. When he had calmed down and regained some breath, we smaller ones were taken out one by one and given our duckings through the rough breakers. The fishermen who up to now had watched my father's antics only with a sort of astounded awe, now gathered together and became openly apprehensive and remonstrated with him, begging him to stop bathing while this dangerous sea was running. This was the worst thing that could have happened, for he was always intolerant of any suggestion that might impugn his prowess as a swimmer or his ability as a waterman when in charge of a boat. His answer was to dive straight into the heavy waves and strike out to sea for one of his foolishly reckless swims. We four children were left shivering on the beach to watch.

We must have strayed apart and become separated. Another fisherman had come down, found the baby Colin alone and miserable—it was now pouring with rain—and taken him to my mother in the hut. Being a fatherly man he had shut the door of the hut and remained inside to help my mother rub some warmth into the small creature. In the meantime my father returned to the shore exhausted by his foolish bravado, horrified to find only three children instead of his four. Instant panic and alarm broke loose. My father shouted to the fishermen, who were scattered now, that his baby was in the sea. A boat was launched and my father dived and searched methodically, getting farther and farther out. The sea was now high with a dangerous ebb running. In the end, he himself was rescued by the boat and in an almost drowned state brought ashore and helped up the beach to the hut, only to be confronted by a Madonna-like picture, the missing infant nestling warmly and nakedly in my mother's arms.

The relief from anxiety and the realization that he himself was to blame caused my father's temper to flare. He was quietly furious with my mother for being in the hut instead of outside, enjoying the rough sea—and of course watching his swimming—and stormed at the unfortunate man who had collected Colin, demanding to know from everybody—the other fishermen were all grouped around us now—if he was not competent to take charge of his own family. By now he was stamping backwards and forwards, and with clenched fists waving above his head demanded of heaven why a man on holiday could not enjoy a quiet swim with his children without all this fuss, interference and womanish timidity. . . . The fishermen's mouths were hanging open by now and convinced that they were dealing with a madman they were galvanized into flight. It was typical of him that later when he had cooled down he sought them all out in their cottages and apologized sincerely.

The excitement and fear that Colin was in the sea of course frightened Wilfred very badly, but he had kept his head splendidly and taken charge of Mary and me and with one in each hand had dragged us along making frantic search up and down the water's edge. We all recovered very quickly and quite enjoyed the safely-past excitement and local notoriety.

Before the holiday was over I was to furnish another excitement in my own peculiarly careless and brainless way. I was standing in the garden of the cottage one evening when I saw a boat beaching, and without looking either way I shot full speed out of the gate and across the road, down which two jaunting cars were travelling at great speed. The drivers were racing abreast. Almost under the wheel, I felt the heat of the first horse on my cheek. Instinct pulled me up dead and prevented me trying to pass the second which would have been impossible. Instead, I turned and passed between the two wheels and ran across behind the second car, making a lightning letter 'S' movement. It had all happened so instantaneously and with such smooth and spontaneous action that far from feeling disconcerted, I had an ecstatic feeling of elation and of something superbly achieved, and I continued to skip along happily towards the boat.

My mother had been sitting in the cottage window and seen every-thing and of course was really frightened. Hurrying across the road, she collected me and, holding me by the hand and scolding me very severe-ly, dragged me back to the cottage. I was now in angry tears for I did not want to leave my boat, but my mother was adamant and continued to impress upon me how impossible my naughtiness was becoming. Once in the room of the cottage my mother changed and became very sweet and gentle and with great tenderness tried to impress upon me how Jesus had saved my life, but my glorious moments had been ruined by her severity so that I did not somehow feel in the mood for Jesus. In any case I thought it most unfair—if there was any praise going at all—that Jesus should have it; I was quite certain myself that it was not Jesus but my own superb letter 'S' manœuvre which had got me safely across the road. My mother's crossness must have made me aware that I had done something wrong, but her description of what might have hap-pened to me, instead of frightening me, only made me think even more highly of my own agility. My mother, perhaps perceiving now that she was only causing me to compete with Jesus for the honours, tried another tactic, painting a frightful picture of what might have happened to me if God had not been watching over me . . . I should have now been a small mangled child, cut everywhere and covered in blood and laid out in a sort of little bundle on the side of the road. . . . I was a bit frightened about God being brought into it. It seemed to me I had quite a fellow-feeling about Jesus, but I did not much like the sound of God; this misgiving, though, was swamped by the vividness of her picture of me spread out on the road. I became absolutely entranced and could see myself quite clearly lying there in a sort of splendid importance of mangled bloodiness. I remember I added a good many more pools of blood myself just for good measure . . . this vision was so splendid to me, I was enjoying looking at myself so much, that something of this pleasure must have appeared in my face and bearing. This my mother misinterpreted and she became terribly distressed and very angry with me. She was of course—so deep was her religious feeling—genuinely frightened for me. I was made to get down on my knees, my mother doing likewise, in order to beg forgiveness from God and Jesus. This I was quite agreeable to do as long as I could leave God out of it, for I badly wanted to get back to my boat. We had just got our knees com-fortably settled when in burst my father demanding to know what on earth we were doing in a stuffy room on an evening like this when we ought to be down by the sea. . . . I was sent out of the room, and later on my father joined me by the boat. He gave me a gruff homily about upsetting 'your mother' so often, told me to look where I was going in future, and then dried up.

He was always amazingly unconcerned about any physical dangers or risks any of us children might encounter, and never became upset or angry over them. It was only some personal misconduct in any of us which made him not only cross with us but really very angry.

Chapter Four

IRELAND

My father and I went out fishing almost every afternoon, rowing or sailing miles out to sea to the dog-fish grounds. The fishermen hated these fish, as they did so much damage to their nets. In revenge they perpetrated horrible cruelties on them. We were line-fishing, and the first we caught were only of moderate size. The men in charge of the boat proceeded with the customary practice of hacking off half the fins and half the tail. This was done so skilfully that the fish could neither die quickly nor get sufficient food, and in this way they died a lingering death; or they would partly disembowel them and throw them back for their own kind to eat alive. My father was horrified at this terrible and useless cruelty and insisted on their being killed outright by stunning and, when senseless, decapitated and thrown overboard. Indirectly this was to lead to something which became of great local interest for many months to come.

On one of these days our boatman, knowing the weather was set fair, suggested that on the following day we should make a dawn start, for if we did this they could take us to another fishing ground much farther out to sea. I was tremendously excited about this, so that when my father came to call me the next morning he found me already struggling into my shorts and jersey. He himself was not much less excited, and so anxious was I not to be late that I could hardly wait to drink our scalding tea, and with our slabs of thick bread and butter still in our hands we set off for the harbour.

For the first few hours we caught only the usual-sized fish, until suddenly my line tore through my hands, burning my fingers badly— I was into a really big fish. My father and one of the men sprang to help me. I refused to let go, but the man forced my hands open and placed them over his own, and later they bound my hands with canvas so that I could hold on. It seemed to me hours while the fish was running until it turned and we hauled in the slack . . . I remember shouting at the men not to let my fish go. . . . After a long struggle it broke surface, threshing the water into a boil ten yards from the boat. I was almost delirious with joy and excitement. The boatman proclaimed it to be a shark. It gave us many more furious runs before it could be brought nearer to the boat, but it was still fighting dangerously. Our fishermen now suggested we should cut the line. They thought it too dangerous to try and bring it over the side and my father, for once, agreed, for these fish unless handled with extreme skill will tear a poisonous bite with their jaws and can inflict severe injuries with a flailing tail.

My cries of rage and disappointment at losing this marvellous prize— caught on my own line too—were so emphatic and so despairing that they all relented and it was decided to get it aboard somehow. After many more runs the men took a turn around the stem with my line and made the fish take the weight of the boat until it began to tire, and the line was gradually shortened until they were able to bring it alongside. Telling my father to look after me, the fishermen with great skill some- how got it inboard, immediately partly smothering it with a heavy sail. The tail was then secured and the head viciously hammered until it lay still. I could barely contain myself, and could not bear the idea of con- tinuing with any more fishing that afternoon. All I wanted was to get ashore as quickly as possible and show my prize to the others, so we put about and headed for the harbour. When we had tied up at the jetty of course the problem of disposal came up, but I quickly settled this by my determination not to be parted from the great fish and demanded that we should take it up to our rooms. There was some demur about this.

The early return of the boat and rumours of a big fish had got about so that we were soon surrounded by everybody near the slipways. My intense excitement and refusal to be separated from the fish infected the crowd and they were touched as well, I think, by my enthusiasm for their own calling. They commenced shouting to one another, excite- ment began to run high, and very soon in their emotional Irish way they had created a sort of carnival atmosphere about the whole happen- ing and were prepared to go to any lengths to see that I had my own way. A rope was secured to the head, a lighter piece of line was bent on to the tail, which I was given to hold to mark my ownership; the men laid on the heavier rope and the parade set off dragging the capture along behind us. Excitement spread and we were soon joined by most of the village men, women, and dogs who, forming up behind us, cheered us on in triumphant procession until we reached our cottage.

My mother and the others were not quite as enthusiastic as I had expected them to be, and the woman from the cottage naturally even less so. She flatly refused to have the dead creature in the wide passageway inside the cottage where I wanted to keep it. However, there was an outhouse adjoining into which it was finally hauled, and the door shut. This was an even better arrangement for me and every half-hour or so I would run out to inspect it. At first one or two of the others would come with me but when they tired of this I would go alone which I liked doing very much, for then I could contemplate it with silent admiration and re-live the excitement of the line running through my canvas-covered fingers. Wilfred showed a surprising interest, making much of my exploit which gave me a nice warm feeling. I continued these visits of adoration until late in the evening. It was on my last visitation before I was to be put to bed that it happened.

It was almost dark now, I opened the shed door, my fish was gone—or so I thought until I heard a wet slithering noise on the stone floor and peering into a dark corner I saw a greyish white upright shape. It was the fish standing on its tail. Even as I drew in my breath and cried out a bit, the wraith-like thing slipped to the floor with a wet slapping noise, but instantly it was up on its tail again so that it appeared to be walking around the shed. When with its next convulsion it lunged towards me it was altogether too much—the transition from death to life was somehow horrible . . . with a sob that was barely half strangled I leapt out of the shed slamming the door behind me. I rushed into the cottage, calling out that the fish was walking about the shed . . . perhaps it was my unfortunate phrasing, anyhow I was met with utter disbelief; I was scolded, too, for making up such a ridiculous story and Wilfred was told to take me up to bed, but I was insistent. In the end—to pacify me—Wilfred came along to the shed, and when we got near he too heard the wet slam of the slapping fish as it fell about. Wilfred didn't like it any more than I did—holding hands very tightly we crept to the door, opened it a crack, saw the ghostly gleam as the thing reared and flopped: this time it was Wilfred who slammed back the door, and we ran to the house calling out for them all to come quickly. My father, excited now, came running out, the fisherman following with a lantern.

Inside the shed the fish seemed weaker; it was still moving about but not so violently. With the shed lighted, the comforting bulk of my father on one side and Wilfred still holding my hand tightly on the other, I was no longer afraid, the creature itself did not now look so fearsome. Its opening and closing mouth and slight gasping noises made me, in a childish way, only dreadfully sorry for it, and guilty that I had brought all this about—perhaps some recollection of my father's anger with the men's cruelty to the dogfish we had been catching was in my mind. As I looked at my fish now fighting to live I could not get out of my thoughts the terrible blows that had been hammered on its head when we had got it into the boat . . . I was instantly consumed with a desire to get it back into the sea and let it live again.

The fisherman at first was dubious but perhaps something in my passionate appeal to my father may have moved him, or more likely he saw in this a permanent and happy ending to the whole affair. The aid of another boatman was secured and, all of us helping, we set off through the darkening village street on the haul back to the sea. It was quite dark when we reached the jetty, but we could just see to slide the fish off the end into deep water. After the water settled we could make out the ghostly grey gleam of it just under the surface as it rolled in the current. In launching it, while removing the heavier line, they had forgotten to take off the light line that had been knotted around its tail for my benefit.

The next morning fishermen in the bay reported that the fish had been seen near the surface swimming weakly but most certainly alive, the piece of line still attached, making identity absolutely certain. Local interest had been aroused over the little English boy's catch, and the amazing fact that it had recovered life after having been apparently killed in the boat and then kept out of the water for over nine hours revived the excitement, and the little boy's fish became a local legend and something of a mascot. It was never molested and was watched with great keenness. I was to see it three or four times swimming more strongly each time. It remained in the bay, cruising near the surface. Some injury it had been dealt by us may have caused this. Altogether it was sighted, but at longer intervals each time, over a period of eleven months, after which it was not seen again.

The interest in the episode sustained itself in the village, as such trivialities sometimes will in small communities. We were to know this because after we had returned home the fisherman got his wife to write to us from time to time. We were told the episode even reached the length of being commented upon in the local press, although we never saw a cutting.

Altogether this special time in Ireland seemed to hold small incidents memorable for all of us in one way or another, and it was I think in many ways momentous for Wilfred, for he was now just old enough to be permanently influenced. It was probably during this time that he became conscious of his allegiance to my mother and of his reluctance to confide in my father.

This of course was a natural enough sequence to our gravitation as a family: my father—because we responded so eagerly to outdoor distractions—looked towards us younger boys; my mother, herself inclining to indoor recreation, tended more and more to encourage in Wilfred his already natural inclination to remain indoors and not join in with us in our lighter outside amusements. In this way it was inevitable that he should be drawn to look to her to provide his quieter interests and this undoubtedly made him—in those early years—unduly dependent upon her. Mary, perhaps because she was an only girl, slipped into a neutral position able to flit without effort from one of these opposites to the other.

It is then probable that it was during this holiday in Ireland that the powerful influence of my mother made its first permanent impression on the little boy Wilfred. Until now he had been too young to be really indented, but it was here that his affection became demonstrative so that he began to seek means of expression for his admiration and devotion, which was tending now towards adoration. Thus, instead of joining us others, he would wander off by himself seeking wild flowers and fern leaves and returning with these he would strew them thickly on the garden path from the cottage door to the gate so that she should always walk on flowers. My father, Mary, and I, on one of our early morning wanderings—he would have us out of bed at five-thirty on these holiday occasions—had found a glade of wild iris growing in beautiful profusion in some boggy land on the banks of a stream. My mother and Wilfred were taken to see them and my mother, who possessed an almost ritualistic passion for flowers, was enthralled with the stiff purple and yellow flags. Wilfred, too, was fascinated by them and until the end of our stay he spent many hours each day collecting them and their swordlike leaves and arranging them around the rooms, my mother helping him. Sometimes the tiny room would have the appearance of being wallpapered with living flowers.

My mother usually rested during the afternoons, lying on an old-fashioned sofa, and Wilfred discovered a special enchantment by persuading her to feign sleep, then covering her completely with masses of the wild blossoms.

I knew later, or at least held the happy conviction, that all this unremitting attention—the flower-strewn paths, sometimes festooned arches in the road itself, the adornment of the sleeping figure—was not entirely original. There was too much of a classical flavour about it to be this; it was the outcome of the mixed stories read to him by my mother and his own advanced dippings into literature. At this early age his desire, which was to be so pronounced later, to experiment, to put into actuality the fleeting conceptions that tantalized his mind, was emerging and showing itself in these demonstrations. This does not lessen his absolute affection for her in these early years, though it does I think explain his obsessional attitude. But my mother never suspected any other motive except altruistic devotion to herself. The truth probably is that it was much of both, but there was a quality about this devotionalism which was too adult in an aesthetic way, altogether too classical and legendary, to have been an original conception of a child's mind.

My father I am sure mildly disapproved of all this, and the obvious segregation which was taking place, and would have preferred Wilfred to join us in our fishing and bathing; but his deep-rooted loyalty to my mother prevented him from actively attempting to stop it. Upon occasions his irritation over it all would flare into exasperation, which always vexed my mother, and although it would be wrong to say these explosions ever frightened Wilfred, they did make him draw into himself and away from my father.

Before our holidays finished, a curious and rather unpleasant experience befell us, a triviality notable only for its isolation. I say isolation purposely for never in the whole of our family life, either before or since, did anything of a similar character ever brush us. It was something, too, which affected us all in exactly the same way, and this in itself is noticeable, so rarely did we react with such similarity; again, it was something which happened while we were all with one another. It was at the very end of our time in Ireland and my father, who was extremely fond of having his whole family together and about him—especially if it was to mark something such as this, the end of our holiday—had with one of his rare shows of determination insisted that we all walk for a few hours together. At the back of his thoughts in his own rather secret imaginative mind he did, I think, want to make a picture for himself of us all in some happy connection so that he could carry back with him to the smoke and dirt of Birkenhead an image that would perhaps give him courage to face the twelve months of anxiety and the constant irritation of uncongenial work which he knew inevitably must pass before another holiday took place. But like so many more of his little plans and projects for our happiness and entertainment, this idea for a final walk together had no success.

It is significant of our family patent that so many of these simple schemes that he thought out for our enjoyment and happiness as a family—if they involved all of us together—seemed to crumble, and only bring him disappointment. This really was a great pity because this wish for our happiness sprang from a sweet stream that ran somewhere deep inside him. Even when circumstances did seem to combine to make things go well, his temperament so often prevented him from putting forward his suggestions in an attractive way; with only one or two of us he would often be quite different. His diffidence made him clumsy in presenting either himself or any of his ideas, and often resulted in his becoming cantankerous and changeable. If there was a journey involved his fuss would approach panic so that he would storm at us all for our dilatoriness—indeed my mother and Wilfred often deserved his censure for they were both of them irritatingly liable not to be on time. My mother could never be clever over this weakness of his—she seemed only capable of adding fuel to his already furious fire. We younger ones secretly revelled in these exhibitions of tantrums, and with great naughtiness did all we could to increase the tempo, very often with most satisfying success. When this happened my father would become very red in the face, he would hold himself very straight and stiff, and with bristling politeness, inquire of no one in particular if there was any chance of getting this expedition started, or had he perhaps made a mistake in the day—might it be tomorrow we were preparing for ... muttering imprecations he would march out of the house stiff-legged as an angry turkey cock, flinging over his shoulder a parting injunction to us to please ourselves whether we came or not, he himself was off. ...

However, this last walk together in Ireland which he had proposed started quite happily, perhaps because we were all a little quiet and sorry that our holiday was over. My father chose a direction with which none of us had so far become familiar. After some time we came to the opening of a narrow lane and following this up we found it brought us to the broken-down entrance gates of a forbidding looking avenue bordered on each side by dense woods. The drive itself was obviously in disuse and heavily over-grown. We walked into this place in quite good spirits until we got some little distance up. It was immensely long and dark; the trees meeting overhead roofed it so that the effect was of a rather dark tunnel. The weather which had been bright with sunshine suddenly changed and became theatrical—great dark clouds must have swept up swiftly and covered the sun, huge drops of cold rain came down, pattering on the foliage with a disagreeable tattoo. Inside our avenue it suddenly became very dark, a bleak feeling seized hold of us all and we became very silent though not fearful at all, and continued on our way, but not very happily—at least I certainly was not, I was disliking it all more and more the further in we penetrated.

It was I who caused the first feeling—not I think of alarm but more a sensation of something strange that caused a curious apprehension to pulse through us all. I brought this about by calling out in a stifled voice that I had seen something large and animal-like moving along a branch high up in one of the trees. Curiously enough, my rather frightened ejaculation was accepted by the others as something almost expected and not with the derision that would have been normal for an outburst of mine like this. Wilfred, following my pointing finger, confirmed me, and almost immediately my father did the same. We all saw it move again, then freeze into immobility as if conscious of our concentrated stares. Horrid cold prickles were running up and down my back which made me long to run and get away from this strangeness and Wilfred was trembling and almost as frightened as I was. I remember we were all instantly frozen into a horrid still silence, which we could not break, and we recalled afterwards that we were all of us holding our breath. It was not until we heard the muffled roar of heavy rain emptying itself from a burst cloud that any movement by ourselves released our paralysis. The violence of the downpour broke our tension and in itself made a curtain between us and what we had seen in the tree. We were uneasy and could not speak, instead we only stared in the direction of the tree. When the rain stopped, the curtain lifted; what we thought we had seen was no longer there, but the space where it had been was frighteningly clear. . . . My father, coming to himself, immediately took charge and with forced hilarity tried to break the spell and cheer us all up with light-hearted explanations of the tricks light and shade could play in trees and how deceptive these could be.

My mother was now quite desperate to get out of this dark wood and return to the friendly village, but my father would have none of it. The rain had now stopped and he was absolutely determined to find out what was at the end of the drive. We children were not now actually frightened but an apprehension and chill oppressiveness had settled on us all. This was emphasized by our surroundings of thickly growing woods which gave us a trapped feeling as we went deeper into the increasing narrowness of the avenue; we were, we thought, getting shut in under this dismal dripping canopy. The water from the cloudburst was now rising up from the warm earth in spirals of pearly coloured vapour which twisted and turned in slow convolutions among the trees and undergrowth. We continued walking along this seemingly endless tunnel, but after some little time it seemed to grow lighter, the trees were becoming thinner and now and again there were open spaces that had only brushwood and no trees. Soon after this the drive, which was dwindling to little more than a rough track, took a sharp right-hand bend and shortly afterwards another—this time to the left. After we had rounded this last curve, we came into open bare-looking ground and were immediately faced with what appeared to be a sheet of water. It was separated from us by about thirty yards of stony foreshore. It did not somehow quite look like real water; instead it had the metallic sheen of polished gunmetal. The whole effect had the eerie quality of a mirage. This was accentuated by a strange high wall of mist which cut across the water in a perfectly straight line. In this way every bit of background was obliterated and in some curious way it seemed that behind this mist there was just nothing at all. The effect was of utter unreality. This dream-like unrealness gave it a weird mystery and some menacing threat of danger that produced in us all a sensation of being warned. So strong was this feeling that we all closed up together and then remained motionless; we did not speak but just stood and stared. I am certain that we remained in this trance-like state for several minutes until my father, shaking himself a little, spoke to us (his voice, I remember, was not quite firm), telling us that this nonsense of being frightened of nothing had gone quite far enough, and throwing some jocular remark that had a merry challenge in it, he started off towards the water. The rest of us were instinctively holding hands and, still under an inexplicable spell of some sort, followed along just behind him. We had perhaps gone half way when we realized that the water and the wall of mist were receding from us at exactly the same pace that we ourselves were moving. The strangeness of this stopped my father—immediately the water and the mist became stationary again, only now the whole scene had taken on a transcendent appearance as if it was not really there at all but superimposed over the rough open space. . . . My father was anxious now and my mother and Wilfred were trembling violently; we younger ones were, I think, more unhappy than frightened. It was darkening now and there was a chill in the air.

My father advanced once more and the same thing happened—the water and the mist again went back, only this time the normal background of trees and sedgy grass seemed in a horrid way to be coming through as if they were real and solid and the water and the mist were nebulous. This was too much for my mother and, swinging around, she turned to get away from it. It was as she turned that for the first and only time in my life I heard her give a stifled scream. This spun us all around to see, standing ten yards or so from us, the shadowy figure of a tall man. This strange figure seemed to radiate the same cold incandescent quality that even now was permeating the hallucinatory lake. For some inexplicable reason the whole attitude of this illusionary being diffused a mute declaration of his intention to do harm to us and this, I know, gave us all a quite unreasonable feeling of desperate insecurity.

My father must have recovered himself and at once addressed this sinister looking person, I have no doubt with some apology for our trespass if we were committing one. The sound of my father's voice had the unexpected effect of contorting the man into a frenzy of fury, and he raised the heavy stick he was carrying with such ferocious intent that attack from him seemed unavoidable. The surprise perhaps silenced my father and immediately the figure relaxed to its original stationary position. After a minute of bemused silence my father tried again, only to produce the same silent paroxysm. Perhaps it was the unnatural muteness more than the gesticulating that created the cold fear that now held all of us except my father. The rest of us were motionless and speechless but he was now very angry and belligerent and advanced upon this thing or man, with the astonishing effect of causing it to walk backwards away from my father, keeping an unvarying distance. It seemed as though the two of them were synchronized, every hesitation or movement of my father was repeated in a backward direction by the figure who still faced us. If my father retreated the figure came forward. This marionette movement continued backwards and forwards until my father, his quick temper rising, strode forward with real determination until he came to the very edge of the wood. . . . It was now that

1. Mother and Wilfred
    Plas Wilmot

2. Father, Mother, and Wilfred

Plas Wilmot

my mother's despairing voice cried out so urgently 'Tom, Tom, come back, come back'.

At this instant the figure, which had been clearly there until now, was suddenly not there any longer. . . . Our tightness left us, and freedom once again was all about us.

My father we could see was standing motionless. It was something in my mother's voice which seemed to awaken some awareness in him, so that he turned about sharply and then walked slowly and tiredly back to us. We were a very subdued family by now and my father was unusually silent. To add to our depression darkness was falling more quickly than usual. Although still preoccupied, my father with great vigour hustled us together and taking a direction right away from the place, herded us along at a tremendous pace. As he turned us away, we all looked back towards the lake. It was no longer there. He had picked up both Colin and Mary, carrying them one under each arm, and my mother had Wilfred and me by the hand. Striding just ahead of us he forced his way through everything until we came to a road—for once my mother had not protested against his rushing haste.

Once on the road he collected himself again and, bustling us along with much cheerfulness, did his best to raise our spirits. We younger ones responded quite well, but Wilfred—very quiet, sombre and absorbed with his own thoughts—seemed unable to do so. My mother, worried about Wilfred, kept urging my father to get us back to the village quickly. I can remember trudging along for what seemed endless miles and then being lifted into some sort of vehicle; after that I cannot remember anything until I woke up in our cottage rooms.

We were, I think, a resilient family. I recall so well while we were having supper with what gaiety we children chattered in our childish way, and how merrily my father made fun out of the strange happenings. Wilfred was in high spirits and was eagerly leading our excited little arguments. In this way all the horridness of the wretched afternoon seemed to melt away and instead took on the brilliant lustre of adventure safely passed, in which we had all played most splendid parts. With immense enjoyment we were vying with each other to claim for ourselves special importance. In the warm cosiness of the fire-lit cottage room, pervaded as it was with the bright cheerfulness of my mother and father, menace could not touch us . . . in retrospect we could feel no threat. . . . Instead, as our excited babblings embroidered themselves, we began to feel as brave as lions. . . .

Down the years it was to turn itself into a fine family legend, to be frequently talked about—but only amongst ourselves . . . we would never speak of it to anyone else.   We were still chattering and quarrelling happily when the fisherman and his wife in their customary way came to our room to wish us goodnight. After a few preliminaries my father and mother began to ask some questions and commenced to recount some of our peculiar experiences. The change in them both was immediate and astounding—their friendliness was wiped away, their faces hardened, and they gazed at us with such frigidity that it became very near to incivility, muttering to one another in a most furtive way. Surprised, my father, realizing that their whole manner forbade any discussion, stopped abruptly. After an awkward silence they relented a little, and both of them together begged him not to speak of it to anyone at all, and to see that we children did not do so either, and in a somewhat peremptory tone implored him to forget all about it entirely. After another long and difficult silence, during which they stared from one to another of us with looks that were full of curiosity and conjecture, they turned about suddenly and without any of their usual courteous ceremony, left the room.

Early the next morning we started our homeward journey to Birkenhead.

Our return to Birkenhead was the beginning of what was most certainly the most difficult era in our family life. It was to last until 1907 when our move to Shrewsbury took place.

It is significant of these years that Wilfred was more settled both in mind and body than he had been in any of the years before, or was to be in any of the years which were to follow. He was firmly and very pleasantly established in his school—the Birkenhead Institute. As I have said, for a very short time I too was attending the school at the same time as Wilfred. This time was so short, though, that my recollection of it can only be hazy. I should like to be able to recount some close companionship with him during this time, but this did not come about; our difference in age helped no doubt to discourage it, but although it was a day school this in itself is not enough to explain why we did not at any time share, as it were, these school days. It was our altogether different approach to the school—mine the less than average liking for any school, Wilfred's attitude already possessed of the intent purposefulness of a serious student—which so strongly underlined and maintained our separateness.

While my own presence in the Birkenhead Institute created from the start minor upsets both in the school and at home, Wilfred's own unbroken seven years there were ones of absolute tranquillity, by which I mean most especially physical tranquillity. I think as well that these were the only years of his life when he had some semblance of peace of mind. Wilfred's entry into this school had been curiously propitious and from the very beginning, in all the time he was there, unlike me, he never ran counter to authority. This is largely explained by his natural extreme gentleness of manner—there was about him, as well, when meeting or being in contact with other people outside the family, something which to me is only describable as an assured diffidence. This gravity of approach, which remained always in advance of his years, coupled as it was with his attractive appearance (not to be confused with good looks), his thick dark brown hair and small delicacy of build—perhaps a lack of robustness even—gave him an air of over-adultness. I always think of it as his 'small dark look'. All this was with him at ten years of age and had an unusual attraction for all the masters and mistresses who ever taught him. His hands, too, were expressive and peculiarly indicative: they were always clean, blue-veined, white and delicate looking. I never once saw him with schoolboy's hands. Indeed in all my recollections of Wilfred when he was at school I can never recall any impression of a schoolboy: I can only think of him—even when he was only eleven or twelve dressed in school clothes with a schoolboy satchel on his back—as a student.

Inside the family and away from his books the impression could be very different, but again, never schoolboyish. His too high spirits, taking the place of childish naughtiness, were also beyond his years. There was about him a wholly unconscious duality which, upon looking back to this time, makes description of him baffling. With us at home he was devoid of diffidence, often touchy and sometimes peremptory, alternating with these gusts of wildly high spirits. When in the company of his seniors, especially his mentors, nothing of this more ordinary demeanour ever showed itself. At these times all of himself that he ever allowed to be seen was this quiet gravity, gravity which not infrequently amounted to solemnity. The perplexing part is that this certainly was not the outcome of ordinary shyness. It was much more as if he, with serious and deliberate thought, decided that this should be the picture of himself that he would like to present. In later years this duality was often mistaken for shyness.

When he entered the Birkenhead Institute he was—most certainly—a solemn little boy, and although he outgrew some of this solemnity, in all his years at the school he never lost his gravity. All this invariably drew the interest of his schoolmasters and mistresses; it also, as I know now, often slightly disconcerted them for they found the unnatural seriousness difficult to place satisfactorily. His diffidence, which was unconnected with timidity, invested him in some unusual way with the power to demand serious consideration even as a little boy. It was I think his expression, especially the expression which would come into his eyes when addressed—always thoughtful and sometimes sombre, with no hint of a childish twinkle—which mostly contributed to this presence: presence of course is too strong a word, but always there was something in his bearing which earned for him an entitlement to be treated in his own right as a person, and could thus single him out from a mass of schoolboys. This being so, it is to me quite remarkable that his passage through the school should have been so smooth and uneventful.

His demeanour during these Birkenhead Institute schooldays, and later when he was at his other school in Shrewsbury, could so easily have been mistaken for priggishness. For all of us at home, of course, this would have been an impossible mistake to make. It is true that although in the language of that day and of our age he was always to us 'the old book-worm', it never did or could occur to any of us that anything in his attitude of mind could contain any hint of priggishness. Indeed his mercurial moods—alternating so suddenly through the cycle of depression to the gayest hilarity—denied most emphatically even the remotest suggestion of anything like this. If anything else was needed to refute it his attacks of bad temper, always brought on by dissatisfaction with himself, made it quite clear—sometimes uncomfortably so—that in him priggishness could not live.

It is true too that he was so often dissatisfied—and never hesitated to say so—with the attitude of mind of us others, especially with mine which of course was a much more usual one. He would often lecture us and sometimes rate us over our casual sort of outlook. In our family life this disapproval, never mild and often furious, was accepted as part and parcel of our old 'Lone Wolf'. We did not lack the ability to give back, in the opposite direction, as good as he gave to us. It was all so wholesome that it became traditional. Later on, in memory, it became something much more which all of us cherished.

Wilfred lacked always the only basis upon which a prig can be formed—self-satisfaction. From infancy, through boyhood and during manhood, dissatisfaction with himself remained inherent in him. Many of his railleries and admonishments of us were, I am certain, only a roundabout way of scourging himself. It is difficult when talking of his boyhood, and more difficult when writing about it, to relate these happenings, and most especially his unboyish attitude, without somehow leaving a faint smear of priggishness. Disassociated, as writing and talking must be, from his warm aliveness at the time, these factual descriptions of him and his actions tend to take on an aspect which is wholly false. Wilfred did quite unknowingly lay himself wide open in this way, which makes it so much more unexpected that his attitude to his schools did not bring upon him normal ragging and harrying. Looking back, to me it is astonishing that this attitude—almost classical in its invitation—did not, even in the early years, make him a prey to this sort of thing. It never did. Of course both his schools being day schools did make an enormous difference. I do not think that in a public school, certainly not during his early years, he could have escaped. I myself was never able to keep out of these schoolboy troubles of one sort or another.

I did not see much of Wilfred while we were at the Institute together. He was preoccupied with his lessons and I was preoccupied with my efforts to keep out of the difficulties which I felt at this time were always lurking around some corner for me. As well as this, Wilfred had formed a close friendship with another boy, Alec Paton. This boy was another of the quiet, studious sort, intent always on his books, and like Wilfred eager to win high places in all his subjects. The friendship, once formed, lasted closely throughout their schooldays, and they spent much time interchanging visits to one another's homes.

While superficially they appeared so much alike, fundamentally they were very different. Alec, unlike Wilfred, was slow and laborious both in his work and all his other activities. Although Wilfred, like Alec, would labour away at his books and on the surface appear equally absorbed, always in him was the hidden fire which once poked would so quickly flare and throw out sparks; but with Alec, poke as much as we did at him, the most we ever got, and that rarely, was a curl of damp smoke. On account of his natural lethargy we younger ones always called him

'Alec Slowcoach'. They went up in the school together, always very close in their subject markings, sometimes one in the lead, sometimes the other. Scholastically they were keen rivals without a trace of antagonism and spent much time together helping each other with their weaker points. It was a good friendship, beneficial to them both, based I think upon mutual respect rather than on any affectionate impulse.

In 1905 they went on holiday together to Rhewl, visiting I think an aunt and uncle of Alec's. It was Wilfred's first time away from home on his own. It was from here that he wrote these three letters.

Glan Clwyd,
Rhewl.

Aug. 7th 1905.

Dear Mother,

Thank you very much for the boots, which I received this morning. It has been so wet here that I changed my shoes and stockings 3 times on Saturday and Alec & I put our feet in hot water when we went to bed. Our feet were only just a little damp, & Mr. Paton laughed & said they were all right, but Mrs. Paton made us change. (Don't tell any one this!) At first, before we got to the farm the place was not what I anticipated, we had to go through, not along, a dirty, wet, muddy lane. But the farm is fine. I am very happy but I am not wild. We are both kept under great restriction. We got up a ladder on to a hay-stack in a Dutch Barn. In case you don't know what a D.B. is, I will draw one.

Well, we made little nests on the top but Mrs. Paton heard us moving the hay & soon called us down. (Mr. P. laughed.) I am asked to thank Mr. Owen for the f.rod. It is useless now! We cannot fish!! No lisence!!! Is it not sad!!! Alec's Uncle broke my rod, it is mended now. He was fishing this morning when a river ~~Bal~~ bailiff came up and told him something about how to fish, thinking he had a lisence! You have to pay 15 or 16 shillings for 1 to fish *I* think. This is a filthy letter, all blots. Thank Mary and Colin for their letters. I slept in chair bed 1st night but I do not now I sleep with Alec.

From your loving
Wilfred.

Aug. 16. 1905.

Dear Mother

I am so sorry you were not well on Sunday. I thought about you very often, nearly all day. We climbed Moel Famma (Varma) on the 14th. I was rather exhausted by the time we reached the top. It was about 4 o'clock, started at 11.30, but when we got home I was hardly so bad as the others were. Alec made a show of sliding down the smooth slippery grass, but he found he could not stop himself. He went bounding on till he was suddenly checked by a sharp stone wall. We thought he had hurt his head, but he had a deep cut on the knee, he said he was able to climb the hill though! I was lying down at the time, resting. Thank you very much for the letter & Turkish Delight. I have had a little bad luck. Up Moel Famma I lost my big fat knife I think. I am very sorry to say I broke the end of your umbrella. We tried to fish with the end of our rods in a tiny stream that runs into the Clwyd. I lent Alec a hook which he lost, & I lost my own, & cracked the tip end of my rod. I have bought a Picture Postcard for Harold which I hope to send tomorrow.

With best love to all
From
Wilfred.

Aug 22nd 1905

Dear Mother

I hope you are all quite well I am eating tremendously. We went gathering nuts this morning I have got, altogether, 113. I am going to bring them home for the children you must not tell them please. Mr. Jones has bought 120 sheep today. They are so tired after walking three days that some will let me stroke them. I can count up to ten in Welsh, & have learnt a few expressions. It will soon be time to milk the cows now. I can milk a bit. I drink buttermilk for dinner, & have cream on the stewed fruit. Indeed I fare very sumptuously, & I wish Mary was here to eat the plums we get off the tree every day. There are nine little piggies. You would be amused if you saw them. Their heads are too large for their bodies & their tails are like curly bits of string.

We are having fine weather now I am very glad of the boots, because in the morning the grass is wet. I have not been to Ruthin yet. When I go I want to

buy a little tiny boat to sail down the Clwyd. It is nearly time for the post now.
With love & kisses always
from
Wilfred.

These letters are indicative of him at that age—the care to enclose in brackets the correct pronunciation of Famma, his intention to learn Welsh, his use of unchildish words like 'anticipated', 'Indeed I fare very sumptuously' and, at twelve years of age, his reference to us as 'the children'.

Out of the general vagueness in my mind of these Birkenhead Institute days, one or two memories stand out clearly. I cannot recall ever walking to or from the school with him. Possibly our times were different, in any case for the going I was most likely dispatched early in order to give more time and space for my mother to deal with the troublesome business of getting Wilfred off. Even in these days he would stop in bed until the very last moment, rush downstairs to the breakfast table and, with a book in one hand swotting something for the day's work and a cup in the other, make a pretence of breakfast, my mother meanwhile urging him to eat and at the same time packing his books into his satchel and trying to get him off. When it seemed it would be impossible for him to get to school in time he would rush out of the house and with surprising speed would get to school. I do not think he was ever late. Unlike Alec Paton, who if he once became late for anything would remain so until the end of the day, Wilfred always had this almost startling attribute of quick and sudden action. It had a startling quality because at one moment he would be deeply absorbed in a book and the next, slamming it down or more likely stuffing it into his pocket, he would take instant and decisive action. We younger ones used to speak of the slow movements and inability to catch up time that was so characteristic of Alec Paton as his 'mooniness', which indeed was an excellent description. There never was anything 'moony' about Wilfred so that all his life, notwithstanding his deep engross-ments and preoccupations, there was always latent in him this un-expected verve.

Our returns from school must have been in character too. I with my liking for finding new ways home and exploring the different streets would set off with this in mind, thinking the time very well spent. Wilfred, though, would tear back from school, thinking only of how speedily he could get home and return to whatever subject was absorb-ing him at the moment. To him transit to and fro was a waste of time. The fears which were to haunt him so desperately in later years had their beginnings here: the dread that lack of time or death itself would prevent him from doing all he must do was starting to ride him.

After his death many people attributed this trait in him to the war, thinking it to be just what assailed all young fighting men—the infinite probability of death. This is wholly wrong. It had its beginning in Birkenhead, and it will be seen later how much these thoughts occupied him—at one time morbidly so—in 1910 and 1911, long before any hint of war came in 1914.

Chapter Five

BROXTON

I HAVE some memories of Wilfred in the playground and they are all quite similar. He would be standing talking to Alec Paton, alone or sometimes in a group of three or four, and it always seemed to be quiet talk for they would remain like this, hardly moving about at all during all the breaks. I never saw Wilfred or Alec play. The pair of them or the small group of bigger and more serious-minded boys were seemingly unaware of the yelling and screaming of the rest of the boys around them. When, as sometimes happened, some tail-end of a horse would accidentally charge them they hardly seemed to notice, but would move quietly out of the way without any interruption. Throughout my term or two at this school Wilfred and I did not mingle much and his attitude to me was one of gentle aloofness; almost at times it seemed that secretly he would like to disavow me. There was nothing of disdain in this, it was much more as if my constant blunderings made him realize that I did not fit in with his own more serious plans. I felt no resentment, but merely put it down to the 'Old Wolf's' funny ways, and it was here that our feelings took a new turn . . . . Even at this early stage we were all finding ourselves as a family—except my father—making allowances for Wilfred's many departures from ordinariness. Amongst us, 'his funny old way' became an expression which explained everything to all of us to our complete satisfaction, and only increased our tenderness—which we healthily took care to disguise—and love for him. The fact is that we were already tending to think and feel that he was in some way different.

One of these memories has remained with me down the years—written down, it does perhaps sound rather silly, but the impact upon me at the time must have been so strong that after his death it returned to me with increased vividness. It was when I was walking about the playground, not thinking of anything special, that I saw some distance away Wilfred and Alec standing talking together. I remember the thought came to me with a rush; there was something about him that made me think how very greatly he looked like a young prince—the thought could not have been an original one, most likely it was connected with some of my childish reading, but there must have been something in Wilfred's attitude which gave foundation for it, and it did rush into my mind as I looked at him standing so very straight and somehow dark and serious. The day was overcast, the asphalt of the playground was wet with rain so that its blackness shone and threw up an illumination around him, accentuating his erect slimness. The contrast between him and Alec was emphatic and striking. Alec, round-shouldered and stooping, very tall and lanky, looked unvital and exactly what he was, a gangling, untidy schoolboy. The small dark Wilfred, although so still and quiet, yet threw around him this fiery quality of vital dignity. I felt a tingle of pride and affection for him cut through me . . . to dispel it I whooped at him rudely.

I was to figure in one more incident during my short time in this school with Wilfred which gained me some notoriety. It came about as usual through my incurable propensity for coming out with my—as it seemed to me—perfectly simple and truthful statements.

Oddly enough, singing was given as a lesson once a week. This was taken by one of the junior masters who I suppose was musically minded. Although I enjoyed so much hearing my father sing I always very much disliked singing myself, and as I had such a distaste for it I could not see why I should ever do it. The lessons had started off with the whole class singing together. I did not mind this at all for by saying the words to myself and moving my lips at the same time, I had no need to sing. But one morning this arrangement was changed and each boy in turn was called upon to sing a verse or two alone. This did not dismay me. Knowing that I could not sing, and anyway that I so disliked it, I had no intention of trying to do so. When my turn came, still quite at ease, I stood up and said, 'Sir, I don't sing thank you very much indeed'. A stunned silence fell over the classroom which astonished me for I had expected my polite statement to be accepted quite ordinarily and without comment. The young master was staring at me in a tensed way in this absolute silence, satisfied, I suppose, that I was not trying to be either impertinent or clever. Then he suddenly collapsed into peals of uncontrollable laughter and hugging his middle with both hands kept repeating between gasps, 'Sir, I do not sing thank you very much indeed. Sir, I do not sing, Oh, my goodness, I do not sing, Sir, I do not sing'.

By thumping on his desk with his clenched fists he made great efforts to control his laughter but it was no good, by now the whole class had taken up the refrain and the noisy uproar became rampageous. I, still surprised at this astonishing effect, remained standing. As soon as he was able to do so the young master staggered out to get help from a senior. When he came back with him, whether it was the sight of me standing up so solemnly, quite unmoved by the hysterical mirth, or whether it was the ingenuousness of my answers to his questions, I do not know, but very soon he was as incapable as his junior and forthwith we were all hurriedly driven out into the playground.

Later on I was sent for and with nothing more severe than sarcasm told that as my muteness seemed of such very high entertainment value, it would seem a pity to spoil it by enforcing vocality. I would therefore be excused any further solo efforts. I was gratified and relieved by the exclusion, but I still did not see anything funny about it. However, as it gained me so much notoriety from all sides I was pleased as a small boy would be. Had I been able to remain in this school for a few years, I think my educational problems would have been very much simplified.

Wilfred taxed me with this singing experience and gave me a solemn lecture about the advisability of conforming to the rules and customs of the school, saying that this habit of mine of always trying to be different should cease immediately. Wilfred would never even then say 'Chuck it, you ass', but would always bring in some heavy-sounding phrase. This habit was to develop into a rather ponderous form of address when talking to me and often included some stuffy quotations. When he did this it made me cross and disagreeable with him. I did not know then or until a long time afterwards that he was even at that age using—with calculated purpose—these long words and heavy-sounding phrases in the form of an exercise in order to accustom himself to the sound and feel of unusual words. Later on something of this was carried on into his letter-writing which accounts for a certain flamboyancy of style.

Wilfred most certainly was aloof with me during this time, but to soften this he would sometimes in his inimitable way lay his hand on my arm or squeeze my shoulder, giving me his little brown half-smile, and when this happened it gave me a warm happy feeling. These gestures were only fleeting, in a moment he would walk off to join Alec or the usual quartet of bigger boys, with the intention, I have no doubt at all, of inflicting on them his cumbersome words and flowery phrases that I myself hated so much.

One final memory remains of Wilfred and the Birkenhead Institute. It must I think have been wintertime while I was there, for the most distinct remembrance I have of the inside of the school is one of yellow-lighted corridors filled with gaslight that came from wall jets which hissed like snakes and flared like ghostly butterflies. We seemed to meet quite often in these echoing passages. I did not like their cold unfriendliness at any time and when they were gas-lit I hated them. If I was deporting myself well he would only hurry past me with a broody look on his face, but if I was careering through as I usually was, to keep my spirits up, he would frown at me with severe disapproval.

I did not think I should remain very long in this school. At home it was constantly being impressed upon me that compared with Wilfred I was doing very badly indeed, and it was an open topic at meal-times whether it was really worth while keeping me there. I cannot remember being resentful about this; I had not had time to get to like the place a great deal, and secretly I didn't think myself that I seemed to be doing so very well. This constant reiteration by the family only confirmed me in my growing sensation that I never should do well at school. I don't think that I minded this very much either; anyhow, I could not under-stand what Wilfred saw in it all. What did rouse my childish fury was when I was blamed for bringing upon myself these 'silly'—'silly' was a family word much applied to me—situations, and when they paraded first Miss Foster, then the 'assault', and now the 'singing business', I would stamp my feet and rage back, for I could not see that in any way they had been brought about by my own doing; to me they had been something that had happened. If my father had not stopped me before I had time to get it in, I would always end by turning to Wilfred and storming at him that he could keep his old school and have it all to himself. This would usually bring down on me the threat that I would be taken from the school and sent once again to a free board school. I did not mind all this very much except that I had now made a friend for myself, and I did not want to lose him.

This was Matheson. I don't know quite what our mutual attraction could have been, perhaps it was because we were both unusually keen on running and got tremendous exhilaration from forcing our small bodies to travel across the ground at the highest speed we could drive them at, and would often make two other boys hold a piece of string as a finishing-tape. As we were very well matched, it caused quite an interest during the breaks. In between times and often in the road when on the way home—for our routes lay part-way together— we would crouch down with immense assiduity to practise getting off the mark, which drew amused comment from passers-by. Running remained my only interest in pure athletics; as it was my one and only feat I am still pleased that seven or eight years later I did the hundred yards in even time, but as the timing was done with naval stop-watches these may have been in my favour.

The boy's father was a professional man with offices in Liverpool and the family lived in a pleasant residential outskirt of Birkenhead. Two or three times I was collected by him with his father or mother and taken to their home for the afternoon. The atmosphere of the smoothly running home, the space in the house, and tea with its silver appoint- ments served from a silver tray, gave me a feeling of rightness and pleasant importance. The way this understanding family made me feel adult and wholly at ease probably kindled in me my first social ambi- tions. It also gave me a vague and obscured knowledge that life held something more than dirty backyards with grimy grey washing flap- ping wetly in the gritty air and inadequate accommodation, and a reali- zation that these pleasant things were to be found and must be sought.

I cannot now remember whether I survived at the Birkenhead In- stitute until we left the town or if I was taken away before we went. I think it must have been the latter, for not only was I showing so little promise but my father must have been finding it difficult to meet the fees for Wilfred and probably impossible to do so for both of us. Which- ever way it was, as it happened it made little difference, for quite shortly all this and our life in the great seaport was to come to an abrupt and unexpected end.

Before I move us all out of Birkenhead there are fragments of our story which should be brought in here to complete the Merseyside period. It is of course an uninteresting detail, but significant in showing the money difficulties which beset my father and mother during Wil- fred's early childhood. During this time the cost of food for our grow- ing family was a constant anxiety. It became habitual amongst us to apportion out the more expensive foods that made up our meals—in this way the dearer items were made to stretch over long periods; at each meal we would fill up the gaps with bread and jam or syrup, so that it was unknown for us to sit down to a meal and just eat the main—and costly—ingredient until we had eaten all we needed. This also serves I think to emphasize the quality of my parents; in spite of their difficulties and the most uncongenial surroundings in which we lived, they were able to exercise a discipline which maintained a quiet dignity wholly out of keeping with the neighbourhood or our circumstances. It brings to light, too, the strength of the Welsh strain in them both, although these separate influences showed themselves in such opposite ways.

In my father it showed in his love of a well-ordered family life, his determination to pursue his cultural relaxations in his spare time, his engrossment with good reading and his absolute passion for music. He had been so starved of this in his early years that music, in any form whatsoever from the most amateurish chamber music to opera, was like water in the desert to him and he would make great sacrifices in order to obtain it. He would even travel long distances by train (which was free of expense to him) in order to hear the Welsh choirs singing on the station platforms while they were waiting for a connecting train to take them to some choral festival or Eisteddfod. It showed, too, in his absolute insistence upon good manners in us in all circumstances, and he would see to it that we never came to the table, no matter how frugal the meal, unless we had gone through the ritual of hand-washing and hair brushing. These things in most circumstances would not be unusual, and in the Welsh valleys where they originated are only an unnoticed part of their beautiful cultural dignity and seemly way of living, but in the back streets of Birkenhead they were glaringly notice-able. Under his weight of worry and anxiety my father could so easily have slipped into conduct less fine, and the fact that at times he was, through despair, tempted to forgo his own way of living and enjoy— if he could—the tawdry glitter of Birkenhead and Liverpool, yet never did, added fineness to his bearing and bestowed immeasurable benefit upon us children. My father, then, represented the softer and more beautiful side of the Welsh, the disinterested love of these things for themselves and the inner consolation they brought him, and never for what the material reward or advancement might be. He was in all his actions never much concerned with his effect upon other people.

The strain of Welsh in my mother came out differently and, I think, originated from the harder streak that sometimes appears in Welsh blood and took the form of a puritanical intolerance of the wider issues of life, with a concern always for superficial appearance. There was a prudery about it as well that demanded the disguise rather than the elimination of wickedness. In this way she was always concerned with our visible semblance, and especially with the effect that our good manners or our misbehaviour might have on other people, and was inclined if not to relax her severity at home at least to fuss less about it. My father on the other hand would when in public let pass or smooth out any childish misdeeds or culpabilities that he would not tolerate in the seclusion of our home.

My father's constant demonstrations of bad temper had a robustness about them which robbed them of reality, so that we—except on the rarest occasions—never feared them; instead we nearly always enjoyed them. My mother's temper, which could and often did flare up rather severely, lacked the obvious justness of my father's tantrums, and was altogether more upsetting. It was I who seemed to bring out in her this exasperated annoyance, much more so than any of the others. I cannot recall any instance of Wilfred ever really doing so. It may have been the incalculability of my actions, but more likely I think it was her recognition of my opposition to her will that made her in those days always liable to be very, very cross with me. At home this seemed only part of our family existence and so did not have a great deal of effect on me. I quite often thought she was unfair but even this, although it fretted me quite a lot, did not bother me much, certainly not seriously.

When, as did happen occasionally, this crossness and upbraiding by my mother took place in the presence of other people outside our own home, I resented it so bitterly that I would become unmanageable and would stubbornly set my will against her own, which of course resulted in a scene which left my mother genuinely disappointed in me and very angry—I did not mind the anger but her disappointment in me would go on hurting for a long time. All this was to be brought into the light rather disastrously. My mother had received an invitation from some rich old ladies living in Oswestry—they were contemporaries of her own parents—and the closest friends of the Shaw family. They had not really approved of 'their Susie's' marriage, and long silences had ensued. Now, however, they wanted my mother to visit them and to bring me with her. One of them was godmother to one of us.

So it was all arranged and I, who was a sociable little boy, was look-

3(*a*). Wilfred with his sword

3(*b*). Wilfred as a soldier, Plas Wilmot. The Hussar's tunic and tent were made by Mother

4(a). Wilfred with the yacht built for him by Father, now in my possession

C. H. Deakin, Shrewsbury

4(b). Mother and Mary

ing forward to the journey and the day in the country very much indeed. The visit entailed a long preparation by my mother and careful admonitions to me as to my behaviour whilst there. I have no doubt at all that these visits were to her always something of an ordeal, as most of the old spinsters were critical and I am sure always hoping to see signs of their own portentous prophecies regarding my mother's marriage coming true. On this particular occasion I expect my mother was overstrung and more than usually sensitive.

I nearly always enjoyed any of these excursions alone with her, first coming the ritual of being bathed and the brushing and combing, and to me the real joy of getting into fresh clean clothes; even at that age being dressed in nice garments gave me a feeling of well-being and confidence that was extremely pleasant. I was usually dressed for these affairs in white cotton sailor suits that had little short knickers with a blouse and square navy collar; the sleeves were finished with dark blue cuffs and emblazoned with anchors. I liked the crisp feeling and the starchy smell of these clothes and the way the sleeves and knicker legs would be slightly stuck together, but not enough to stop you pushing your arms and legs through and getting the glorious feeling of stiff sharp cleanness. If I had the blouse with the sleeves that were very close fitting around the wrists and just exactly the right length, then I was delighted.

All these nice things had happened on this special day. The train journey had been splendid and the forenoon and lunch had gone off well. The old ladies had been exceptionally kind to me, and I had a fine feeling of being liked by them. I had removed my hat at appropriate times and risen and trotted along to open doors when occasion seemed to demand it. Altogether I felt a success. It was at tea-time that my childish impetuosity was to overtake me and ruin my day. After lunch I had been turned out in the grounds under the care of the gardeners. These men entertained me splendidly by taking me around the stables, kennels, and gardens. They had reserved one special surprise for me as a sort of finale before delivering me back to the house. This took the form of releasing from a loose box a gigantic St. Bernard dog. This delighted me intensely and when I was allowed to fondle it, and then was picked up and mounted on its back, my bliss and enchantment knew no bounds. After walking around the paths, still mounted, we loped in fine style up to the lawn in front of the drawing room. My excitement completely overcame me and I longed for my mother to share this great pleasure with me. Thinking of nothing else except the wish to bring her into this great event, I tore as fast as my little legs could carry me up to and through the open French windows in a mad rush to my mother who rose in horror at my wild and unbidden entrance, snatched off my wideawake hat which, in my excitement, I had not had time to remove, and catching me by the shoulder shook me rather severely. So wrought up was she that the shake was probably harder than she really meant; in my rush it had caught me off-balance, my feet slipped from under me and I went spinning on my hands and knees across the polished parquet floor. What should have passed off as an ordinary scolding now—through the accident of my slipping—took on the look of a rather ugly little scene. There were cries of 'Susie, Susie, you mustn't.' My mother, now terribly distressed, ran to pick me up but I had already gathered myself together and while doing so experienced my first cold anger, for I had thought, as indeed so had the old ladies, that my mother had struck me. I was frightened too by the complete unexpectedness of this sudden twist from pure joy to sudden disaster, and taking my hat from my mother's now unresisting fingers I fled out of the room into the garden.

I had not minded the shaking so much: it was the shock of thinking—so wrongly—that she had struck me, and the indignity of the sprawling that scalded me. It was my mother's rebuff to me by not only refusing to share my pleasure but spurning my offer of it which wounded me so deeply. The dreadful humiliation in front of my nice old ladies was more than I could bear. I stubbornly refused all their kindly pleas and bribes, and resisting furiously my mother's now repentant cajolery, refused to enter the house again. My mother, ashamed of me and the way the unfortunate happening—so trivial really—had developed into something serious, was near to nervous collapse; but by now she could do nothing with me. When sweetness failed she tried sternness to break down my anger. With a sorrowful repentant child to show, her mortification would have been lessened so that something for her might yet have been retrieved from the ruined day, but I could not soften—yet. She was hurt and baffled by my refusal to yield to her. There was nothing that could be done except to take me home. A dog-cart was ordered round and, with my mother quietly weeping now, we drove to the station.

Once more I had spoilt everything, for indeed about her must have lain her shattered hopes for the day, so that in her thoughts was the bitter belief—real to her—that I had disgraced her. She had most likely had a trying time with the old ladies, probably spending the whole of the afternoon in loyal defence of my father and, what is certain, in high praise of her children. It is not improbable that my unbidden plunge into the room came just at the moment when she was eulogizing my well-trained gentle behaviour. She was all her life over-inclined when we were children to build up our virtues too idealistically, not so much in her own mind, nor yet to us ourselves, but in the minds of other people, especially relatives and the old friends from her maiden days. In this way if, when one of us was visiting with her, we defaulted in some way and came short of her ideal, it seemed to her that we fell farther than we really did, and this made her unduly sensitive to our behaviour as she felt any falling away threw a reflection upon herself. On this unfortunate day the climax must have been especially galling for her, as she was, as it were, showing me off, and this for the first time, to old family friends who had so lugubriously prophesied disaster for her marriage.

On the way home my mother's gentle crying and distress and her sweet efforts to win me back in the end melted my stoniness, which was never very hard to do—my emotions seemed to me always to be just at the back of my throat ready to burst out in a flood of ready acceptance of any overture. Once back in the hurly-burly of our family life these tenser moments soon lost importance. In the robust activity of our house they healthily faded away.

There is, though, no doubt that the constant anxiety of looking after my father and us four children, with the ever-present nightmare of bills not yet paid and coming expenses always in the offing, was tautening her nerves severely. It accounted for her intolerant outbreaks over our childish misdemeanours which nearly always seemed to be mine, but then I was always looked upon as the toughest and it is likely that, this being so, I came in for some of the others' share. My father undoubtedly realized how worn and overtired my mother was becoming. It may have been chance or my father may have had something to do with it; whichever it was, a girlhood friend of my mother's from the Plas Wilmot days offered them the use of a small furnished cottage in the hills around Broxton. It was impossible for my father to get away so it was arranged that she and Wilfred should use the cottage; but for the first part all of us were to go together, my father only for a day or so after which he would return home, taking me with him for company.

I can remember so well our journey and arrival at the cottage; for both Wilfred and myself, it was our first realization of summer. Up till now our summers had mostly been days of hot uncomfortable sun, striking up from burning pavements, and hot walks and the warm meaty smell of ashbins spilling over with refuse and rotting tea leaves and vegetables, and the swarming flies. But our first view of the little house gave us a feeling of sweetness and a sense of loneliness. The cottage itself nestled warmly brown in the sunshine and seemed a part of the friendly little green hill that it leaned against. The weather was lovely, with hot sunshine drawing up a greeny brown glow from the bracken ferns that undulated on other little rounded hillocks all about the tiny building. I remember so well the delight I felt when the sweet damp fronds brushed so wetly against my bare knees as we walked up the stone-flagged path to the door. The garden had no boundary and seemed just to reach out as part of the hill-land. The only real things seemed to be the path that helped itself up to the tiny porch with successions of warmly red and green crumbling brick steps and, almost the best of all, the pig-sty with the enormous pig that chortled and grunted at us in such friendly fashion.

That afternoon Wilfred and I wandered in and out of the shoulder-high fern or lay side by side on our backs when we were tired and stared happily at the fat cotton-wool clouds that moved so slowly across the blue sky. That night we were put to bed together in a room so low that we seemed to be lying with our faces on the ceiling instead of our backs to the floor. My father and mother tucked us in with a tenderness that was unusual, and blowing out the candle tip-toed away. We were warm and happy and very sleepy.

The next morning we ran out into thick white night mist that the sun had not yet burned away and we ate our breakfast on the hillside with the vapour swirling about us. In the afternoon my father and mother went to the village to buy provisions for her stay. Wilfred and I gathered the delicate blue harebells and twisted them into sprays with the half uncurled bracken fronds and massed them on the table in the cottage as a surprise for them.

That evening my father and I left them. I can see them now as I saw them then when we turned to wave goodbye—both of them, the little boy and the young-looking woman with her arm around the child's shoulder, both looking so sad to see us go, their two dark heads at such different heights lit up with a warm goldenness that streamed across from the lowering sun.

There was a magic about this day and night in Broxton that spread a softness over us all. My father and mother were gentle with each other, Wilfred and I forgot our bickering and enjoyed each other, fussing together over the two little ones, Mary and Colin, to make them happy . . . it was as if the little house reached out to enfold us all . . . gone were our strifes and small irritations and in their place was only this indescribable welling up of affection which flooded over us. . . .

Years afterwards when we were both on leave, he from the Western Front and I from a battleship in the North Sea, we were to recall with nostalgic bitterness the purity and innocence of those few silver hours.

The woman and the young boy we left standing outside the cottage were to live full, happy weeks in and around it. The weather was perfect and they spent long days in the open and long evenings in the lamplight. Something in the little boy was beginning to stir and quicken. His reading continued, encouraged and uninterrupted, and the restless stirrings were able to emerge with doubting delight. It was in Broxon among the ferns and bracken and the little hills, secure in the safety and understanding love that my mother wrapped about him with such tender ministration, that the poetry in Wilfred, with gentle pushings, without hurt, began to bud, and not on the battlefields of France.

There was I am certain something epochal about these few weeks in Broxton, certainly for Wilfred and I think too for my mother—for him the beginning of realization of a power within himself; for her it marked, I am sure, the absolute establishment of Wilfred's love for her. Until this time he, like the rest of us upon occasions, had rebelled against the strength of her sometimes insistent will. From the Broxton weeks onward there was, between these two, only unvarying accord without interruption. It was a beautiful time for them both. My mother free from the burden of family house-keeping had time to think and perhaps for the first time since Plas Wilmot peace to enjoy and guide the little Wilfred. He, free of the nurse-maiding of us smaller ones, had quietness to stand and stare and the sweet companionship of my mother. They spent many hours either on the warm hillside or in the cottage reading to each other. It was a time of delight and although other happinesses were to come to them together I do not think that any of these ever quite equalled the perfection of Broxton.

Although I had wanted to stay at the cottage very much and did not want to go back to Birkenhead, just the same the few weeks my mother and Wilfred were away were happier than usual for me at home, for instead of the grimy slut or dirty charwoman who was usually imported into the house to look after us during my mother's absence, my father had secured the services of a merry, boisterous young Liverpool woman he had heard of through one of his seaman friends. She was the daughter of a sailor who had been wrecked and drowned, and the sister of four other sailors. She had been a waitress in sailors' cafés in Liverpool and came to us between jobs which she always seemed to be losing. She was I think Liverpool Irish, her rollicking, easy-going, slapdash way of dealing with everything was extremely infectious and she diverted us all very much. I became particularly attached to her, and she to me. Her warm affection and constant good humour released a boyish pleasure in me and I enjoyed her immensely. She was a large young woman and everything she did was in a large way too, and her skill in handling plates of food was a perpetual source of fun for us. She would slam down one loaded plate after another so that they skated along the table and came to rest in exactly the right position opposite each of us, and when, as occasionally happened, one would slide right off the table either into my lap or on to the floor, then the fun became uproarious. She would remain with us all day until my father's return, when she would leave and come back before we were up next morning.

She begged my father's permission to take me home with her for one afternoon and evening, and promised me a sailor's tea. When the day arrived, it was all great fun. We set off in great spirits and by devious trams and walks arrived at her home in the shabby seaport street, but inside the home everything was warm and friendly. A tremendous tea was laid out with eggs ready to boil and bacon being fried by a huge man in a blue jersey. This was one of the brothers home from sea. This man, like his sister, had a great roaring laugh and, sitting us both down, served us and himself to a magnificent meal of bacon and eggs and muffins and buttered toast and cakes and jam, all accompanied by gales of laughter. After tea, the sailor pulled up the sleeves of his jersey and showed me his tattooing. I was tremendously intrigued and demanded to see more, whereupon he pulled off his jersey and shirt and exposed to my fascinated gaze a full-rigged ship in full sail across his chest. His arms and shoulders were covered with butterflies and pictures of ladies without any clothes on. I think my excitement must have been infectious, for telling his sister to turn away and turning his own back to me he dropped his trousers to the floor; I was entranced to see curling out from between his buttocks a huge blue and red snake that, encircling his waist with its body, brought its head around and reared up in a striking position in the small of his back.

After this I was entertained by being shown models of sailing ships of which the whole house seemed to be full. As a final treat I was taken into a small upstairs room and shown a superlative but only half-rigged model about four feet long, and I was told without any laughter now how their father had worked on it between voyages and was hoping to finish it on his next return, but the ship had foundered when rounding Cape Horn and their father had been drowned. His last instructions had been that it was to be dusted but otherwise left undisturbed. Although he would never return, they had carried out these instructions and proposed doing so until the end of time. Every thread-reel was in place and even the loose thread ends were kept exactly as they had been left. They both showed great reverence when speaking of their father, but I became a little confused over it all and I remember wondering how he was going to finish the model if he was lying dead at the bottom of the sea. However, their sad mood did not last long and we were soon back to the old gaiety and fun. On the way home they made a detour into their local shopping street and they went in and out of the brightly lit shops buying me sweets and other little gifts until my pockets were loaded down.

Although Elisabeth, for that was her name, was such a great success from my point of view, she evidently did not impress my mother in the same way. After she and Wilfred returned from Broxton and life in our street resumed its normal course, Elisabeth was never called in to look after us again. Her noisy cheerfulness and levity did not, I think, meet with approval, but I expect my too vivid story—with anatomical details—of the tattooing was finally to seal her unsuitability. She came round to see us twice or three times after this but the visits were not encouraged and soon ceased altogether.

Something else happened before we left Birkenhead: this was the foundation of a 'family phrase'. It came about during a holiday in Cornwall. This particular year my mother and father had taken rooms in the tiny hamlet, as it then was, of Carbis Bay. The holiday had followed our usual pattern; my father in his most carefree mood looked happy and nice and jolly in his white jersey and flannels. We were the only visitors there so we had the sea and the beach to ourselves. As usual I was roused out at about half-past five in the mornings to go clambering over the rocks or walking along the cliff tops or just standing as my father was fond of doing and staring out to sea. Always if the fishing boats were in we would go down to them and buy fish for breakfast. It was one of our very best holidays; the weather was perfect and when we were not on some modest excursion or another we spent all day on the sands swimming or playing at the water's edge. It was chiefly momentous for supplying us with this family phrase.

Embedded in the sand on the beach was an enormous ship's boiler that had been washed ashore at some time or another. When the tide was in it became almost submerged. Even before our bathe on our first morning my father had immediately spotted the possibilities of this: it would of course make an ideal diving platform. He soon had Wilfred, Mary, and I out to it to encourage us to dive. Our diving efforts were most childish but it was enormous fun, and with my father treading water ready to fish us up again we felt safe and enjoyed our jumps and flops into the sea with great abandon. Colin, little more than a baby, was naturally left out of this and stayed with my mother. For some reason or another, most likely seeing and hearing the glorious fun we were having, the small Colin suddenly demanded to be let dive as well. This delighted my father and cradling the tiny child on his chest he swam on his back the short distance to the boiler; placing him carefully on it with his little arms poised above his head, my father told him to dive. Colin just lowered his arms, looked calmly all round and down at the water, and completely unconcerned said in a detached little piping voice, '*Not today, tomorrow I will*'. The seriousness of the little creature set us all off into uproarious laughter. Something in the moment had caught all of us and we loved it. It might have stopped at this—a fleeting moment of pure delight—indeed nothing more was said and before we had finished our after-bathing coffee that my mother always brought for us it had passed from us, but that night when Colin had been put into his pyjamas and was padding around to give us all his goodnight kiss, to each of us in turn with comical solemnity he said, '*Tomorrow I dive off the boiler*'. We all followed the lead of my father and each of us as he came to us answered, '*Yes, tomorrow you will for certain'*. Satisfied that he would, he went off to bed.

It became a ritual and every day of the holiday he had to be taken out to the boiler and placed in the diving position. This done, without any prompting he went through precisely the same procedure—lowered his arms, looked round gravely, and came out with his *'Not today, to-morrow'*. And every night on his goodnight journey to each of us the same confident assertion, *'Tomorrow I dive off the boiler'*. Of course the expression became a byword amongst us almost at once and remained for all the years that we were to be together our 'family phrase', so that if any one of us was inclined to say he would undertake some project far beyond his scope, showing over-confidence or any tinge of boast-fulness, it would instantly bring forth cries of *'Tomorrow I dive off the boiler'*, which gradually shortened itself to *'Dive off the boiler'*. If, as not infrequently happened, the phrase shot out in front of other people it led to much mystification, but we never explained and it remained always our secret family code phrase.

Another family personality who influenced our lives while we were small children living in Birkenhead and Shrewsbury was Cousin May Susan. I have never been clear about the exact relationship. She was, I suppose, a cousin by remove of my mother's and more distantly of us children; to my father and mother she was always May Susan—to us children Cousin May. She was a person of such sparkling vitality and strong personality that when she came to us for her annual visits she enlivened us all with so much gaiety and light-hearted happiness that her stays came to be looked forward to for weeks ahead. Her fascina-tion for us became trebly enhanced when my mother, in an unguarded moment, took us into her confidence and, having gathered us around her, with lowered voice and conspiratorial solemnity told us that while of course Cousin May was everything that was good and virtuous she *did* paint her face (it was thus described in the early 1900's), which was a very wicked thing to do; equally wicked was Cousin May's predilec-tion for the stage and her constant theatre-going: at this Wilfred and I pricked up our ears. Wilfred immediately demanded to know 'Had Cousin May been an actress'; my mother's horrified emphatic denial made Wilfred look disappointed and made me feel so. I am sure that my mother was genuinely concerned about these supposed foibles of Cousin May's, and incredible as it seems seriously alarmed lest, if we were not warned to be on guard against such ungodly practices, our young morals would be endangered.

Thinking back about Cousin May, remembering the years of brisk gaiety and bright happiness that she brought to us—especially when recalling her innate goodness as a person—it is fantastically difficult now even to imagine how her innocent attempts at beautification and her wish to make the best of herself should have been looked upon as bordering upon actual immorality: it is indicative of her remarkable strength of character that in the early 1900's, when such views were so widely held, she did insist, in opposition to her friends and family, upon applying to herself these gentle arts. The effect of this knowledge upon us children was electrifying, Cousin May's rose-petal complexion —which of course we had not as yet even noticed—was actually painted on: to us this was something too magnificently fascinating to be true, the delicious air of naughtiness about it all intrigued and excited us and in abandoned moments we would innocently whisper to one another with only the barest audibility, '*the painted lady*', which made us feel terribly wicked and almost as splendidly daring as Cousin May herself. It inspired in Wilfred and me an awed respect for her defiance of the proprieties and her unbelievable indulgence in what had been so solemnly impressed upon us as such wickedness. We were both unable to prevent ourselves gazing at her countenance with irresistible enchantment; speculation must have been obvious in our eyes, but as this was mistaken for fond admiration we escaped reprimand for staring.

Whatever arts she may have employed, the result was more than justified and the creamy rose skin made a fine setting for her brilliant blue eyes. She was a woman of some means, which fluctuated according to the success or otherwise of her gambles in the money markets, for she had a dangerous addiction to speculation which brought her some bad moments; but her luck—it was little else—held surprisingly. In other fields she was competent in an amateur way as a business woman; she was much given to launching quite surprising enterprises, always with the highest hopes that they might add to her income. One of the earliest—and to her family and friends quite the most startling of these ventures—was her single-handed setting up of a clinic, of all extraordinary things, for the removal of unwanted hair from hirsute females: she invented her own instruments, devised her own original but risky treatment processes, rented a room, and fitted it up as a surgery. From the beginning it went well, clients flowed in and so did the money, which was all that Cousin May cared about, until catastrophe struck—one of her 'patients' developed blood-poisoning and skin-disease. She was threatened with legal action and a claim for heavy damages; once again her amazing luck held, the patient made an unexpectedly rapid recovery; with the aid of a clever lawyer she was able to extricate herself—a small lump sum in total settlement was agreed upon and the case never reached the courts. Cousin May, very badly frightened, threw away her instruments and abandoned hair-extraction for ever.

After giving up this mad scheme she fell back for some years upon pure and simple Stock Exchange speculation until a series of heavy losses made her look around for something else with which to recoup herself. This time she hit on the idea of starting a private school for girls, bought a house in some east coast town, had her stationery, prospectuses, and curriculum printed, advertisements inserted in suitable journals, and waited for pupils to arrive—they soon did. She herself had no experience whatsoever of teaching, or any specialized qualifications, but this did not deter her in the least. The school flourished in a modest way for a number of years.

As well as the longer stays with us, Cousin May would sometimes descend on us for short flying ones and during these she would make special efforts to arrange some treat for us children, whisking us off somewhere if only to a pleasanter part of Birkenhead. We never minded what we did—just to be with her and enjoy her brisk aliveness was enough in itself. She was never silent; even when taking us younger ones out alone she would keep up the most lively chatter, full of sparkling fun. She was an adept story-teller and could hold us spellbound with sheer entertainment for hours on end. Wilfred and I became particularly attached to her and shared an appreciative admiration for her smart clothes and sophisticated appearance. Cousin May in turn sensed—and liked—our naïve enthusiasm for worldly glitter and she probably had something of this in mind when she became obsessed with the idea of taking Wilfred and me to a theatre in Liverpool.

In her impulsive way she immediately told us of her plan, working us up as she did so into a state of fevered excitement about the glittering proposal. This of course only made our disappointment all the more bitter when my mother without equivocation refused to countenance any such idea. Her prejudice against the theatre and all to do with it was unbelievably inflexible. Cousin May pleaded and cajoled, promising only a suitable play or even a circus and finally lost her temper, but all to no avail, my mother remained adamant. Wilfred in his grave way was deeply disappointed for he was old enough to regret the missed opportunity for actually seeing a play as such in a real theatre. At this time to be able to do this was I think one of his most cherished longings. My own younger disappointment was only for a treat denied to me and not as was Wilfred's for an opportunity missed. My mother's attitude was all the more difficult to understand for she had fostered in Wilfred from his earliest infancy his passionate love of toy theatres, helped him to construct his home-made stages complete with curtains and candle-lighting, and encouraged him in his love of make-believe and dressing up, helping him to write and act parts of his own devising.

Cousin May was not a person to be easily thwarted. Cunningly switching her arguments from entertainment to necessary educational value, suggesting a Shakespearian play—by this time she was prepared to take us up to London rather than be defeated—she might still have won the day if she had not appealed to Wilfred to add his persuasion to this fresh approach and help to salve my mother's conscience. Wilfred, full of his youthful and engaging loyalty to my mother, would have none of this, refusing to place her at a disadvantage in the argument with Cousin May, so the whole project was dropped.

Perhaps to make up for my disappointment, for I had been less accommodating over this than Wilfred, Cousin May was allowed to take me on a lunch and shopping expedition to Liverpool. This was a tremendous event for me, constituting as it did my first essay into society unaccompanied by my family. Cousin May was in one of her reckless spending moods, carrying a purse crammed with sovereigns and half-sovereigns, and these she spilled out in payment as we rushed from shop to shop. The lavish unconcern with which she spent all this money fascinated me; and as she insisted upon consulting me about the various purchases I felt I was gloriously helping to spend all this money myself. Best of all perhaps was her delightful insistence that for this day I must deport myself as her squire. Selecting the best restaurant, she made me precede her into the dining-room, choose a table, and with her help order lunch. Lunch over, she left me with a handful of sovereigns, telling me to settle the bill. With grave help from the head waiter I managed this difficult task apparently satisfactorily. Altogether the day was an enormous success for us both. Cousin May made our return home triumphal for me by her enthuasiastic report to a slightly astonished family, who had been a little dubious concerning my zest for unpredictable behaviour, upon my comportment as an escort.

Wilfred's initiation into the theatre came after we had left Birkenhead, and then it was only to see an extremely poor touring company doing—very badly—a series of Shakespearian plays. Wilfred was reading Shakespeare heavily at the time and my father had insisted upon taking him, but as I could not qualify on educational grounds I was not taken. (My own plunge into this wickedness came when I was lying in the Pool of London. Going ashore in the East End, I had walked about looking for a theatre and went into the first one I found, which must have been a music hall. The audience was rowdy and salaciously vocal, the show was crude, lurid in lighting, cast, and atmosphere—indeed the air was fetid. I did nothing to lessen this by burning through several Trichinopoly cheroots which I had brought back from India and was enthusiastically trying to teach myself to smoke—as I thought it behoved me to do as a 'brassbounder'. I was not yet sixteen years of age. I loved every minute of the heat, noise, and howling ribald disorder. I found another one to go to the very next evening.) Wilfred and I both saw the early moving pictures before we saw anything on the legitimate stage.

A pleasing custom of Cousin May's which she unfailingly maintained was to send gloves as presents to all of us every Christmas; she never got the sizes right, but as there were six pairs, they could be shuffled round the family to fit. Always they were perfect barometers to indicate her financial successes or failures of the previous year. A good year would bring astrakhan of the finest quality, a medium year plain leather, and a really bad one woollen ones of the cheapest possible sort. Her financial rashness very nearly brought extreme poverty to her in her old age, but once again her incredible luck held firm and by a risky manipulation she just saved herself.

When once I had gone to sea I did not, through force of circumstance, see Cousin May again for a great many years. When I did at last make a special effort to visit her, I found her in a cottage in Yorkshire—her eccentricity as marked as ever but fortunately her vitality as electric as it always had been. This was just as well for I had to have tea with her in a room in which her companion-friend lay speechless and very close to death; as well as this gruesome corpse-like occupant, there were seven beautiful white cats—Cousin May's latest diversion. It was a warm spring afternoon, every window was closed and in an old-fashioned grate a roasting fire was burning, but Cousin May's vivacity and pleasure in seeing me surmounted the grisly atmosphere. Her bird-like cheerfulness never left her as every five minutes or so she hopped up from the tea table to make sure that her funereally sheeted companion was still breathing. Her hair I saw was white, the intense blue of her eyes had faded, but I was freshly charmed as my enchanted gaze noticed the perfection of her complexion—she had not lost her art.

It must have been 1907 when we finally left Birkenhead and for us children the move came as a complete surprise. One morning my father failed to go to his office as usual. This in itself was peculiar as he never missed going, but what struck our young minds most was that although he was not going he should be in such a bad temper, because on the days that he did not have to go he was always gay and frolicked about with us in fine style; but this special morning everything was wrong. He was irritable and cross with us all. After a hurried and disagreeable breakfast, for he had driven me upstairs to brush my hair properly and stormed with more than usual violence at Wilfred for being late, as he always was, he finally flung the wooden pepper-grinder, which one of our hands had made sticky with marmalade, across the small room, breaking one of my mother's pet vases. Lamentations and sharp words followed. In a towering rage he crashed out of the room, muttering that if he couldn't have a comfortable breakfast in his own house on the one important day of his life, he would go without. The mystery deepened when he reappeared in morning clothes and a silk hat, which he proceeded to brush with great care. After this my mother had to examine him and remove every speck of dust from him. A frenzied search for his only gloves, a last-minute adjustment to his tie, a friendly and repentant kiss for my mother, and he was out of the house and gone.

It was the mystery only that unsettled us, for we were well trained to his harmless outbursts of temper. The evening made up for every-thing, for my father returned jubilant and happy, and taking my mother aside whispered a few words to her, after which he demanded that his family should be assembled around him. When we were seated to his satisfaction—he was very fussy about this—he, still standing, proceeded with his delivery of one of his set speeches. The gist of it was that we were to leave Birkenhead almost immediately to go and live in Shrewsbury. He then went on, still in his speechifying manner, to whet our appetites for the delights to come, and in his own excitement and enthusiasm over-gilded the prospects; but we drank it all in and begged for more and he supplied it with visions of life in the country, boating and fishing on a river, early morning excursions, bird-watching, walks and, above all, a better neighbourhood, better house, and more and nicer food, and wound up by thrilling us with the news that he himself henceforward would be a much more important person than hitherto-fore—his own words those. After making us all very happy with a read from 'Uncle Remus', he took us all into the tiny kitchen and, finding his dripping and bread, he boiled his kettle and proceeded to make celebration for us—and for himself—with his famous lobscouse.

My parents of course had known of this possibility for some weeks, and the day of mystery that had started so badly and ended so happily had been the day of the final and deciding interview with the directors of the company who were to appoint a man to the post in Shrewsbury. My father had rather unexpectedly come into the running at the last moment; the post, though badly paid, was an important and a very responsible one. It was known as Assistant Superintendent of the Joint Railways, and was directive in nature rather than one of a series of prescribed duties, such as he had previously held. After my father's meagre opportunities it was something of a triumph for him, and although financially it was wretched, yet as a recognition of ability it was considerable.

My mother's reaction to all this was probably relief and pleasure, but, as always, it was tempered and spoilt by an unnecessary dread of the upheaval, and the sorting and packing it would mean, and indeed with four small children and the perpetual lack of co-operation between her-self and my father, especially over the small and unimportant details which would have to be decided upon, changed, and be decided again a dozen times in a few hours, it did present a period of indecisions, petty worries, and nervously frayed tempers that could not be looked for-ward to.

Wilfred, after the first excitement had worn off, realized that it meant leaving the Institute and the abrupt abandonment of his pleasantly-established position and progress there, so that he became moody and a little resentful of the move. The thought of leaving Birkenhead was unsettling him too as he began to realize that it would probably be the end of his music lessons which were, on account of expense, always in the balance. But they had just attained some security through an arrangement with the young woman who came to give him lessons. She was a pleasant, rather boisterous person, always in good spirits, who entertained us all with stories of herself and her other pupils. She could only come in the evenings as she worked at something else all day. She usually shared a meal of sorts with us. All her stories were amusing and some I believe—for those days—were near the borderline. There was one special one which, although it really shocked my mother and father, never failed to have them helpless with laughter. We children were not allowed to hear it properly but we were able to gather that it was something to do with a dark night, a ditch, and a man with too much beer. Her personality must have been strong for her to survive my mother's prejudices. After the first few terms my father found it impossible to manage the fees and had to ask her to discontinue the lessons, but by now she was interested in Wilfred's serious eagerness to make the most of her instruction and told my father quite frankly that she enjoyed her evenings with such an odd family as we were, and she would come anyhow. In the end, minimum fees and longer evenings were arranged, and the arrangement remained permanent until now when we were about to leave Birkenhead.

My father, realizing perhaps that it might be difficult to settle Wilfred again both for music and in such a suitable school, and one that would also be within his means—a public school was of course completely out of the question—tentatively put forward the proposal, which he previously made sure was possible, that instead of Wilfred coming with us to Shrewsbury, he should remain in Birkenhead during term time and live with the Paton family, who were delighted with the idea and welcomed the thought of companionship for their only son Alec. By doing this, he could also continue with his music lessons. Wilfred might have fallen in with the scheme readily enough if my mother had been agreeable, but she was adamant in her refusal to countenance such an idea and would not even discuss the suggestion with my father, so his plan which was solely evolved to secure continuity in Wilfred's education came to nothing. This lack of agreement over Wilfred was discouraging to my father so that he was becoming more and more inclined to withdraw from serious discussion about him. It also made him disposed to be impatient with Wilfred, which was a pity.

I myself was glad and excited at the thought of leaving Birkenhead and its misery of dirty streets and the gloom and horridness of our dark and dismal little house; and above all I wanted to be free of the anxiety ever present in my journeyings alone through the streets, for I was always liable to attack from the small and large ruffians who inhabited our neighbourhood. I had early developed a technique for dealing with attacks—singly or in pairs—by these boys of my own age, for I had found out that a rush towards them with an attacking blow or two evaporated their aggressiveness in a most satisfying way, and the ensuing struggle was merely a face-saving scuffle which would end by one side or other seizing a cap or school satchel and flinging it into a garden or the road, after which we would each be glad to go our ways. But the marauding gangs of bigger boys who lay in wait for small defenceless boys were dangerous, as I had found out when I tried out my early technique on one of these bands. The six or seven bullies would smother the victim, three or four holding him powerless and the remainder raining blows until blood flowed—nothing but blood satisfied them. By violent struggling, biting, kicking, and butting, it was sometimes possible to hurt one or two of them and make an escape, but being caught nearly always meant a really bad fight. What I disliked more than anything else about these mauling scuffles was the disgusting physical contacts, the filthy mauling hands, and the bitter sourness of the smell of their bodies nauseated me to fury—this was fortunate for me, for without this fury I should have taken some bad bruisings. Getting mixed up with these gangs was largely my own fault, through my incurable liking for walking about alone and this practice of exploring strange streets. To these quick-witted sharp-eyed little Birkenhead boys this habit was enough to mark me down. I was beginning to dread these disgusting encounters and they were by now a spoliation of the fleeting moments of happiness I had been able to snatch in my journeyings through the miserable streets. In my childish way I had thought all this to be a local unpleasantness and that a move away from it would leave it all behind. My father's eloquent appraisal of all the good things in store for us in Shrewsbury had helped in this and made me look forward to going with an impatience I could not contain. I did not have long to wait, either for the going away or the disillusionment that was so soon to come.

My father now had a few days to himself, and early one morning he told me he was going to take me for a long day around the docks and ships to have a final look at them. I think he had a feeling that this migration inland away from a port was cutting his last link with his beloved sea and he wanted to bid it farewell. As it happened it was not to be his last contact, but at that time I feel sure he thought it would be. I am certain as well that he wanted once more to have lunch in his dock-side café and restaurant. It was an eating-house frequented almost exclusively by ships' masters and officers. He had quite often taken me there for a pot of tea or coffee on our earlier sojourns amongst the ships, and on this day as he always had on other occasions he reminded me to show no surprise or make any remark when he was addressed by the proprietor and waitresses as ' Captain', which they invariably did.

After we had finished our meal we left the eating-house to wander round the docks to look at the steamers. My father I could see was thinking about something and presently suggested that we might journey to the outlying sailing-ship dock to see if by any chance our lovely Norwegian barque was in. He was muttering rather shyly to himself that of course it wasn't very likely that she would be there, but we might go and see just to make certain before we left Birkenhead. I was entranced at the idea for I was longing to see again the jolly giant of a Captain and his warm yellow-haired wife, and of course my splendid friend, the Negro cook. On the way to the sailing-ship basin I asked my father to tell me again the Norwegian words of greeting and I rehearsed them to myself all the way. As we neared the berth we were both of us searching to catch a glimpse of the tall spiring masts with their delicate spiderwork of rigging and the graceful slant of her topsail yard-arms or the gleam of her gold-painted trucks that tipped the slender mastheads. We could not see them. As we rounded the warehouse and fitting-out sheds we knew she could not be there. Lying in her place was a squat ugly little brig grimed with coaldust, a collier in the coasting trade. We turned away immediately and went straight home.

Years later when my father came to visit me in one of the ships I was serving in we went again to this ships' officers' eating-house, only this time I had taken him, instead of as before him taking me, which pleased us both. It was then he told me that he had first commenced using this place in order to listen to the sea-going talk, and to see close at hand the men who commanded and officered ships. On his first visit he had immediately been mistaken for a ship's captain. He somehow failed to rectify the initial misunderstanding and the conviction and the illusion remained sustained. This suited his purpose in visiting the place very well and his enforced, rather silent evasiveness and refusal to be drawn by the other habitués gained him a reputation for a hard-case ship's master.

The mistake is easy to understand, for his general appearance at that time was very typically seamanlike. He was around his early forties and his short stocky figure with the breadth of shoulder and deep chest gave him a rather savage bearing resembling a small but uncertain bull. The effect was one of physical toughness and strength. His dress, too, quite accidentally seemed to conform, for he always wore dark blue serge suits with white shirts and stiff white collars and dark ties, which seemed to be the universal shore-going rig of masters and mates, more especially from the sailing ships and cargo steamers. The liner captains were, except to very close observers, indistinguishable from ordinary professional civilians. The build of his face and head always seemed to me to suggest the sea with its brickish red complexion, the general weather-beaten look, and the network of fine lines and wrinkles that surrounded the eyes. The eyes themselves had the fluctuating quality of the sea and could change from the steely grey fierceness of anger through the ordinary coldness of blue-grey to warmth and tenderness difficult to resist or describe.

Thinking there might be some fun for me over this 'Captain' business if I asked him to order the meal, I did so. He at once assumed an icy disdainful manner, and snapped out his orders in a most commanding fashion which certainly was entertaining for me. Occasionally one of the younger officers would tender him a deferential formal greeting. My father would return this with a piercing look, a curt nod, and the shortest possible rejoinder.

Not long after my father's return from his interview with the railway company's directors he received his orders to take up his new post in Shrewsbury. This set our whole house in a turmoil, but things began to happen quickly. Somehow the sorting and packing had been got through; the main lot of furniture loaded in a van outside the house. The next morning our last day in Birkenhead had arrived. Perhaps because I was so excited about going I have a vivid memory of the early part of this day. It started with the loading up of the remaining pieces which we had had to keep for overnight use. The whole business of moving had been entirely to my liking and gave me a great feeling of exciting adventure. The others had been less responsive to the alluring side and were not able to share my high spirits. They did not appreciate my insistence upon helping the men to carry out the small pieces and odds and ends. I was still fearful in case anything should go wrong and we should be prevented from going, so I wanted to hasten everything up.

At last the things were loaded and the van rolled away to the railway yard, leaving us—the family complete and altogether—in the empty house waiting for the cab which had been ordered to take us to the station. I remember it all so well; we were dispersed around the tiny downstairs room, using broken packing cases or the window-ledge for seats. My father, still a youngish-looking man, was, as always, turned out nicely in a dark suit and well-polished boots. He was nervously agitated as he always was when any journey was imminent, especially a railway one which he loathed and detested; this made him querulous, short-tempered and just slightly inclined to panic about details and he was now working himself up as to whether the cab would arrive in time. He was quite capable of outrageously blaming my mother—or any one of us—most unfairly if anything went wrong and kept pacing the room like a caged lion, constantly opening the street door and looking up and down the street, muttering annoyed imprecations.

My mother was also still looking young, although the years of hardship and the difficult task of rearing us had taken a heavy toll of her early beauty and freshness. But the masses of dark, almost black hair still remained lustrous and unfaded, and although her once blue eyes had taken on a tired greyness they were still a prominent feature. I cannot recall how she was dressed but, knowing the importance she attached to outward appearance, it would be with care and suitability but most certainly just behind the prevailing fashion in time. She was always rather averse to wearing anything that even nearly approached the mode of the day—she would have looked upon doing so as 'fast' and not quite nice. In her puritanical parochialism she would have deemed it sin. With this same thinking she would never wear full evening dress except—and then only under protest—when it was important to my father that she should accompany him to some function. All her life she was sincerely to believe that evening wear for women was something immodest.

I remember very well on one of these rare occasions my father, very proud of her, had taken me up to see her. I was rather overcome with wonder and hardly knew her, and in my pleasure admired her white shoulders. But I had said the wrong thing and I was sent out of the room—but not too harshly this time for she was I think secretly rather pleased by my notice.

We were still in the empty house waiting for the cab. My father was by now in one of his real states of fluster, pulling out his watch every few seconds and openly accusing my mother of not having ordered the cab at all or, if she had done so, then of ordering it for the wrong time.

My mother meanwhile was fussing quite a lot herself, trying to keep the small Colin not only amused while we waited but, almost more important to her, in a reasonable state of repair for the journey. This further irritated my father who testily demanded that she leave the child alone. With considerable tactlessness—considering my father's attack of nervous irritability—she not only took no notice of this but commenced to fuss over us others as well.

Wilfred was hunched up in a corner deep in some book or other, seemingly impervious to the fretted tempers snapping around him. He was dressed in a Norfolk knickerbocker suit, much in vogue among schoolboys at that period, of some brownish material, with stockings and boots, and a narrow stiff white collar with a stringy-looking tie that would never keep closed up to the collar itself. His very dark brown hair was falling untidily but attractively over his forehead: it badly needed cutting. Another source of irritation to my father—of which we three boys were all guilty—was our aversion to visiting the barber often enough to satisfy him. Wilfred had slung over his shoulders his school satchel containing his current exercise and text books from which he refused to be parted. In his hand was the book he was reading and stuffed into his pockets were other books. He seemed unconcerned and calmly indifferent to the event, and only raised his head to admonish one of us if he thought we were making things too difficult for my mother. His preoccupation and air of neutrality was an added friction to my father who would have liked him to have co-operated and shown interest in what was going on. Wilfred had absorbed from my mother the settled mode of thought towards my father which, while refusing to assist him materially over any arrangement or necessary action, nevertheless held him responsible for all that might happen. There was a slight disassociation about this, probably not realized, that hurt my father and made him feel left out, which he hated, for he longed for affectionate sharing of these petty troubles as well as pleasures.

Mary, who was still a little girl round about twelve or thirteen, was already quite domesticated, helping in the general work of the household and quite an efficient little cook. My mother had preconceived and very strong views upon how little girls should be brought up, the strongest of which was the unshakable conviction that their sole purpose was to be useful and devoted to their parents. This attitude was not so unusual then as it sounds now. Mary's niche in the family was and always remained peculiarly unbiased to the alternating factions that surrounded her. Being the only girl may have helped. Her love and real affection for my father were very strong, but her devotion—in the sense of service—tended towards my mother. This naturally came about through my mother's state of semi-invalidism and the necessity for Mary to take over many of her responsibilities. As well as this, my mother, again influenced by her era, was disinclined to consider Mary as a person in her own right but—very fondly of course—as a daughter whose only function in life would be, as it was said in those days, to think of her parents. My mother, however, had gone further than this and had inculcated into the little girl such a powerful sense of duty and the need for filial devotion that it amounted to a form of self-sacrifice, an expression which my mother was inordinately fond of using—she was very fond of expounding to us all the absolute need always to practise this. I myself could never see to what end all this self-sacrificing business was meant to lead, and when I asked her she would either be cross with me or tell me I must pray more before I could see the light. As I liked neither of these answers, especially the one about praying and seeing a light (I was really beginning to be afraid that one day I might see this awful light and I did not like the idea at all), I soon stopped asking.

For Mary the effect was different; she accepted the doctrine only too easily and as a consequence became obsessed with an unnatural and far too adult sense of responsibility towards my mother's comforts and well-being, a sense which was later to develop into a self-effacing devotion of service to her, and much later still to turn to a nursing dedication, all of which left so little time to her for the cultivation of herself. In spite of this, from a very early age she showed a strong little personality and an individuality of her own which caused her to distribute her unselfishness among other members of the family; but solicitude for my mother was always dominant and able powerfully to colour her thoughts and actions. My father adored his only daughter.

My mother's self-absorption was, I think, so strong that it prevented her from becoming truly aware of the power of domination she was exercising over Mary. When she did realize something of what might be happening, she would I know have combated it successfully had her own sincerity not been so repressed by this overlay of evangelism. Instead she would excuse it to herself and others on the grounds of the necessity of instilling filial love and a sense of service into young children, even to the exclusion of their own development, and would vigorously attempt to sustain her point with religious vehemence.

Some of the solicitude already present, and the anxiety Mary was to develop so overpoweringly later, showed itself while we were waiting for the cab, as she trotted back and forth with cups of water to refresh my mother. Colin at this time of leaving Birkenhead was still a very little boy. He was idolized by my mother and Wilfred; being so young and amenable he was a joy and satisfaction to them both. In a few years' time he was to become my companion and co-adventurer, Wilfred retaining his more remote admiration and affection for him.

The cab had at last arrived, the only suitcase and the many bundles and parcels and odd packages, so dear to my mother and so infuriating to my father, were stowed inside or on the boot. We somehow packed ourselves in. My father, after directing the driver, managed to squeeze himself in too. We were on our way to Shrewsbury.

Chapter Six

SHREWSBURY 1907

THIS Birkenhead epoch that we were now leaving had woven itself into a curious pattern for all of us—the drear years in the dismal streets came and went, the insecurity of it all warmed only by the prevalence of our family love. The dreariness of the day ate into us all in our different ways, except Wilfred, perhaps because he was happy in his school, but more I think because he was already so sure of his direction. His road lay clearly before him—the pursuit of knowledge and the determination that literature and the other arts should take precedence over all else in his life. In this way he acquired an immunity, almost an invulnerability, to the difficulties which beset the rest of us—my father hating his work but worried and anxious about retaining his post; my mother and Mary overtaxed to keep the house going. For me the memory of the general background of the daytimes of these years is certainly sombre and I think unhappy. The memory of the evenings is not like this. When we were all shut up in our little house with the blue gas-jets burning—except on special occasions always turned low for economy—I remember only safety and happiness and often high gaiety. My father and mother did make great efforts to bring joy and happiness to us in these candle- or gas-lit evenings. Looking back I can see that it was an unconscious patent of the family that while in the daytime we must all stand on our separate feet and fight our own battles, quarrel among ourselves and give way to bad temper, in the evening the family had to be indivisible.

Occasionally my father would take Wilfred and me out with him just to walk about the lighted shopping streets. Wilfred, when he would come, always enjoyed these jaunts and at these times he and I would be friendly and close, happy in the secure feeling that being taken charge of by my father gave us both. Wilfred would not come often, he would not leave his books. I have a clear recollection of my father taking me out at night during some national celebration—it might have been the end of the Boer War—right over to Liverpool. I could not have been more than five or six. I remember getting caught up in the wildly excited crowds so that we could not get home. I loved every minute of it; he must have carried me most of the time.

In memory, all this weaves itself into a curiously patterned tapestry, a tapestry in which for me the background is certainly sombre and unhappy but interspersed, as it so surprisingly was, by these rare but brilliant patches of colour—the Irish holiday, Carbis Bay, Broxton by the hill—and the silver threads that are woven into it by the visits to the docks, criss-crossing with the golden ones that are our evening times in the different shabby little houses in which we lived. The tiny jewelled patch, that must be looked for to be seen, was the beautiful Norwegian barque that my father found for me.

It was my father squeezing himself into the overloaded four-wheeler that broke the final link with Birkenhead. This epoch was finished . . . all that had happened here was to be left behind . . . as the cab rolled away down the mean street both my father and mother looked back at the small empty house. Mary and I looked forwards . . . in front of us was a new beginning. The little Colin wedged on the floor could look neither way. Wilfred looked at his book.

Tonight we should be in Shrewsbury.

It was dark and pouring with rain when we arrived in Shrewsbury, and I can remember being packed into a cab and rattling and jolting through the streets until we stopped and were unloaded outside a very small house, one of many in a dark little road. The door opened and a tall thin old gentleman with very long and pure white moustaches helped us all into the house. These magnificent white moustaches of his attracted my fascinated stares to the exclusion of everything else. I had never seen anything like them before and it was probably my intense interest in them which made me notice other things about the stately old gentleman, his shock of tousled very white hair and his cold icy-blue eyes that I soon discovered were piercing right through me in a most uncomfortable way, and his extraordinarily transparent skin stretched tightly over his prominent face bones. The bones seemed to hold an illumination that glowed through the skin itself so that it made me fearful and unhappy. Presently, he placed one of his bony hands on my shoulder and, speaking to me, broke my spellbound absorption. It was only then that I noticed the really tiny little old lady who immediately smiled very sweetly and warmly at me, at the same time handing me a mug of cocoa with a biscuit. We were bidden to drink up quickly by my mother and immediately afterwards hustled up some narrow dark stairs and put to bed.

These two white-haired and white-faced old people were my paternal grandparents, whom I had not seen before. They had, however, seen me. They were not spoken of very much and usually a slight mysteriousness enveloped them. This was most likely owing to their permanent state of just not having quite enough money, for even by exercising the most stringent economy they were still left on the borderline of insufficiency. My grandfather and grandmother were very proud people and difficult to help. My father had persuaded them to allow him to augment in a small way the minute income that my grandfather possessed. This was something which my father with his own financial difficulties could ill afford to do, but he and my mother always agreed that somehow it must be managed.

These ageing parents of my father's, in whose house we now found ourselves, were living in Shrewsbury at this time and my father had dumped his family on them while he looked for a house to settle us in. Houses were not difficult to rent in those times and in a few days he had found what he wanted and we were able to move in. As there were only two bedrooms in my grandfather's house, this was just as well. Wilfred and I shared a mattress on the floor of one bedroom. It was dark and cold and our discomfort made Wilfred very big-brotherly and affectionate towards me. I whispered to him how much I hated this house and wanted to get out of it and would rather go and sleep outside. This warmed his natural affection, and perhaps his own assumption of indifference could not quite withstand the indescribable and uncertain atmosphere of this horrid little house. Snuggling close together for warmth and company, we hoped we would not stay long here; doing this, we whispered ourselves to sleep.

The house my father had found was in the same road and no great distance away, but although we were so close I cannot remember that we children saw much of these grandparents. I was too young to express it even to myself, but while not actively disliking them, as their kindness when we did meet was extraordinarily evident and showed itself in small acts and presents calculated to please young children, yet with all this I could never overcome a strange antipathy to being near them. I could not connect either of them with my own childhood and could not realize any kinship. They were at this time already ageing over-rapidly; they too had lived through a lifetime of anxiety and struggle for which the years were now taking their heavy toll.

My aversion may have been caused, without my knowing it, by a childish prescience that they were finished with this world and an awareness that they were drawing nearer to another. Not very long after our arrival in Shrewsbury they became rapidly enfeebled. The un-pleasant small house was given up and they went to live with my father's now widowed elder sister. Decrepitude rapidly encompassed them both and they faded out as gently and unobtrusively as they had lived. I never saw them again.

On the morning after our first night I awoke before Wilfred and rushed to the window, eager to see for myself the delights that daylight would reveal to me, for I had taken my father's version of the joys and happiness that were awaiting our arrival in Shrewsbury too literally altogether and was convinced in my small mind that I had only to look out of the window to find it all in glorious actuality.

I climbed up on to a chair and after clearing a patch on the grimy misted windowpane with my hand, I peered out and was deluged with disappointment. What I saw was not in the least what I had expected. It seemed much the same as Birkenhead. The same narrow sort of street with what seemed to be the same drab and dreary little houses opposite. Actually it was not so, for the houses, though mean and small, were not squalid and were in no respect similar in character or inhabitants to the slummy districts we had left behind in Birkenhead. My disillusionment was bitter. The grey morning and the sooty rain which was falling with such steady monotony blinded me to any difference. My feeling of de-jection was increased as I saw that the roadway was littered with rubbishy oddments, and became complete when I noticed that here too, like Birkenhead, were the familiar discarded newspapers caught up in corners and lying in sodden pulp. Here as well were the same old shreds of coloured posters torn off by the wind which flattened them-selves with such wet obstinacy against house walls and garden railings. Even as I gazed out of the window a long blue streamer billowed along the road and wrapped itself with clinging wetness around a lamp-post.

Getting down from the chair I turned away from the window and going over to the mattress on the floor tried to rouse Wilfred, hoping he would get up and look out of the window and share with me my lowering spirits, but he was tired and cross, his warm friendliness of the night before had disappeared and he petulantly told me to come back to bed. I was cold as well as miserable so I lay down and worked myself in between the blankets again, but I was careful not to let my cold feet strike against Wilfred's.

In two days' time our furniture arrived outside our new home and we settled in to live there. The excitement of watching our things go into the house and the turmoil of arranging the furniture cheered us all up, and I began to feel there was a lot to be said for everything and that perhaps my father was right about our better prospects in Shrewsbury after all.

While we were settling in, the problem of schools for us children came up and much discussion and some argument floated about perpetually between my mother and father. A great deal of it was in front of us and, I have no doubt, some more when we were sleeping. Once again Wilfred, being the eldest, was the subject of most of the discussion and argument, but it was eventually decided that as he could so safely be left to pursue his own studies the need for finding a school for him was not immediately urgent, and that it would be better to wait, rather than risk sending him to a wrong one, until they knew a little more about what could be found for him. I was given much shorter shrift and again dismissed as not being of sufficient promise and ability to warrant unnecessary expense, so it was decided that a free board school was the solution for me. The other two, Mary and Colin, could well wait until Wilfred and I were established somewhere. The paramount necessity seemed to be to get me fixed up somewhere, if possible satisfactorily—there was much open doubt among the family about the possibility of doing this, and even more secret doubt in my own mind. One Saturday afternoon my father told me he had arranged an interview with the headmaster of one of these board schools in the town and that we would go along there then, and if things went well I would start school the next week.

The interview was accorded to us in an empty classroom which seemed huge to me; indeed my first impression of the whole building itself was one of immensity, a feeling which I found cold and disconcerting. The interview was a lesson in brevity. The headmaster proved to be a sarcastic and waspish little man—he had a dash of French blood somewhere—and he disposed of me very quickly by asking me to spell some impossibly long word which of course I could not do, but I did try and thereby provoked his scorn and sarcasm. This began to make my father angry with me for not being able to answer correctly and with the headmaster for his sharpness, and the visit was abruptly terminated with ill-feeling in all three of us; but not before it had been decided that I should start attendance on the following Monday. The headmaster's parting shot to me was not to forget to bring my tuppence.

Although this was a board school some pupils had to pay a few pence a week, probably something to do with parents' incomes. I started at tuppence a week and before I left had risen to fourpence. The pupils required to do this had to take the pennies and deliver them to the class master every Friday morning, and woe threatened for any boy who forgot. It was less heinous and far safer to remain away from school on a Friday rather than admit having forgotten the pennies. Both boys and girls were taught in this school and, although in the same building, were entirely segregated during school hours.

So on the following Monday morning I was dressed and sent off to launch myself into my new school, this time entirely alone. I did not like this going off by myself very much. For one thing the school was right the other side of the town and I was not at all sure that I could find it as I had only been there the once with my father, and on top of this doubt I dreaded the prospect of having to introduce myself into this huge, gaunt, prison-like building. However, clutching my penny and two halfpennies in a hot hand I set off hoping, not very cheerfully, that everything might be better than I expected. I did eventually arrive at the school, but only after I had hopelessly lost my way several times. So of course I was very late and instead of the crowds of boys I was prepared for I was confronted with the immense and completely deserted playground; and the great red building itself seemed to me coldly forbidding and very menacing in its profound silence.

I did not know what to do and very nearly turned around to go back home, but after this first hesitation I decided to find my way in and walked across the playground, my small boots echoing hollowly in a noisy and alarming way on the hard concrete. Inside I fared even worse and wandered along the passages hoping to find an open door, but failing in this, I timidly knocked on a closed one. After some seconds this was opened and a seemingly furious master demanded my business. I stammered out some sort of explanation and before I could finish was dragged roughly by the shoulder into the classroom and sarcastically ridiculed to the gaping form as the new infant who aspired to join the sixth form—standard I think they called it, not form—after which I was thrust out into the corridor again and told to find my own standard and to be quick about it. As I did not know to which standard I was supposed to belong, this was a little difficult. However, a mistress came along and I was ushered, more kindly this time, into the right class-room. This was another very large room, but divided into smaller spaces by wood and glass sliding partitions. I had to negotiate through three classes before I arrived in my allotted one. Here I was sat down on a form next to a large, fat, pasty-looking boy who welcomed me with a vicious dig in my ribs with his elbow. I retaliated by telling him he looked like a lump of lard and started a feud which never died.

My entry was made conspicuous by being a new boy in mid-term and by my late arrival, and at break-time the junior boys ganged up, led by my fat neighbour, and mobbed and mauled me horribly. But because I had to reappear in school, it was confined to disarrangement of tie and cap and hair and rolling in the dirty playground, and blood-chilling threats and promises of what would happen to me when we were finally let out of school at four o'clock.

When school for the day ended we were spewed out of the classroom in a howling yelling crowd. I found myself hemmed in on all sides by jeering boys, big and small, and my secret hope that fleetness might aid me disappeared. Once outside, I was carried along to some waste ground and a concerted attack on me began. I was soon taking a bad bruising and I began bleeding profusely, but I suppose I must have made some resistance for I found myself temporarily with a clear space round me, and it was then that uncontrollable rage and some inspiration once again helped me. In a flash I had picked up a large quarry stone and hurled it with all my diminishing strength straight at the face of one of the big boys. Luckily for him, and for me, my aim was low and the stone struck him in the ribs. Had it hit him in the face it would have laid his cheek wide open. As it was, it sent him down gasping and twisting in horrid pain. The effect was miraculous and after a few seconds of frightened quietness, all the boys, except two bigger ones, fled in all directions. The two remaining boys and myself helped the smitten boy to his feet when he became disgustingly sick, but otherwise he seemed all right. My anger had subsided now, and fear at what I had done gripped me. I was glad when the two big boys ordered me to get off home quickly before someone came along.

On my way home I stopped by the river bank and with my handker-chief sponged off what I could of the mud and blood and straightened up my clothes and combed through my hair with my fingers, for I did not expect sympathy, let alone understanding, of what had been happening to me, and could only hope that by preening myself I could disguise the seriousness of it and so lessen the blame and scolding which my appearance was bound to bring upon me.

When I arrived home my dishevelment did cause some consterna-tion, but when it was found that there was no serious hurt to me, the concern switched—as it so often did—from alarm to recrimination. My mother and Wilfred, after extracting from me what had happened, were disinclined to believe my story; instead they were both comfort-ably certain that it was only my own stupidity and ill-behaviour that had brought my troubles upon me. Perhaps from a feeling that I could not stand having any more unjust guilt being thrust upon me, I said no word of the final stone-throwing action. Later Mary tried to soothe and comfort me and continually administered first aid to my cuts and swollen nose and give me all her stored-up chocolate. I could not be comforted, though, for I was tired and very frightened, not of the future but of what I had done by throwing the stone at the boy. The guilt of it nagged at me and I longed for somebody to unburden myself to and to share my secret misgivings.

I still had a hope that my father when he came home would let me talk to him and that I should be able to tell him everything and be believed. I was sent to bed early and my father came home late and I expect very tired, and when he did come up to see me it was only be-cause my mother sent him up to give me a serious talking to and threats of punishments if I did not mend my ways. But he was weary himself and in need of his evening meal; he seemed elusive and far away and could not help me and, after a few stereotyped phrases about trying to be good in the future, left me and went downstairs. This to me was the final heartbreak after the long and bitter day, for my own family had now succeeded in doing what the masters and boys in the whole of this first day at the school had failed to do—brought a lump into my throat which I could not force back, so that tears brimmed into my eyes.

I went back to the school next day and to my relieved surprise found myself left entirely alone. This of course was not due to ostracism, which in better-class schools would have come about through my un-orthodox and dangerous rock-throwing. In this school and all its like there never was any recognized code of school behaviour; such terms as 'playing the game', 'sporting', 'good' or 'bad form' were absolutely unknown. Had anything like this been even heard of it would have been scorned as 'soft'. The only known criteria were bodily strength, lying, and low strategy. It was quite simply catch as catch can, all-in, and nothing barred. In this way my unpremeditated violence in hurling the rock, although an act of desperation on my part, was an inspired one—this was something they could understand, and out of this under-standing came the realization that it could be dangerous to molest me. Something of this kind must have happened, for without much further effort on my part a quite erroneous legend grew around me that I was to be feared in a fight. This could not prevent involvement in minor brawls but it did free me from ganged-up molestation. In this way I was able to maintain my aloofness and when my previous nickname of the Birkenhead Bull-Fighter caught up with me the illusion that I was dangerous was built up even more strongly, which suited me very well.

I found these other boys even less pleasant than the tough, stringy little Birkenheadites who at least were alert and could think and act for themselves. In comparison these Shropshire boys seemed fatter and heavier and altogether more bovine and stupid, and what ruminations came to them seemed foul and beastly after the Birkenhead boys' brighter, cleaner, and harder evilness. No doubt the agricultural com-munity and atmosphere of the country town had much to do with this. Some hint of real foulness did throw out its weaving tentacles to suck me in, but fortunately I was too young to be receptive to salaciousness and some instinct warned me of danger. As well as underlying vice among the bigger boys, there was a disgusting vulgarity prevalent in this school, so that the boys vied with each other in producing from themselves prolonged eructations and worse animal noises and mani-fested coarse hilarity and entertainment and pornographic pride in their pubescent efforts.

My first few visits to the latrines were without incident except for my overwhelming repulsion at the sour filthiness of their smell. They were loathsome with slime and beastly pools of urine and nasty pieces of paper littering the flooring. Unless I was pressed beyond endurance I never went in, preferring to suffer the discomfort until I was released from school and could dart into a public urinal that I had found in the street on the way home. One cold morning, through being under a bigger strain than usual, I had to visit them and was confronted by five or six of the bigger boys giving each other exhibitions of their naked-ness and promise. I was shocked and revolted and was only just able to escape before I too would have been forced by them into semi-nudity. As long as I was in the school I never again went inside these latrines, and if I could not wait I would slip through the school gates and into a disused alleyway. It was lucky for me that I was never caught at this for it would have meant accusations of indecency and I could never have explained my desire for cleanliness but instead would have brought all sorts of horridness down on my head. I became quite clever and trained myself to stop instantly if anyone came along, and would pretend satis-factorily to be playing about.

I was not at all happy in this school and made one or two efforts to talk to Wilfred about it, and especially about the latrine happenings, in the hope that I might be taken away, but Wilfred in his moody way could not be helpful. I do not think he really believed me and in his rather preoccupied manner dismissed my dislike of the place and told me I was really very stupid and I must not speak of such happenings and that I was being extremely tiresome and difficult. All the same in his quiet way Wilfred must have thought this over and spoken to my mother about me, for shortly afterwards she herself brought up the subject with me. My mother, especially in those early years, did possess an extraordinary facility for dismissing from her mind ugly truths, and, doing so, was content with the make-believe that they really were non-existent. For her what was not nice must never in any way be acknowledged.

She opened with an approach that made it quite clear that it must be me that was wrong in not liking this school, telling me that what God had ordained—which was my attendance at this school—I myself must not try to put aside but must instead put my trust in Him where-ever I was. I could not quite see, as it was I and not God who had to go to this horrible place, why it was that I should be left out of it so much. I started to tell her that if God really thought this school was a nice place then he could not know what he was talking about, so I did not see how I could trust Him at all. This not only shocked her profoundly but genuinely horrified her so much that she tearfully accused me of wilfully hurting her. In a reverently lowered voice she told me with frightening solemnity that if I went on like this—speaking of these things that were not nice—as I had done to Wilfred, then my feet would be set on a road which could only lead to eternal hellfire where I should burn everlastingly . . . as I could never bear the remorseful emotion that always welled up in me when my mother accused me of wilfully hurting her I remained silent, managing to keep my thoughts about God and my own doubt of his trustworthiness to myself.

My mother continued to exhort me to try and be a nice little boy, and not take any notice of anything nasty I might see or hear . . . good little boys did not see or hear these things . . . and then God saw to it that no harm came to them. . . . If I did not try harder to be nicer I should not only displease God but break her own heart as well—so I must promise to stop speaking of these things even to Wilfred . . . and of course none of these things could possibly be true . . . I must stop making things up. . . . Rather hopelessly I tried to tell her that I didn't want to talk about God but only about the lavatories and what happened in them . . . this only made things worse . . . it was no good, my mother in her failure to convince me was losing patience with me; so, forecasting doom for me, she sent me off.

In my childish mind I reasoned quite simply that if God's idea of looking after me was only to make me stop at this school, then I did not like the arrangement very much and if, as my mother said, he was displeased with me about it all, I thought I had much more reason to be displeased with Him—if He did have anything to do with it—for letting me be there. Altogether I did not think that God or Jesus seemed to be managing things at all well. I found it difficult to connect either of them with the school lavatories which after all, I thought, was the only thing I had tried to confide in Wilfred about. I had not spoken about the roughness—for this was something, I knew now, that I could deal with myself. I began to see that I would have to rely on myself to steer through this other sort of thing as well—which made me feel a bit lonely. I had to count out Wilfred as being too vague and too liable to misunderstand me, and leave out both God and Jesus as being so unreliable that they certainly were not to be counted on in any way at all. From now on, I thought I would rely only on myself in my own way.

I was to remain at this school for some time. I suppose I must have learnt something but it could not have been much. As far as the lessons themselves went, I soon discovered that if I sat quietly and did not fidget little notice was taken of me and it did not seem to matter whether I paid any attention or not. I found this to my liking because

I could safely think of other things. Now and again my interest was caught but it was never held. Any attempt to seek enlightenment was quite obviously discouraged; a quiet and well-ordered classroom was the only concern of the mistresses and masters who undertook the teaching.

One mistress did seize my imagination, curiously enough with arithmetic. So far this had been completely obscure to me, but one morning she spent half an hour with me explaining the intricacies, and there seemed to me to be something about the neat and orderly way the figures sorted themselves out to give a clean, exact, and correct answer that intrigued me, and after a few simple, unaided successes, I became very fascinated and would have liked to have pursued the long divisions and reductions for hours for the pleasure they gave me; but I caught up too quickly with the meagre instruction and the mistress who had interested me could not devote the time to individual guidance. It was the same with all the other subjects. Apart from these very few fragmentary bits of knowledge that stuck by accident, I was learning absolutely nothing. What little exercise book work we did always seemed to be good and kept up to date, but I soon realized that this was looked after by the mistresses and what we did not know we were helped to put down under their guidance. They were responsible for very large classes and of course had their own records as teachers to think about. In none of the lessons did I in the least understand what was supposed to be going on or have any inkling of what I was doing. It was not a case of losing interest but one of never having found it.

Of all the hundreds of boys in the school I can only recall one individual, the rest I can remember only as a belligerent noisy mob that I could not like. It must have been near to the end of my time in this school and I would have been about eleven years old. This boy was only important to me because it was through him that I first became— in a way I could recognize—aware of compassion and pity and, perhaps more important, alive to the knowledge of the power that was born with the possession of this understanding over the person to whom the sympathy was shown. Until now I had, I expect, been only occupied with my own reactions and my own struggles to maintain some semblance of coherence in what was happening about me. This boy changed all this in a marked way. He was considerably older than me, tall and very delicate-looking and the idol of a doting mother: so much so that he became literally a figure of fun in the school, to such an extent that his passage through it was fairly easy—he experienced very little physical violence for he seemed only able to evoke absolute contempt from the other boys and was merely the object of derisive and ribald mockery. It was most likely this, to me, extraordinary capability of accepting so many foul insults without resentment that made me first notice him, and his degraded helplessness was so immense that in some way it brought to me this realization of extreme pathos so that I felt drawn to behave with kindness towards him. His gratitude was appalling and poured over me with such avid hunger that his lack of restraint overwhelmed me. He attached himself to me with a limpet-like eagerness which I found embarrassing. When I attempted to discourage him the abject hurt which came into his eyes forced me to relent.

His mother overdressed him atrociously, and I remember with a pang when he appeared in the most frightful pair of bright yellow boots. These wretched boots were too much for my newly born sense of sympathy, so that I was ready to spurn both them and him, but he forestalled me by drawing my attention to the atrocities with such genuine pride and pleasure that my hardening heart melted and instead I outshone him in my admiration and simulated envy. Once again his gratitude and obvious pleasure were so inordinate that I had a most uncomfortable feeling of responsibility towards him and a quite puzzling sensation of power, and began to see that by manipulating words and assuming attitudes—which were false—it was possible to control reactions, especially happiness . . . I remember it gave me an obscure sensation that I had somehow received knowledge . . . it was my first hazy realization of the separation of knowledge and learning. While I was much too young to clarify it for myself I also experienced a vaguely frightening realization that this potent power could work in reverse. . . . Beyond these unbidden glimpses of barely apprehended knowledge I could not go.

The boy himself was unimportant to me at the time; it is only when I look back that I can see that he was the vehicle through which came to me the awakening of a receptiveness which could be stabbed by pity, and an awareness that to encounter pathos could scorch. Our relations never developed into friendship, his own tragic humility prevented this happening, yet he remains the only boy that I can remember anything at all about. He persuaded me to go to his home two or three times to meet his mother, but her over-sweet sentimentality made me feel rather silly so I did not like her or enjoy the visits. Soon afterwards the boy's illness developed more acutely and he was taken away from the school and quite shortly left the town.

I suppose I must have become temporarily resigned to this school; anyway I had perfected my techniques for dealing with the noisy and often violent roughness and my scheme to avoid using the lavatories continued to work well; but my detestation of everything to do with the place increased. I found I was able to make it bearable during the hours I spent in it by concentrating my thoughts upon how I would use the time once I was away from it. Each week, of course, there was always the freedom of Saturday to which I could look forward. My father, I think, realized that I was not learning anything and outwardly blamed me with some severity for this. His censure was his way of relieving his own anxious fear that the school was really no good to me. However, I must have given the impression that I was fairly settled and if my father had his doubts my mother was content that at least I appeared to be satisfied. That the education itself might not be satisfactory did not bother her in the least for she was convinced by now that I was such poor material from this point of view that it made little difference where I might be. Her lack of ambition for me at this time was truly astonishing.

A little private school conducted in a sitting-room of a small house had been found for Mary in an adjoining road, to which she was sent each morning; later on Colin was to join her there. It was for a few pupils only, efficiently run by a Miss Goodwin, a young woman who became a great friend of our family. 'Goody', as she was known to us all, eventually came to the house to give piano lessons to Wilfred, Mary, and Colin. She was a first-class French linguist and did good work with Mary and Colin in this direction; unofficially during her visits to us she helped Wilfred quite a lot with his French. It did not look as if it was going to be easy to find a suitable school for Wilfred and we had been in Shrewsbury some little time before a solution was found to this problem. He it seemed was the most difficult to fit in anywhere. Mary was fixed up in the day school. Colin would follow when the time came. I was—it was thought—secure in my board school for some years to come, but the right place for Wilfred did not easily present itself: to send him to a board school, as had been done with me, was somehow never considered. Wilfred himself would have liked to go to Shrewsbury itself, but this of course could not be contemplated.

Wilfred was unsettled, difficult, and moody, and showed a studied, lethargic, disinterested indifference to any suggestion from my father, and a nervous disregard for his opinion, but at the same time expressed almost fanatical liveliness about any ideas my mother held for him. These were many and utterly impracticable—all of which hurt and irritated my father and caused unnecessary and very wearying arguments between my father and mother. These not only led nowhere but entirely fogged the issue until it became a haphazard two-sided groping.

There were numerous so-called high-class private schools in the town. My father sent for prospectuses, which all contained the same claim—as being for the sons of gentlemen—and visited one or two of the owners of these establishments. Others visited my father in the evenings and gave a strong impression of gross canvassing. My mother and Wilfred were both very impressed with one of these last and my father took Wilfred for an interview with the owner and principal. Wilfred was anxious to be sent to this one. My mother, though knowing nothing at all about the school, wanted very much that Wilfred should be sent there, really only because he seemed so pleased with the idea and she argued hard and lengthily to persuade my father to send him.

My father's perspicacity, which was so much greater than my mother's, told him clearly that this school was no place for Wilfred, and with one of his rare stands of firmness he vetoed it and the rest of the private schools with it. My mother was vexed and Wilfred became more moody and displayed a most difficult attitude towards my father. He was much later to realize how right my father had been and how much he owed to him for not weakening in his decision. As it transpired, the school was no doubt admirable in many respects, especially for a slightly superior bucolic type of education, but no person in the establishment was concerned with scholarship in its true sense or even in the pursuit of learning. Besides the futility of its aims, Wilfred, with his sensitive, highly attuned mind and his small body that rebelled against physical exercise or violence, would have suffered intolerable misery in it at the hands of the young gentlemen who inhabited the place. These were drawn from well-off families (for the fees were considerable) whose aim in life was pseudo-gentility but who remained throughout in thought, word, and deed forever plebeian.

An uncomfortable hiatus followed after my father's adamant decision, and although he remained vexed and unhappy in the lack of co-operation and understanding between the three of them, his genuine love for my mother and natural affection for Wilfred caused him to keep seeking the right setting—within his means—for Wilfred. This eventually led to his discovery of what was known as the Technical School in Shrewsbury. This time he made full inquiries and interviewed the principal alone. There were I believe one or two formalities to be complied with or got over, which may have been something to do with age of entry. It was of course a fee-paying school and although these to my father were considerable, they were within his means. The upshot was that a further interview was arranged at which Wilfred was to be present. If this went satisfactorily he would be able to start his studies there at once.

This meeting was thoroughly successful and both my father and Wilfred—their past tense differences now forgotten—returned from it pleased and happy. Wilfred was unusually jubilant at the prospect of once again commencing organized work and he indulged in one of his moods of buoyant fluency, amusing us all with his description of the evening. My father joined in and contributed to the fun. Wilfred and I were sharing a bedroom and when he came up to bed that night he at once set about sorting and arranging his text and exercise books until he had them to his satisfaction (for he was to begin at the Technical School in a few days), after which he regaled me with choice bits about his plans and hopes for the new school and persisted in reading long stanzas of poetry. But I was sleepy and more than a little envious of the care and trouble that was being devoted to him to ensure his ease of learning, and my own prospect of my board school tomorrow with its obscurity of teaching and the wearying daily combat to maintain my independence amongst the other boys seemed frightening and futile and I had a feeling of smallness and unimportance. I was awakened some time later by Wilfred in order that I might listen to him reciting a long piece of poetry that he had learnt while I was, to quote his own words, 'wasting time in hog-like slumber'. These disturbances of me to gain an audience were a nightly practice of his and were followed by a further waking up when he flung back the bed clothes, letting in the cold air, and tumbled his frozen little body into bed next to my own warm one. It must sometimes have been the early hours when he finally blew out the candle. In the mornings he would be peevish and morose and impossible to arouse and waken, often rounding on me for my inattention to his discourses of the night before.

Wilfred seemed to settle down comfortably and easily in his new school and again did not seem to encounter any difficulty or unpleasantness from the other students. These were a little different from the average run of schoolboy and in almost every case were attending for the express and serious purpose of gaining knowledge, so that his intent application probably went unnoticed and was certainly never resented. The school, too, was quite unconcerned with games or sport of any kind, but outside pursuits and interests of educational value were much encouraged and were even woven into the curriculum itself when sufficient interest was obvious. Later on this adaptability of the school encouraged Wilfred enormously in his awakening interest in geology and antiquities and especially in his collection of Roman remains. There was a mistress here too who took English, whose influence and guidance were extremely important at this time to Wilfred. I think she was much taken with the small dark boy with his polished unobtrusive good manners and his immense concentration and determination to overcome the difficulties of attaining scholarship and knowledge. For Wilfred encountered difficulty in these scholastic technical achievements, and it was sheer hard work and not brilliance that finally gained him ascendancy over them. This often led him into long and deep depression and bouts of doubtfulness that at times crossed the verge into morbidity.

This English mistress—I think her name was Wright though I cannot be quite sure—exerted a strong influence over Wilfred which did much to offset his doubt and feeling of unsureness in himself. I think she realized the young boy's inherent distrust of himself and by judicious praise and encouragement and a great deal of extra coaching in his weak subjects she was able to restore his flagging confidence in a way which no master succeeded in achieving. Many people have claimed to have influenced or helped Wilfred in his early years, usually with little or no justification. It is certain that Miss Wright brought real understanding and appreciation so that her sympathetic guidance during those formative years at the Shrewsbury Technical School were of significant help to him. She became friendly with us as a family, but later we lost touch altogether.

With Wilfred happily fixed at the Technical School, myself now uncomplaining in mine, and Mary and Colin suitably arranged for in Miss Goodwin's sitting-room school, my father relaxed a little and set about seeking for some entertainment for himself and his children. This, on account of our schools and his work, had to be fitted into the early mornings or the evenings. The early morning was his favourite time; in the evenings he was sometimes jaded and irritable.

At first these early mornings did not seem much fun and I did not much like being got up at half past five or earlier, especially if Wilfred had kept me awake the night before, and the washing in cold water which my father insisted upon was a shivery business; but the hot tea and nice thick piece of bread and butter that he would have ready downstairs made it almost worth while. To begin with, I was the only victim. Once only my father had made Wilfred get up, but he was lethargic and tired and altogether disinterested in these early morning excursions and unwilling to have anything to do with them. My father made one or two more unsuccessful attempts to get him out of bed; my mother, though, intervened with some heat over this unnecessary disturbance so he rather angrily gave up trying. Mary at this time was too delicate and Colin too young, although they both joined us later on.

After the tea and bread and butter, we would steal quietly out of the house and set off for the fields and river which were no distance away. My father took great pains and interest in pointing out to me the birds in the air, the fish in the river, and the crops growing out of the fields, about all of which he had considerable knowledge stored up from his boyhood. These excursions were not a daily practice and although I rebelled about getting up when the morning came, the nights when I went to bed with his promise of an early morning were my happy ones, and I would fall asleep thinking of the new delights we might find in the morning. My father was good, too, at helping me to get up and if I was very sleepy would lift me out of bed wholesale and, standing me up at the bedroom basin, would start me sponging my face.

The river was always a source of interest and we came to know the swims of the roach and where the fat, coarse chubb lazed just underneath the surface. The big, cruel-looking pike lying so cunningly dangerous in the waving reed beds and the flashing little jack were all looked for and noted for other days. Sometimes a lovely speckled trout would be found sucking down with greedy selectiveness the mayflies as they floated down the river in their fragile dresses of transparent silky gauze.

The country around was heavy with uncut hedges and small clumps of bush and trees, and in the nesting season my father would find—and mark down for watching—many different kinds of birds' nests and was always seeking to add new species to our list. In the breeding season we would go out almost daily and if a nest was expected to hatch out, would return in the evenings to mark progress. Sometimes we would take one particular nest for watching and, hiding ourselves in the bushes nearby, would stand motionless for long periods watching the parent birds rearing their young. Other times on warm sunny mornings we would walk straight down to the river, my father looking for two suitably secluded alcoves in a hedge. Having selected these, he would repair to his and get into his bathing costume. I would go to mine and put on short swimming trunks. My father was always very particular about all this and although I was so young would never let me bathe in the nude. Although there was never anyone about at this early hour except an odd farm labourer or two, he would peer about anxiously and fuss terribly to make sure our improvised dressing rooms could not be overlooked. I enjoyed splashing about in the water and swimming short distances in deep water with my father, but I always felt a little weak and hungry when I came out and the walk home seemed rather long. On lucky days my father would fish out a bar of chocolate from his pocket or sometimes just a dry crust of bread. If he did not produce anything, I would not dream of asking for it or even reminding him but would trudge along by his side contentedly disappointed. Once home, he would revert to his nervous manner and would be brusque and cross again and storm up and down if breakfast was not ready—as it never was until Mary grew a little older and bigger—and he would be fantastically cross with Wilfred, shouting at him with angry disgust for not being dressed or, as it mostly happened, not even yet out of bed; I myself had only to make one slip or be negligent in manners to bring a tirade down upon my head.

It was sometimes hard to believe that this stormily petulant person was the same gentle man who a few hours earlier had so skilfully widened a nest without damage so that I might watch a minute baby wren peck its way out of its tiny egg shell. If he was in a particularly irate mood Wilfred would take care not to appear at all until he had stormed out of the house on the way to his office, which meant that Wilfred had only time to drink some tea, usually on the stairs as my mother met him half way up with it, taking it to him so that he could be hurried away by her and get to school without being late.

It was my turn again to upset the household with serious illness. All my short life I had been subject to acute attacks of sore throat, and I went down with one again, only this time much more violently. Our usual doctor was away but after some days the locum tenens was called in and diagnosed severe tonsilitis. I became alarmingly worse and was segregated in a bedroom where my mother nursed me. I recovered a little and was allowed to get up and managed to totter about the room, being kept in bed when the weakness was too marked. After two or three weeks of this sort of thing, I suddenly became dangerously ill. Our usual doctor had now returned. Swabs were taken—this had not previously been done—and a diphtheric condition pronounced.

Some days later the doctor told my father that my chances of survival were nil. I was still more or less conscious for I remember a table being rigged up in the centre of the room and a mirror placed at such an angle that when I was propped up in bed, my reflection was visible to anyone standing in the passageway. This was arranged so that the others might have a last look at me without actual contact. I vaguely remember my mother giving me some preparation for the next world, and promises of going to heaven. This puzzled me a little but did not bother me at all as I was too young to accept the import of the words or apply them to myself, and of death I had no knowledge or perception and it carried no threat or meaning as I could not associate it with my own person.

I was a tough little boy and pulled through, even though I did not bring much with me in the process except skin and bone. After a short —too short—convalescence, I was up and about again as usual. However, I was still too weak to walk very far and for the next half term I accompanied Mary and Colin to Miss Goodwin's. I was not a success here—I was already too sophisticated by my board school experiences. A good thing came out of this, though, for Miss Goodwin with great concern reported that in the school I was at it was impossible that I was being taught anything at all. This confirmed my father's fears and awakened my mother to the truth that in this board school I was learning just nothing at all, but I went back there at the beginning of the next term.

My return was miserable and unhappy and I had all the anxious business of re-asserting myself in the school. My nice mistress had left and some young master whom I can't even remember had taken her place. I was, I expect, low-spirited; I hated the noisy vulgarity of the place, the meaty noisomeness of the other boys, the constant bucolic

harping on the pornographic, and above all the perpetual physical jost-
ling which was unavoidable among so many boys. The smell of improperly washed bodies bothered me: the way we were squashed up
together in bodily contact during class-time made me feel sick so that
I elbowed and fought for space around me, causing innumerable fracas
and bringing anger down upon me from the masters. I was becoming
a trouble maker and I did not mind—the boredom of sitting through
the school hours without any interest was making me difficult and
sometimes mutinous. Notes between the school and my father were
exchanged but before these could result in any action my tonsil trouble
hit me again severely. This time it was decided to cut them out, the
thought of which frightened me very badly. The operation was under-
taken by a G.P. and took place in the back bedroom. I was seated on a
kitchen chair, a female of sorts pushed her fingers into my neck, my
throat was lightly sprayed—no injection was given—and the doctor
commenced tearing and sawing at my right-hand tonsil. The pain was
excruciating. Three quarters of an hour had to elapse before the second
one was attacked. This dreadful wait, with now absolute knowledge of
what was at the end of it, seared into me horribly. All that afternoon
and evening I bled so profusely that I was fainting every hour. The
doctor did not come again until late at night at which time I was
mercifully oblivious. The blood I was swallowing caused constant
vomiting which in turn tore at my lacerated throat. My bed was a
shambles. The haemorrhage and vomiting stopped the next day and I
gained strength.

When I was recovered sufficiently I was again sent back to the school,
but this time I had had enough: I became intractable and after more
exchanges of notes and some interviews my father decided to take me
away. He had by now made some useful contacts in Shrewsbury and
he decided to try and get me into another school, a small day school,
apparently of some standing in the town. Under certain circumstances,
if not all, it was free of fees but was not in any sense a board school. It
may originally have been established by some bequest. I was never to
find out. The entry was by influence and nomination and my father
somehow achieved acceptance for me. The school was very small and
run entirely by the headmaster and his wife and daughter.

I had been shaken up rather badly lately and my infant confidence
was not nearly so sound as it had been; as I grew older, self-conscious-
ness began increasing uncomfortably. It was a pleasant surprise when I

made my first, somewhat timid, entry into this school to be accepted agreeably by the other boys. During my not very lengthy stay here I enjoyed them all very healthily and had fun with them during break periods and after school hours and made a number of temporary friends. One of these in particular I liked very much and continued the friendship after my dramatic exit.

His family and my own became very friendly, visiting each other's houses frequently. Wilfred thawed out to this boy's elder brother who was rather a serious person and they discoursed together. Later, after serving in the war, I believe he took Holy Orders. We younger ones (for the boy—my companion Herbert Oliver—had several sisters) consorted together to form merry parties always enjoying terrific hilarity in whichever house we happened to be, the fun always running high with noisy card games or charades. My father nearly always came with us when we went to see them, joining in with whatever we might be doing. He was enormously popular and we all enjoyed his youthful spirits. My mother never came with us but joined in the gaiety in our own home. The youngest sister Nellie, a gay and happy creature, was a great favourite with us all and she attached herself to us as a family and would spend many informal evenings with us. Herbert was a year or so older than me and went to sea in the Merchant Service shortly after I did. During the 1914–1918 war his ship was sunk by a raiding cruiser and he and the rest of the crew were cast adrift in open boats in mid-Pacific. The boat he was in made a romantic landfall in the uninhabited Galapagos Islands where they lived on turtle. Afterwards, as no help was forthcoming, half the boat's company volunteered, Herbert Oliver among them, to sail the small boat to the mainland two hundred miles distant. They achieved this successfully and a ship was sent to pick up the other survivors. I met him again when that war was over, looking terribly ill and emaciated. He had contracted some tropical disease while serving as an officer in a tanker. Eventually he had to abandon the sea as a career, after which, in my own fight for survival, I lost sight of him and his family until one day when I was a post-war student in London I ran into Nellie in Piccadilly who promptly took me to her rooms for tea in St. George's Hospital where she was a sister. She had taken up nursing during the war and, liking it, had stayed on permanently and very successfully.

Chapter Seven

UFFINGTON

THE new school, though in an altogether higher class than the one I had just left, was not to prove a happy one for me, at least not for very long. I had settled down comfortably with the other boys and was beginning to take an interest in the work, especially the drawing classes. In these I excelled and in this subject I almost immediately went to the top of the school, which made me feel encouraged. However, after a term or so I discovered to my dismay that I had irretrievably aroused not only antagonism but most violent dislike in the headmaster. As far as I can recall he was the one and only master, the classes being shared by his wife and daughter. I was not alone in this; I had seen already how easily he would work up dislike for the whole school and a fanatical hatred for individual boys. I had begun to sense that this man was cunning and bad-tempered. He was not so much given to favouritism, although he had a few of these; it was more that he liked selecting one or two of the less promising boys on whose heads he delighted to vent his ill-humour and sarcastic malice. He revelled in scheming to get these unfortunate victims in compromising positions and predicaments and would derive abominable joy from watching them try to extricate themselves. There was method in his tryannical madness for although he cared nothing for the individual boy's welfare he was intensely interested and concerned about the school records to a degree which was not quite normal. This bullying attitude may have been his method of winnowing; if it was, then I was certainly fair prey for him, for too obviously I had nothing to bring in the way of gaining future laurels for the school. My wasted time in the other schools had of course handicapped me very badly—here, though, I was working seriously but naturally I could not make much of a showing. The blistering tongue and savagery of the teacher nonplussed and bewildered me, so that I probably did appear to him not only quite hopeless but also a menace to his school records.

144

I cannot remember just how long I survived in this school. It may have been two or three terms or most probably even less before the inevitable and, as it happened, the final storm burst about me. He had for some time been bullying and selecting me for his butt and was persistently finding fault and flashing out poisonous gibes to incite me. Eventually, by odious machinations and taking advantage of my bewilderment he so contrived that I should stand apparently guilty of downright lying and gross and continuous prevarication. I resented this fiercely and so added further to his real or simulated rage. I was called out in front of the school and ordered to take six strokes with the cane on the hand. I walked up to his desk and when ordered to hold out my hand I refused to do so. Seizing my arm, he attempted to extend it by force but I wrenched it free, pushing him away at the same time; with this he lost all control and set about beating me with the stick about my neck and shoulders. I was tigerish now with anger and I warded off his savage blows with a fury and determination that enraged him to insensate fury; but I was frightened too for he was big and dangerous-looking. I dodged around his desk and picking up a pile of heavy books I was just prepared to hurl them at his head when with a sort of grunting noise he lunged at me, overturning the desk as he came. He must have lost balance in his rush towards me for he spread-eagled over the falling desk, knocking the breath out of himself, which was very lucky for me. The crash of the falling desk and the general uproar in the classroom, which was beside itself at the unpleasant spectacle, brought his wife and daughter on the scene and they took the lunatic in hand and restored quietness. Brandy and water was brought for him by his wife, for he was now in a state of emotional frenzy. The daughter seized me and for safety shepherded me from the classroom into the street, telling me to go home.

My refusal to take the punishment had nothing whatsoever to do with the gross injustice of the accusation. I would have refused just the same had I merited it. Neither was it fear of the pain; it was something in me myself, a part of me, which was inherent then and has remained so ever since, that prevented me from accepting a blow from any source —even if this was a recognized and accepted disciplinary measure. I preferred the consequence of a complete overwhelming by superior numbers, or the anger of official superiors, as the case might be, to the gross indignity of docile acceptance. This did not come from my own reasoning—it was something I could not help—I never had any choice.

When, years later, I was serving as a midshipman in a battleship I committed some trivial technical offence and I was ordered the usual gun-room punishment of six of the best. I defied the sub-lieutenant and owing to the fracas which resulted the matter went to the Captain and later Flag level. I was given the ultimatum of accepting the customary gun-room punishment or court-martial. I chose court-martial. Of course the whole thing had become ridiculous in the extreme, and could not, or at least never did, come to anything. A very senior officer concerned with it admitted to me some time later when he invited me to drink a glass of wine with him that I set them all flat aback with the very devil's own conundrum.

When the schoolmaster's daughter hurried me out of the school I took my time going home; I was feeling rather wretched; the splendid glow I had felt in defying this crazy man had evaporated and now I only felt small and deflated. I could not see how I could explain what had happened when I got home; I knew I should never be able to do so. I knew that this was the end of this school for me and drearily wondered what was to come next. I cheered up a lot when I remembered that I had a drawing that I had started and would now be able to finish.

When I got home I told my mother and Wilfred—who was at home with a cold—that I didn't like this school any more and had tried to throw some books at the headmaster. Eventually, under persuasion I tried to give my version, but I did not seem to be able to put it very well and before I had finished I was confused myself as to just how it had all come about, so that my mother thought I was prevaricating again and she was upset, too, at the thought of further trouble over me. Wilfred tried to give me a wry grin, which was nice, but it did not comfort me much for I had the feeling that he thought I was being quite impossible. The whole thing was then deferred for my father to sort out and settle when he returned in the evening. He, too, showed nothing but annoyance with me until I came to where I had been set about with the stick. After he had satisfied himself about this he left me and went straight to the school house. What exactly transpired there I never quite knew. But the man was, I think, too clever for my father's rather direct simplicity and by adroit misrepresentation extricated himself; and after some discussion it was decided that I should not return to the school. I was undoubtedly sacked. After this, although my father did not openly blame me, I am sure the smooth tongue had further convinced him that if I was not entirely guilty, at best I was proving most unsatisfactory.

A week after this I was sent off to another board school, a smaller one and this time quite free, not even pennies a week need be taken here. I found it tucked away behind one of the main streets of the town and it had to be approached through a slummy alleyway. This smelled most abominably in the summer time and was lined in all seasons by filthy slatternly women with protruding stomachs idling in their doorways and wearing men's caps on their ill-kept heads. They would call out to us boys, as we passed through the narrow passage, with coarse and foul language and bandied lewd and repulsive jokes between themselves mostly as to our respective promise as future males. One or two would always be openly feeding a dirty infant at the breast. One of these women in particular whenever I passed would purposely expose her free breast and, cupping it with her hand, waggle it at me, but I would pretend not to see and hurry past.

My settling in here was almost precisely similar to what had gone before. The same struggle to prevent submersion, which if not effected meant perpetual bullying by the bigger boys, with the usual disgusting wrestling and struggling and with the occasional more serious bouts of real fighting. Sometimes the bigger louts would gang up and give us smaller ones some bad maulings, but on the whole I held my own somehow and retained my independence throughout.

The boys were lower in type than the contingent in my first board school and some were in fact the sons of the slatterns who dragged out their sordid existences in the surrounding dark alleyways. The remainder were drawn from the lowest dregs of other unsavoury parts of the town. The school was known as the poorest in the district and generally possessed a bad reputation. I knew afterwards that these children were salacious and obscene, revelled in lewdness and exchanged their jokes, stories, and practices almost unchecked. Although I was so much in this unchoice atmosphere, I was as yet unaware of sex and instinctively feared and avoided obscenity and so it glanced off me quite harmlessly.

The teaching was carried out a little differently. The classes were smaller and were conducted by masters, or teachers as they were more usually called, with no mistresses at all. I seem to remember I got on quite well with them in a negative sort of way; the interest on both sides was lethargic. There was one youngish man who became very intrigued with my ability to draw. My efficiency in this was actually very much in advance of my age and I was deriving intense pleasure from it. I am sure he was not interested in art at all, yet he took a curious pride in my efforts and would bring various objects from his rooms for me to draw; and if one of my drawings did not quite come off he became really upset—not annoyed, but disappointed as if an expected conjuring trick had failed. He would show these sketches to the other masters with great pride. It is likely that in this dirty school of muddled inefficiency my spark of dexterity and keenness may have afforded him refreshment and a slight return for his unrewarding work. He did not stay long and nobody else continued the teaching of drawing.

On looking back I can see that it could have been only in this school that I was able to pick up such fragmentary learning—that is to say scholastic knowledge—as was to come my way by means of tuition. These odd bits of rudimentary teaching were my only educational foundation; for the rest I was soon to have to rely entirely upon myself. This was to be my last school in the ordinary sense. Soon after this, and before I was twelve years old, I decided not only to get myself out of this time-wasting place with its unpleasant associations but to finish with ordinary schools altogether. I did not at all see how I was going to be able to do this yet I was curiously confident that somehow I would bring it about.

However, before this happened I was to spend some time yet in this school. I was by now well into the dreary routine and by continuing to practise my technique of using the school hours to plan what I would do with my free ones I managed to avoid any further major incidents. My conviction that I would be able to get myself out of it gave me a hopeful feeling and with this to look forward to I expect I gave the impression at home that I was at last settled.

Another thing which helped was that here in Shrewsbury our family life was much happier in every way than it had been in Birkenhead. For one thing there was so much more scope for all of us, not only in the house, which although very small could be by co-operation just adequate, but also in the freedom outside the house with our nearness to the countryside and the field interests and fishing which my father had instituted. I was learning the trick of being able to live just in the future and projecting images for myself of delights to come, and if these failed to materialize quite satisfactorily at least I had the joy of the images and I could always project just a little further and so smother any present disillusionment. My drawing and painting was becoming important to me and my reading, if somewhat diverse in character, gave me not only recurring delight but escape from the thought of the school as well. I became absorbed in Scott and Dickens and read both with unsatiated appetite.

Wilfred was liking the Technical School and had by now once again established himself very firmly as a promising student. He was sixteen or seventeen now. My father was becoming restive about Wilfred's future. For some time now there had been discussions about what Wilfred should do. My father was very genuinely worried about him and, it must be admitted, not a little disgruntled with him for he found it difficult to reconcile this unnatural absorption in his books with his apparent lack of design for his future. When my father taxed him with these things Wilfred would reply only vaguely, or sometimes with gentle despondency would mutter that unless he could go on to a university he didn't see what he could be except perhaps a third-rate schoolteacher. This characteristic of his, muttering his replies, always angered my father and usually evoked some testy comments which he did not really mean, whereupon Wilfred would become moody and difficult and my father would huff-up—he himself now muttering that what the boy needed was more fresh air and exercise and less of these infernal books.

As well as sincerely believing it might be good for Wilfred to be started on some sort of career, if only to break up his preoccupation with his books, he had another reason for wishing that Wilfred might be launched into something through which he would be on the way to earning some money. My father could not see how in our circumstances literature, much less poetry, could possibly make a living for Wilfred. He found it difficult to share my mother's utterly unfounded and rather uncalculated optimistic view that everything would turn out all right somehow, and that if it didn't then it was further proof of God's will for all of us.

Wilfred himself, although day-dreaming on the larger issues, was as fully aware of these immediate necessities as my father; but at the moment he was content to gain time, if only from year to year, to prolong his period of whole-time reading even under the prescribed education of the Shrewsbury Technical. My father was once again worried about his job and the security of his family must have seemed, as it was, precarious to him. There was still with him the anxious knowledge that a sudden illness or accident could deprive him of his powers of earning. This anxiety was never really understood either by Wilfred or by my mother who were rather inclined to think that he despised Wilfred's application to reading and study. In fairness to them, my father's irritation with Wilfred for not living a more boyish life and his general refusal to take any exercise or be a companion to him in any way did lend colour to this idea, and of course my mother's perpetual championship of Wilfred's aspirations and equally strong disregard of my father's tentative suggestions sustained an unnecessary friction.

Wilfred himself was sensitive to all this and fell in rather eagerly—this at least would be writing—with a suggestion that a journalistic job, perhaps starting as a boy reporter on a local paper, might be obtained for him. I do not think this idea appealed at all to my mother who was secretly cherishing a hope that he would be able to enter the Church, and the reporter's job was not pursued with much determination. My father made some inquiries, but he had little or no influence in this direction and soon found that such an opening was impossible to come by without some powerful friends and he had none of these.

My mother was much taken up with surface religion and cultivated the various parish Church of England clergymen who seemed to abound in this town, and would encourage their prayerful visits to the house. (My father disliked them all except one who seemed to be much more interested in cricket than the prayer book. My father still played a little when he got the chance, which was not often, and watched every match whenever he could, so the two of them would converse with great amiability and much enjoyment. Prayers—except mock ones to bring about a much-desired win for an England or county eleven—were at a great discount in these conversations.) It is little wonder that Wilfred should fall under the spell of my mother's religious fervour. Indeed, at one time and for a very considerable period the effect was to give him a false vocation. This was to become quite strong and lasted until his own fine intelligence made him aware of the circumstances that had occasioned it.

An early result of this feeling was what was known in the family as 'Wilfred's Church'. Aided and encouraged by my mother, Wilfred would on Sunday evenings arrange our small sitting-room to represent a church. The table would be moved away, all available chairs collected and arranged for pews, an armchair turned backwards making a pulpit and lectern. At first it was all very simple but as his enthusiasm grew and his imagination took wing, it became more and more elaborate and my mother was kept busy making altar cloths, stoles, and a perfectly fashioned small linen surplice, all most beautifully worked, for she was a superb needlewoman. Finally she made a bishop's mitre. This was most extraordinarily effective; it was made from Bristol boards, white and glossy and cunningly enscrolled with gold paint. Wilfred would spend a long time arranging the room, after which he would robe himself and, looking very priestlike in his surplice and mitre, would call us in to form the congregation. He would then conduct a complete evening service with remarkable exactitude and would end by reading a short sermon he had prepared with great care and thought. The whole of these unusual proceedings were conducted with absolute reverence throughout, naturally so by Wilfred and my mother, but surprisingly also there was no hint of levity from myself or the other two who formed the congregation—perhaps not so surprising, for the hour or so had a solemnity and beauty that could not be withstood. The only lighting in the room came from the candles on the beautifully arranged altar. The sideboard was improvised for its construction and gleamed with white damask, a table cloth broken in the centre by the lovely coloured embroidery of my mother's cloths. Silver candlesticks were so arranged with reflecting mirrors that the lighted candles were multiplied a hundred times. Behind and flanking these would be banked masses of wildflowers and fern.

My father could never quite make up his mind about all this and I think decided to let the practice fade out itself for, although he would not often be part of the congregation, he was not antagonistic. The cessation was, I think, hastened by Wilfred's mounting demands for more embellishment and I think my mother feared it might develop into Popery. It was of course the obtaining of the effective setting and his own unconscious acting in his role as priest which really intrigued him, and not the religious value or importance. From beginning to end there was no hint of priggishness about the proceedings.

There was much insistence upon real family church-going at about this time and each Sunday morning we would have to accompany my father to one of the churches in the town, for we seemed to change churches with an extraordinary rapidity and for no particular reason. We began by attending as a complete family unit but we soon tailed off as my mother found the walk to and from the churches too much for her. Wilfred became too engrossed with his school work and the preparation of his own sermon, Mary was required to help prepare the mid-day meal, and Colin was too young to come very often. So it frequently happened that my father and I went alone, which was rather strange as we were the two least influenced by religion. However, my father was missing his docks and ships and I think found some relaxation in the services. The music appealed to him and he enjoyed exercising his voice during the hymns and intonations. I went mostly under protest, especially to the morning services which made me feel self-conscious and bored. The evening services I liked better, particularly when I found out, as I soon did, that my father only went if he knew there was to be a voluntary organ recital afterwards. These only occurred in the two larger churches in the town, one of which was the beautiful Abbey Church which very nearly approached cathedral dimensions. I would sit quite happily through the service looking forward to the recital afterwards. The vast building would be only sparsely lit during the usual service and this gave me a covered-up, comfortable feeling, so different from the revealing morning light. When the ordinary service was over and the congregation had filed out, leaving perhaps only six or a dozen people dotted about the church, more lights would go out, leaving a radiant glow from the organ-loft and only a few gleams of mystic light elsewhere. This gave me a floating feeling of unreality with an awed sense that God must be very near indeed and made me feel dispassionately for the bodies that I knew lay buried beneath our feet. I felt sorry for the dead people and in my childish way somehow felt that they themselves might have escaped, leaving only their bones beneath the great slabs of stone, and be even now, at this moment, floating around unseen in the darkened mystery of the church. I hoped they were, for the atmosphere made me feel companionable to them. If the organ was boisterous and thundered and boomed, the spiritual mystery faded and my thoughts applied themselves to myself and were much concerned with valour and achievement. It was when the music softly echoed with seemingly distant trumpetings or shrilled quietly with a lovely high trembling reediness that the mystery wholly enveloped me; when it trembled in clear fluting tremolo, then little cold shivers ran up and down my backbone and my hair seemed alive with tingling, and my mind would float away always seeking gropingly something that I dimly knew I could not find. My absorption in the music and disregard for my father during these recitals puzzled him for he could not attribute it to the music, thinking as he did that I had a profound inability to acquire any sort of musical efficiency. However, I made a small companion for him on his lonely Sunday evenings when he sought to find ease for his mind and satisfy his hunger for melody.

On the walk home through the dark streets my father would question me about the pieces that had been played and discourse one-sidedly upon the merits or technicalities of the rendering, often humming his own version, but once out of the church I was dead to it and could not answer intelligently or remember anything to say about it. He thought that I was rather stupid about it all, even allowing for my entire lack of musical talent; and he was really rather disappointed and quite a little annoyed.

I was still at the same school; and although I was absorbing some very rudimentary knowledge—I believe this process was known and currently spoken of as the three Rs—in any true sense I was learning nothing and disliking the foul-smelling little school more and more. I would sit through the boring school hours in a state of numbed futility and somehow get through the four walks to and fro to morning and afternoon school. In the summer they seemed hot and wearying and in the winter cold and wet. It was possibly a two-mile walk to the school. I was becoming more and more absorbed in my own private pursuits at home. Drawing and painting took the foremost place and I was learning to relegate the school and its unpleasant associations to a background which had to be endured. By shutting down my thoughts about it I could largely obliterate the unliked hours, which was good for my drawing and my childish attempts at carving but very bad for my three Rs. But even so this abominable school was never entirely negatived and its lewd and physically dirty atmosphere still loomed too large for my childish liking and endurance.

My hatred of this place was becoming acute and rather forlornly hopeless, for I knew now that there was no hope of my family reprieving me from it. It was by accident that I discovered an escape and set about securing this for myself. This was a diversion that was soon to overshadow the effects of the bad schools so that they no longer mattered to me at all, and eventually to sever me so decisively that I was able to free myself and finally force my way out of the school altogether, leaving it to its odorous fate with immense satisfaction and gladness. My partial escape happened quite soon although my ultimate severance was to take another year or so.

It happened one summer afternoon when I was loitering rather lazily home from school that, in passing Wilfred's school, I saw that a notice board which had always stood near the main entrance was freshly painted and varnished. The cream-coloured background and cerulean blue lettering held my attention and I went idly up to it to study the information displayed. It contained notices about the School of Art and my interest became riveted: I stretched to tip-toe the better to take it in, and my heart commenced to beat hard with excitement when I found they were beginning evening art classes on Mondays, Wednesdays, and Fridays. All at once an irresistible desire overcame me to attend these classes as soon as possible, and with it a clear picture of what my action must be in order to succeed. I knew that to propose it at home would receive sympathetic non-attention and my project would be added to the long list of things that might be done when I was older. As I stood peering at the board I knew what I must do, though I quailed at the demand for I was not a bold little boy, especially not in thrusting myself into strange buildings or houses or meeting strange people; so before my resolve could weaken I had opened the iron gates and rung the bell of the main door. By this time my heart was thudding painfully and my throat and my mouth were dry. The door was opened by the janitor and I stuttered out my request to see the head of the Art School. Years of contact with boys had made him soured and sceptical although he was afterwards to become one of my most valued friends. At the moment, though, his appearance was forbidding and he gruffly tried to send me away, but my anxiety was mounting and with it an incoherent determination. My appearance and eagerness must, I think, have conveyed a sense of urgency and I was reluctantly admitted. In a surprisingly short time I was ushered into the Principal's studio-office.

A small-made dark man with brilliant merry brown eyes came forward and after an astonished stare at his small visitor immediately set about making me feel comfortable. He did this by fussing about and chuckling to himself most infectiously. Very soon he invited me to look at a water-colour he was working on, and friendship between us was immediate. My nervousness disappeared. It was not until this happened that he inquired how he could help me. I told him my story and he was intrigued with it and at once became my avowed ally. He demurred a little about age, but I knew it was all right, and he progressed to fees. Here, he felt he could hardly conclude negotiations without consulting my father who, I must remember, knew nothing about this idea; but comforted me with an audible quip to himself which sounded like 'small boys, small fees', followed by more merriment. He was much given to these—always kindly—asides. After showing me some of the school he made a final suggestion that I should bring my father to see him one evening to try to fix things up. He ushered me out, escorting me through the door with some ceremony. All the way home my heart sang with happiness at the thought of the evening classes that might lie before me.

When I arrived home I rushed to my mother and blurted out my news. This created more of a flutter than I had expected and brought upon my head disapproval and scolding for having so impulsively approached the school without first consulting my family, an independence that was thought to accord with my exasperating and unpredictable behaviour. Wilfred was told about it and showed marked annoyance that I had dared to approach his own school in such an unmannerly way and without first consulting him, and he did not in any way welcome the idea that a child like me—his words—should become a co-student. He huffily told me privately that if by some unlikely mischance I should manage to get myself accepted, I would have to alter myself and behave with great circumspection; and he at once digressed lengthily and I thought tiresomely upon the meaning and derivation of the word 'circumspect', at the same time saying that of course with my multitude of interests—which did not include English—it was unlikely that I knew what the word meant. I wasn't at all certain, which quite spoilt my answer to him and I had to fall back on my stock rejoinder, telling him not to be such a stuffy old book-worm. Mumbling something about it being better to be a book-worm than colossally ignorant, he took himself off upstairs in something of a nervous huff over what he called my School of Art effrontery . . . calling down from the top landing that I was indeed an optimist . . . did I know what that meant . . . if I thought I should last long in it . . . Thinking again of the merry twinkle in Mr. Weaver's eyes I had my own very confident ideas about this and for once did not call back to him.

Actually, the School of Art and the Technical School, although housed in the same building (a pleasant stone-built one of Georgian type) standing attractively near the river, were run separately with entirely different staffs. I never knew under what authority the schools were run, but I imagine it must have been some government department. They were certainly not private enterprises, although the Art School always gave out the feeling and impression of being so. Wilfred always felt this about his section too.

When my father came home from his office it all had to be recounted again and another family council convened. Nothing of course was settled but neither my mother nor father were averse to the idea, only a little nonplussed at my not first consulting them. They really thought it would be a good thing, if the fees could be managed, and both stressed very hard that it was such a good thing to have a hobby and, as long as I did not contemplate it as a career, they could see no harm in it.

My mother and Wilfred were both very concerned at what had taken place during my interview; Wilfred was specially bothered as to how I had comported myself and was not at all hopeful that my behaviour had been satisfactory or that it would not in some way reflect back adversely upon him. My father did not share this misgiving. However, my first independent social contact outside the family turned out well, for the next morning there arrived an extremely pleasant note for my father from the Principal, suggesting a meeting and putting me in a most favourable light. This bumped me up in the family estimation and, better still, solidified my plan, and even Wilfred began to look at me more thoughtfully and show reserved respect for the proposal in general.

A few evenings later, my father and I went along to see Mr. Weaver. After some hesitation on my father's side and some discussion by Mr. Weaver about how the problem of my age was to be got over, it was decided that something could be done. Mr. Weaver was extremely adept at arranging things; he said he would manage it somehow and the fees too, and suggested I might start next term, but this did not suit me at all and I begged to start at once. After more hesitation, this time on Mr. Weaver's part, he said with a chuckle that he would fix this as well and that I might present myself the following Monday evening. On the way home my father was thoughtful and quiet; I was exhilarated and triumphant. At bedtime that evening as I went to kiss my father goodnight, he told me that he would call me at six o'clock in the morning and we would start building a model ship.

My father's thoughtfulness on the walk home was brought about by the realization that here was yet another son of his pursuing the arts, and a lessening of the chance—perhaps a serious one—of getting me started on a sea-going career. The model boat-building, although it had failed so noticeably with Wilfred, might yet influence me. He had accepted without any resentment his disappointment over Wilfred; his hopes for breeding a seaman now centred in me. This School of Art nonsense could be a serious menace; to offset it he must get me interested in building a ship. My childish enthusiasm for drawing and painting, culminating in my impetuous attack upon the School of Art, must have made him wonder if he must not again prepare for further disappointment.

The almost astonishing thing about this deep wish of my father's was not the desire itself, which in an island race is after all ordinary enough not to excite much comment, but in the fact that it never took really definite form in the way of action of any sort. It became almost secretive and was referred to obliquely and never put before Wilfred or myself with its advantages and disadvantages openly laid out for our inspection. In Wilfred's case, he was so undeniably unsuitable that this was understandable; in my own, less so. This trait of his was the commencement of a future fatal inability in my father to help and advise his sons by placing before them through his own experience and greater knowledge of the world any definite results that would be likely to follow certain defined actions. Much of this was caused, too, by my mother's absolute aversion to the thought of any of us going to sea or doing anything even mildly adventurous which might lead us into temptation and in any case would certainly lead us far from home and religious influences. This no doubt made it difficult for my father to plan or even openly make serious suggestions. In the end it was more of an accident of circumstances coupled with some determination of my own that actually sent me to sea. Or perhaps my father was cleverer than any of us appreciated. I don't know.

The boat-building began, as my father had suggested it should, the next morning. This model boat-building was to be quite a part of our lives for several years to come, especially for my father and me. Wilfred never took any part in it but the other two, although not doing much of the practical work, were always keenly interested in our efforts and would always want to be with us when we were working, content to watch and be useful in handing us things. The fashioning and shaping appealed strongly to me and one of my efforts was a full-rigged, four-masted ship completely clothed up to skysails and stunning sails, with all running parts free and all spars and booms properly made. My mother made her suit of sails, some thirty in all, out of linen to my paper patterns, beautifully made with reefing lines and bolt holes, all eyeletted. Great care was taken in selecting the small log of yellow pine, which we were able to buy from a friendly builder, from which the hull was hollow carved, and afterwards decked over. I would work hard with paint and sandpaper on the outside of the hull to get a perfect finish, filling all the grain of the wood, until it gleamed like satin. The moulding of lead for the keels was rather a ritual and much looked forward to, as it meant bringing old pieces of lead piping to boiling point in a saucepan on the gas stove, then skimming the dross from the boiling liquid and casting the refined molten metal into a carefully prepared clay mould. This operation was pleasantly dangerous as the bubbling, spitting lead could be vicious. Often four or five recastings had to be done before the exact size and weight could be obtained. Already the craftsman's lure of seeking perfection and discounting time or labour was seizing hold of me. The moment of completion was always the least rewarding of all. This ship I had built, I launched and christened—with proper ceremony—the *Mary Millard*, in honour of Mary. Later, she was very nearly to be the cause of drowning the small Colin.

It happened while my mother and Mary were away from home on one of their periodic visits to her sister. Wilfred was in charge of Colin and me during my father's absence. One day Wilfred had retired to his 'study', a table in his bedroom, and I decided to take the *Mary Millard* and sail her on the river and of course take Colin with me, for by now he was becoming my devoted and most affectionate little adherent in all that I did. When we got to the river, we found it in full flood and running very fast and high. To have launched our boat from the bank would have been to lose her at once, but higher up-stream we saw a disused flat-bottomed pontoon. One nose of this was fairly near the bank and we saw that if we could board her, we would be able to sail our craft in the triangle of water between the side of the pontoon and the bank. We successfully negotiated the difficult embarkation and sailed the *Mary Millard* happily for some time until suddenly Colin over-reached, fell, and without a sound disappeared in the deep water. The next few seconds were nightmarish for me. My father had taught me sufficient water-lore for me to be able to appreciate the danger of this treacherous current—for a few seconds I must have panicked. I can recall a disconnected scream as if coming from someone else, whether it came from me or Colin I shall never know. I can remember nothing of those bad moments until suddenly my brain cleared and without effort on my part I was galvanized into immediate action. I remember a sensation of exhilaration seized me as my body responded to my brain —years afterwards I was to realize that this was my first experience of this almost ecstatic exhilaration that is only possible in the presence of immediate danger. I can only describe it as a standing still of time.

In after years, while I was at sea I was again to experience many times, when faced with emergency, this extraordinary sensation of the negation of time and self. It was as if after the first split second of blinding shock—which always came—I somehow jumped out of myself, a clarity of thought and a co-ordination of brain and body replaced the consciousness of ordinary living. It was only in these moments of peril, it seemed to me, that it was possible to really live vitally; it was as if the intensity of these flashes of living was concentrated and funnelled into one burning shaft of realism that was absolute and sublime. In this sublimity, neither the past nor the future was at all relative, only in the vacuum of the halt in time was there any significance. Consequences had no relation to the exquisite awareness of transference from ordinary living to this high plane of reflex action.

As well as this intense exhilaration there was an illumination of spirit that transcended ordinary thought. In this way every action of my body was controlled with a surety and a conviction of rightness that could leave no place for doubt or even consideration. Only spontaneity could survive the intenseness of quality of these experiences. Always for me the presence of danger was a spiritual experience.

Suddenly, Colin's body appeared somewhere and I grabbed at it, but lost it and endured hours of agony in that split second. What else happened I do not know but suddenly and miraculously I had hold of Colin and I pulled frantically, but current suction was spinning his body under to the bottom of the pontoon. His own instinctive kicking may have freed him for I could do nothing except hold on and pull. Terrible waves of despair and hope were alternating over me, until they were dispersed by finding I had him safely in the pontoon. The poor little boy was in a bad way; he could not speak and could hardly breathe, his eyes were closed and his face was mottled blue. I somehow got him ashore from the pontoon. I tried to remember my father's life-saving instructions but they all seemed to have vanished. In my despair and fear I may have pummelled and shaken him and I could recall afterwards rolling him over on his tummy when he ejected a lot of brown muddy water, after which he recovered rapidly and was soon tottering about on his short legs. Dragging and half carrying him, I stumbled off for home. When I got out of the fields and into the street an unknown and kindly man picked up the dripping shivering little creature and carried him to our gate. Both our teeth were chattering, his from his half-drowning and mine from reaction to fear.

When I had got Colin into the house I called out urgently for Wilfred who came tearing down. He gave one look at Colin and to me gave a terrible glare of furious anger. Between us we rushed him upstairs and Wilfred stripped all the small garments from him and we started to rub him down hard with towels, standing him on a chair to do this more effectively, Wilfred all the time muttering to himself, 'pneumonia, pneumonia'. After a lot of rubbing Wilfred sent me down to boil some milk, saying he could finish the rubbing. When I took this upstairs, Colin was rosy all over, but Wilfred thought it would be a good thing to roll him in a blanket. This we did and lifting the cocoon-like little object, put him in a bed and Wilfred fed him with hot milk. Colin was quite docile over all this and if anything seemed to be enjoying the fuss. Wilfred told him to go to sleep, and me to go downstairs and keep out of the way. This I very miserably did and wandered about listlessly and presently felt very cold. When Wilfred came down I was shivering uncontrollably. I suppose this drew attention to my own wetness for although I had not actually been in the water, my struggle with Colin had soaked me almost as much as if I had. This brought more angry words from Wilfred, who sent me off to change. My feeling of relief at having got Colin safely home was giving way to the feeling that I was to blame. When I wandered downstairs again Wilfred was waiting for me and immediately attacked me with a lot of long-worded recriminations for my careless irresponsibility in allowing Colin to fall into the river while he was in my charge—after some more of this I was just ready to come back at him with a good answer, which I had thought up during his peroration, when he shocked me into silence by saying that of course it was quite certain that Colin would contract pneumonia and die on the eleventh day and went on to describe the medical course the illness would take. If this happened I should be responsible.

My guilt was now established in me and I was too overwrought at the certain knowledge that Colin would now die to retaliate in my usual healthy way to Wilfred. Instead, without a word, I ran out into the garden. Wilfred followed me far enough to call out and forbid me to go near Colin and that he would look after him, I could only do more harm. I expect in my distress some of our religious influences came up in me, for I started saying in my head 'Please, Jesus, don't let him die, please, Jesus, don't let him die', until the words became a refrain that worked automatically and would not leave me. All day I was miserable and by the time my father returned, I was sullen and silent with despair.

When my father returned Wilfred told him what had happened to Colin. Of course he at once sprang up the stairs to satisfy himself that all was well. Colin was lively enough and still enjoying everything and, being a tremendously loyal little boy, had made the best of the story to my father as far as I was concerned. Wilfred, in his strangely aloof way, had asked me no questions at all about what had happened; instead he had immediately assumed that whatever had happened was just another proof of my utter stupidity.

It was a curious attitude that Wilfred brought to bear on me in those early years. It is difficult to relate, but I think perhaps there was something—wholly unconscious—in me which must have appeared inimical to him. His behaviour to me was not deliberate unkindness, and although his constant censures were calculated, they were sponsored by a genuineness of conviction which robbed them of any tinge of spite. Wilfred could not be spiteful, but where he was convinced of irresponsibility or stupidity he could be ruthless. In these years—only these years—he sincerely believed that I was naturally stupid and unnaturally irresponsible and because for some unaccountable reason he exaggerated to himself these traits in me I quite often had to pay an undeserved penalty.

The pneumonia idea and his over-eagerness to entertain the suggestion of death sprang from a concern for and an unhealthy absorption in his own state of health. This was beginning to grip him dangerously and his violent outburst towards me was possibly only an outlet for his own suppressed anxiety. Keats was ever-present in his mind, and he was given to this absorption in the life and work of men in all the arts who had died young; he was also wont to compare the histories of these talented short-lived lives with his own plans for his writing of poetry.

He could never divest himself of the parallel this comparison implied. I know that Wilfred was beginning to be convinced, and deeply convinced, in his own mind that high attainment and the expected period of life were impossible to combine, and he was inclined when working well to fear it denoted early death; and when feeling robust and healthy to fear that this was a signal of lack of talent and a negation of all his hopes for literary achievement. This vicious and disconcerting mental see-saw never gave him relief, so that one moment he eagerly sought signs of permanent ill-health and looked forward to finding them to prove promise for himself and at another sought to encourage his robust feeling and the promise this held of a normal length of life. He was also young enough and just boyish enough never quite to know which to choose or welcome.

None of this was helped by my mother's attitude of over-anxiety concerning his physical well-being and her downright encouragement of an acceptance of delicacy and a lack of general robustness. This physical state, although he was not muscularly powerful, never existed organically. At the back of his mind, too, I think lodged a nagging fear that he might miss it both ways and that he might be seized with fatal illness before he had completed his projected work.

None of this mental consternation bothered me at all at this time—which may have accounted for some of our inimicality. I found my own immediate difficulties and problems quite pressing enough without adding to them by peering too deeply into the future, but I think perhaps my immediate and lesser ones hit me harder than Wilfred's lesser ones hit him. He had greater immunity from trivial emotion than I had. When my father came downstairs again from seeing Colin, he hurriedly sought me out and, gripping both my shoulders with his hands, squeezed me to him and with his eyes and voice full of lovely tenderness and emotion whispered to me, 'That's the good old bach you are.' My father in his unbelievably rare and so quickly suppressed flashes of emotional tenderness always lapsed into a sort of hybrid Welsh in the choice of his words. His voice and inflections at these times were purely Welsh and very beautiful indeed.

This unusual praise from my father broke down my stubborn silence. I could nearly always withhold tears of misery but happy relief or high praise always surged up in me in a barely controllable lump and I ran up to Colin's bedroom and kicked away at the iron bed leg until I felt the danger of tears had gone. Then I ran back to my father, and begged for assurance that Colin would not die on the eleventh day. He was mystified and concerned about my frantic appeals, so Colin was brought down and my father instigated and encouraged wild hilarity, I expect to convince me of Colin's unquestioned longevity. Wilfred would take no part in this, but muttering something inaudible went off to his bedroom to read. My father made no attempt to stop him.

Although Colin was none the worse for his near-drowning in the swollen river, Wilfred's bitter attack and tirade against me had bitten into me more deeply than usual, for my own affection and love for the baby of the family were certainly no less than his own and may have been more unselfish. Wilfred's terrible description of what would happen to Colin and his convincing certainty of calamity had impressed me too gravely, and I would find myself searching little Colin's face for the dread symptoms. I could not be happy again until the eleventh day was safely passed. After this I very soon forgot the whole incident.

In the meantime my little ship the *Mary Millard* to which I had not given a thought, must have sailed herself into the floodstream, no doubt rejoicing in her sudden freedom. She must have squared her yardarms, filled her sails, and taking advantage of the tide, set her own course down the Severn for Bristol—the home of her forebears. My father, Colin, and I searched the river banks for many miles and many weeks. I searched only half-heartedly, for now I was in imagination following her adventures and liked to think of her negotiating the port and making for the open sea. I had no wish to find her dismasted and crippled in the debris of the river bank.

Before all this happened I had made my début into the School of Art. On the Monday evening that I was to attend my first night class I asked my mother for permission to wear better clothes than I always wore to go to school. This was readily given and set a precedent which I always adhered to and which gave me so much pleasure in the few years to come. On my way home from the day-school I would hurry along very gaily looking forward to the evening. Once tea was over I would scrub my hands and wash myself very clean, whitening my teeth by rubbing on soot which I gathered straight from the chimney. This was a secret process of mine that I had somehow heard about and it was most effective. I liked the taste of the soot too. My hair, which grew in a fringe over my forehead, I dealt with by putting my head under the tap and flattening it down while still soaking. We were not allowed to use any hair oil. I took great care and trouble over my appearance and enjoyed the confidence and freshness that the whole operation brought about. My mother was splendid in keeping our clothes nice and could patch and darn almost invisibly.

On this first evening I had taken special care and set off feeling pleased and happy. I had no real qualms, except for twinges of natural nervousness, about entering yet another school. For one thing it was my own special find and I knew I had no need to continue unless I liked doing so, and I was firmly convinced that it would be all I expected and not in the least like any of the other schools I had been to. How right I was. When I arrived Mr. Weaver himself was looking out for me and escorted me through all the classrooms, gravely introducing me to all the young art masters and two young mistresses and a few of the students, and altogether made my entry quite delightful. As I had thought, there was no new-boy nonsense and I was accepted with warmth and friendliness and best of all without any exhibition of curiosity.

Some of the students seemed very old to me. The youngest of them must have been six years older than I was. I was set a free-hand drawing test and I was soon absorbed and interested. I had the lovely feeling that my drawing was flowing through my pencil perfectly. There was an official break at 8 o'clock when we would congregate on the ground floor to stretch ourselves and talk and, as I found out later, to enjoy some pleasant sky-larking and healthy horse-play, but this was incidental and nobody was dragged into it unless he showed enthusiasm. The school was small and the classrooms pleasantly largish so there was plenty of room to work. Nobody was allotted any special table or desk and we would work where we pleased, the masters and mistresses moving about giving individual instruction. I later found that the students were allowed to work, or not, just as they pleased and could wander in and out of the room at will. The only restriction really enforced was the ban on any sustained conversation except during the break period. I was surprised when nine-thirty came. I did not think that the time could possibly have passed so quickly. I was told to remain behind until the other students had gone when Mr. Weaver and the other three would assess my test work. I was happy about this as I knew I had been drawing very well indeed. It must anyway have been satisfactory, for Mr. Weaver ordered primary instruction to be cut out so that I could go straight into advanced work. I was particularly pleased and excited about this, so that when I set off in the dark for the walk home I had a nice springy feeling in my legs and I was looking forward very much to the specially nice supper my mother had promised to have ready for me, and very much hoping it would be pork pie.

My return home was greeted with warmth and friendly approbation and sitting alone to a meal so late in the evening gave me a nice feeling of importance, which was added to by the questions fired at me by the rest of the family, even Wilfred unbending and showing interested curiosity. But later he annoyed me with a lecturing address upon the necessity of working hard, for otherwise—so he had heard in his department of the school—students were not allowed to stay on. I created further misunderstanding between us by telling him—again with simplicity—that I was not going to my School of Art specially to work but much more to enjoy myself. This had true meaning for me because I just could not imagine drawing and painting as work, but it made Wilfred look triumphant and all the others a bit chagrined. This curse of mine of stating without thought what to me was so very true caused much misapprehension and sometimes led to these misunderstandings. I felt a bit disappointed about this and wished I had not said it. I was still, of course, going every day to my board school in the day-time but this unpleasantness I found I could now more easily disregard. With my Monday, Wednesday, and Friday evenings to look forward to, I found for the time being that I could manage to put up with this offensiveness —later, I had to change my mind about even this.

Quite soon after my beginning at the Art School I conceived a passionate affection for everything about it; the very building itself and above all its rather dry, slightly sour museum smell fascinated me, with its suggestion of turpentine and paint. This was at first only a suggestion as the oil-painting room was at the far end of the building and well away from our drawing rooms. This was reserved entirely for day students and the evening-only people were never allowed even to see inside.

I spent hours as well in looking at the many drawings and designs —beautifully framed and hung—that lined the rooms and corridors. These were by past and present masters and senior pupils. They had a dragging attraction for me, not so much for their aesthetic appeal but wholly—as it appeared to me—for the almost incredible power of draftsmanship and impeccable execution, so that my admiration and genuine envy could hold me spellbound for minutes and I came to be pleasantly but unmercifully teased by the others for my unconcealed adoration. The young master was a Gold Medallist in design and his winning design was displayed prominently. Strangely enough, it was the one work that had no appeal for me, but there is another story connected with that and it will crop up later.

These evening classes brought to me my first awareness of what real happiness could mean: the delight that could be wrested from gloating over work already accomplished and the even greater joy of premeditating work planned but not yet executed. My absorbed interest in these evenings became stronger and stronger and I would spend most of the time in between evenings in drawing at home, all this at the expense of my ordinary education that was supposed to be proceeding at the board school; but I had no enthusiasm for any subject that was presented to me there. However, none was sought for or even expected and I plodded through the days without caring in the least. From time to time my father became suspicious that progress in this school was impossible and would set me test papers of his own construction. My unwilling efforts to answer these papers always drove him into exasperated bad temper and were always followed by one of his speeches of condemnation and exhortation, equally always followed by the same worriedly muttered promises and resolves that he must do something about it. Nothing was ever done and anyway some other family matter would usually arise and the whole subject would be set aside again until such time as panic swept him once more. In truth there was little that could be done about it. Colin had now been placed in a preparatory private day school in the town, Mary was attending another private girls' school, and the expenses of Wilfred at the Technical were always mounting. All three of them, as well, were receiving music lessons for which fees had to be found, so that to embark upon a better school for me and therefore more fee-finding seemed impossible; so I was left to go on as best I could where I was. In any case it was thought I was not coming to any definite harm and in those days this was always held to be a good argument against any suggested change or betterment.

I was now turning more and more to Colin for companionship, and as the little boy responded so warmly and co-operated so loyally in the various schemes we devised between us for our own entertainment we became, for the next few years until I went to sea, quite inseparable. One of these plans which we were so often to carry out together was the spending of our Saturdays—on which day we neither of us went to school—in long days away from home, taking our lunch and tea with us, carried in our school satchels.

At first these were not entirely a success, but the failure lay only in our misjudgement of time. After all we were both very young, and of course had no watches. We commenced by setting forth about 8.30, the time my father would leave for his office. We would quite soon be in fields and country lanes and after an hour or two of wandering about would think it must be lunch time, and feeling very hungry would attack our food with great gusto. A little more rambling about and we would be sure it was time to go home, only to find when we got there it was only one o'clock and lunch had not yet started. This caused amusement at home and of course more lunch for us. But we did not like it ourselves and always had a flat feeling which spoiled the rest of the day. After a few more bad timings, one or two of which were over-late ones which caused anxiety and a scolding reception, we became cleverer at this and from then on were able to judge our timing pretty well.

At first of course our legs did not carry us very far, but we were adventurous and soon began to get farther and farther afield; some-times, too, a passing trap or cart would give us a friendly lift. We never cared much in which direction it was going as long as it would set us down some miles farther away from home. Occasionally, we would allow ourselves to be carried too far and getting ourselves home turned itself into a task which called for resolve and determination and for frequent rests before we could urge ourselves onwards, but this, too, we learned to judge better through experience. If it was midsummer when we were caught like this, we would arrive home very weary, smothered and choked with the greyish white dust that lay so thickly about the country roads and hedges. As we plodded along, the dust, disturbed by our lagging feet, would spiral up into our mouths and nostrils. In those years the dusty lanes seemed to be summer itself and I loved walking through them, and especially the way the dust muffled the sound of our footsteps. If I was sitting on a bank I liked pushing my hands deep into its lovely close warmth, trickling it out idly through half-closed fingers. Glorious, too, the fun and entertainment when a sudden summer shower falling on its dry velvety thickness spun it into enchantingly perfect little dust balls. These rolled and ran in all directions colliding so gaily with one another and, still unbroken, would unify into bigger ones until the weight of water would burst the fragile film and a tiny rivulet would be born. I shall always regret the dusty rutted lanes.

It was during one of these days that we discovered my lovely village of Uffington. The day we found it we could not penetrate into it for between us and it lay the river. I had not on this day the pennies necessary to use the ferry. But we resolved there and then to save up our weekly pocket money—at this time Wilfred had 6*d.*, Mary 3*d.*, and Colin and I 1*d.* each—and worked out that we could do it in two weeks' time.

I had fallen in love with the look of the village from my side of the river, but I was not impatient and enjoyed the thought of the tantalizing wait at the end of which I knew with absolute certitude that I would not be disappointed. Before we got home again I had sworn Colin to secrecy about it, for I did not want to be given the extra pennies, which would have been instantly forthcoming if I had explained what they were for. This might have meant being taken to it. I did not want this to happen. I wanted to find it myself and so in my mind possess it. I had infected Colin with my enthusiasm to penetrate into and explore this place by ourselves. Two weeks later, this time armed with our ferry-fare pennies, we started off early and, very pleased about our prospect for the day, we trudged along steadily until we came to the river bank and the ferry. This had to be hailed from our side of the water and we enjoyed piping our calls in unison to attract the ferryman's attention. This was never easy to do, but eventually we saw him emerge from his cottage, lumber slowly down to the landing steps and, throwing out the securing chain, push off towards us. These boats were long, flat-bottomed, heavy, punt-like contraptions and were propelled across the river by the ferryman hauling hand over hand on a light wire hawser that was stretched tautly from one bank to the other, the one side of the punt being fitted with two iron stanchions mounted with steel rollers clipped securely but freely around the suspended wire. Normally, it was a simple operation, but when the river was running fast with heavy flood water, it needed great skill and long experience to manœuvre the clumsy craft safely across.

Colin and I, arriving on the other side, felt the day had started splendidly when the kind boatman told us that as we were so small he would only charge us a halfpenny each, which left us with an extra penny each to spend. Both full of expectation about the newly found village, we climbed up the steep and narrow alder-lined path, past the ferry cottage and so into the dusty village square, around which the cottages and farm buildings leaned and nestled so warmly. We were

enchanted with it all and wandered around happily, now and again
exchanging polite words with the men and women who slowly moved
about their business. They welcomed our staring interest with kindly
regard.

Our bewitchment was completed when the immense black water-
mill wheel with thunderous clankings and muffled inner clangings and
groanings commenced ponderously turning its creaking bulk. With its
first half-turn it drove out in mock alarm hundreds of gaily coloured
pigeons from the whitewashed cobweb-encrusted lofts. The birds
wheeled and tumbled and spiralled above and about our heads in lovely
confusion of black and white, blue-grey, and blue and slate, their backs
and wings glistening in the sunlight.

Rather dizzily, from watching the churning cascading wheel and the
rapid whirring of the birds about us, we made our way out of the
village to find a quiet field in which to lie on our tummies and eat our
lunch. After our meal, which Colin and I ate as we always did with such
hungry happiness, we wandered back towards the village. On the way
we found a pump at which we stopped and after drinking from our
cupped hands, took it in turn to pump water over each other's heads,
for the sun was blazing down. We found another lane leading out past
the back of the mill house, which we saw to our delight led us to a
hump-backed brick-built little bridge that carried the lane over a canal.
The strip of water, fringed on either side with bulrushes, lay sleeping
with glassy stillness.

We had not expected this surprise and at once made our way down
to the towpath that we might look at the canal itself more closely.
We soon found a narrow cutting which curved steeply down to the
water level. One side of this constricted passageway was lined with the
minute village shops, placed here no doubt to attract the custom of the
passing narrow boats and the bargee families they always housed. The
windows of these very small shops were so low that their uppermost
panes of thick green bubbly glass only reached our eye-level, so that
even we small boys had to stoop to see what was mistily displayed
behind them. In the few summers to follow we were to come to know
these small shops and their owners very well and to spend many pennies
with them. We started then and there by investing a halfpenny each in
pear drops and acid drops which we ate alternately and with precise
exactitude from each other's paper bag until they were all finished,
when we blew up the bags and burst them.

We were getting tired now and I thought it must be time to be going home, for I remembered the long way we had to walk after we had crossed the river again. But there was still one more unexpected happening waiting for us. I had noticed the tiny church with its little exposed bells and on the way back looked for it again, but this time it was not the church which caught my attention but the garden adjoining it. I was astonished at the massed array of colour that seemed to flow along in such dazzling brilliance. It was most likely my first look at a really beautiful summer border. It was certainly my first conscious appreciation of one and I remained just mutely staring. Presently, unseen by me, a gentle hand was laid on my shoulder and an old old voice asked me what I was looking at. With some trepidation I replied as politely as I could, I suppose saying something about liking the flowers. Whereupon, brushing aside our rather shyly uttered excuses, an old clergyman ushered us into his garden and, escorting us around, showed us all of it with great kindliness. He disappeared into the house and came out with two glasses of milk which we drank very gratefully and after pressing huge slices of cake into our hands allowed us to express our rather timid thanks and set us forth on our way to the ferry. Fortified with the milk and still existent cake and the pleasant feeling of good-will the kindly vicar had inspired in us, the way home did not seem so long as usual. I was day-dreaming too of paint boxes and sketching easels, so that I did not notice the miles. I was enchanted to have found this village for myself: there was an exact rightness about it that in a curious way supplied a need in me—perhaps it was the sun-warmed peacefulness of the crumbling brick and tiled cottages, the farm smells, and the undertones of quiet sounds that drifted through the air from beasts and birds mingling with the muted vibrations that came from the noise of pails and country tools being used in farmyard and cottage garden.

Mr. Weaver had already shown me some David Cox reproductions and the lovely water-colours had inflamed me instantaneously with ambition to paint similar pictures. This village of Uffington, I thought, supplied everything in actuality that the David Coxes had given me in imagination; even the mill and water wheel were there. Walking home, I made up my mind that soon I would go there and paint. . . . We were late getting back that evening but all of them at home were used to our roaming excursions to undisclosed destinations, and while our belated returns would sometimes cause vexation, they rarely caused alarm. By now both my mother and father had great trust in me to take good care of the younger Colin.

Once at home again my one wish was to discourse upon the happenings of the day and persuade the others if possible to share in the joys of my find. Over supper I found I had an appreciative audience, especially my father who liked hearing about anything in the way of a new find. Wilfred as well was interested and really became rather impressed. I remember he stopped eating to turn towards me with an open-eyed stare when I started talking in a rather hesitant way about David Cox and the affinity I thought existed between Uffington and his water-colours. My father chuff-chuffed a bit at this trend and promptly asked what I thought the prospects for fishing would be, suggesting at the same time that it might be a good thing if we took a picnic and all went to see this place on his next free Saturday.

I can see now—and look back upon it with pleasure—that in our family any proposal that was mooted, such as this, was always carried through and never allowed to drop or be forgotten. Fuss and to-do there was in plenty when the time came to start, even last-minute changes of detail, but no project was allowed just to fade out. So it was with this one, only this time there was much less of the usual disagreements and indecisions that were so often the forerunners of a family exodus. As it was thought to be too long a walk for my mother, my father had arranged for a hired carriage to take us as far as it could by road, which was within two or three fields of the ferry on our side of the river. These family days were a very pronounced feature in our life together, most especially through the six years from 1907 to 1913, and were a powerful influence in binding us together as a unit—the very fact that periodically we insisted on and looked forward to doing something all together struck a happy balance which offset our individual interests, which in our 'house' life were always divergent and so often dissentient. As I have said, they so often started badly and sometimes continued well into the day with argumentative humours and ruffled tempers, but they always finished well, so that at the end of the day trivial antagonisms—if only temporarily—would be put aside, and we all enjoyed one another with tranquil happiness. I cannot remember it otherwise. They were important to us all in many ways, perhaps not least in the unconscious discipline which they engendered in each one of us in our different behaviours.

Although Wilfred was always the most difficult to enlist into these goings-forth, they were, I think, of even greater importance to him than to any of the rest of us. Because of the significance of these family days together Uffington village became in a way a part of our lives, for not only did we often go there but we used the village as a point of departure for other penetrations into the surrounding countryside. This particular day when we were to visit Uffington all together for the first time was one of our best days.

My father and the rest of us were very considerate and thoughtful about my mother, especially about not allowing her to overtax her strength, as this was considered to be an undertaking and even an ordeal for her. An unspoken family loyalty helped as well, for although my father had arranged the outing, it was realized that Colin and I had actually found the place and for this reason the others made extra efforts to make it all go well for our sakes. Wilfred was quite humane and really quite enjoyed himself. The weather was perfect and my father was skilful in boiling the kettle without loss of either temper or water which was unusual enough to herald a success in itself. By common consent it was agreed that we should keep well away from the church as I dreaded meeting my nice old clergyman so soon and in such increased numbers. This disappointed Wilfred who had been intrigued by my vague description of the church and extremely cross with me for not being able to provide him with architectural details, or even approximate period, and he wanted to find out these for himself. After some discussion it was agreed that if he went alone and avoided contact with the old gentleman there could be no possible connection between Wilfred and ourselves, and he happily walked back to the village to interest himself with the church.

He returned in an hour or so with his own carefully documented notes giving a suggested history of the building, its origin, and various additions or alterations, together with quick diagrammatic sketches of the windows and the stained glass, which he told us he thought very poor. He proceeded to transfer his notes into a sort of lecture to us all, hinting all the time at my lack of enterprise in not having secured all this for myself last time, driving home his not unkindly barbs with slyly malevolent glances in my direction. None of us minded him doing this at all. We were used to these dissertations, thinking only that the Old Wolf was off again and, taking little notice, we went on with our own thoughts or conversation.

Half-way through Wilfred's discourse my father had wandered away to engage in talk with a likely-looking man he had noticed, in the hopes of gleaning local information concerning possible walks in the surrounding countryside. He returned to us with the news that large tracts of woods and fields were open and free from restriction. He had in mind further scope for Colin and me to explore. As there was still time before we need start to return to our waiting carriage, he took us and showed us where we might go without fear of trespass; in particular he showed me the entrance to a lovely avenue of trees which he assured me led to a beautiful wooded hill over which we might roam at will and from the top of which, if and when we could manage the climb, a superb view of the surrounding counties could be seen. He was especially anxious to do this because, although he would not stop Colin and me going off on our own, he was worried in case we got into difficulties. We had already had one or two frightening experiences of being crudely and roughly ordered off land, and one dangerous one when a drunken brute of a farmer, returning from market in his gig and seeing Colin and me sitting quietly just inside one of his grass fields, had slashed out with murderous viciousness with his long driving whip, the wicked thong only missing our faces by inches. It was only the fact of being alone in his gig with a horse already almost uncontrollable from his drunken handling that saved us from a dreadful thrashing. As it was we made good our escape across fields where he could not follow with his horse. I remember we trembled violently most of the way home from the shock of the sudden gross assault.

Chapter Eight

'BLESSED WITH GOLD'

Another happy outcome of the finding of Uffington was an escape for me from having to go to the dreary town churches on Sunday mornings. My father suddenly thought how nice it would be if we went instead to this little village church. I liked this idea tremendously and abetted him in every way, for besides the church service, which I thought must—in my village—be much easier to sit through than in any other church, there was the lure of the walk through the fields in the early freshness of the mornings and of course the ferry crossings. More than anything else, perhaps, it was just because it was Uffington—I find it difficult to describe the enchantment that this village had wrapped about me; in some unknown way it satisfied a need in me and in return I had immediately loved it.

At first my father would take one or two of us with him. By starting very early we had time to loiter slowly along the riverside watching the fish—of this my father never tired. These were the only churchgoings that I ever enjoyed or looked forward to. This was not altogether due to the interest of the country walk for during the service itself I was never restless or bored; instead an awareness of tranquil spirituality seemed to descend upon me that in some way enveloped me with a feeling of protection. Inside the friendly little building I felt secure from anything disagreeable. During the morning services I enjoyed the musty warm smell that was driven out of the stone walls by the hot sunshine that burned its way through from the outside. I loved the shaft of transparent golden light that blazed through the square made by the always open door. All around me were splashes of blue and green, rose and amber, that filtered through the stained glass in rainbow beams to make suspended pools of warmth that glowed under the dark arched roof. The sparrows and finches flew in and out as they wished; swallows also would dart in, inspect the interior, flash around with a perfection of speed and timing, and not finding what they wanted glance their way out again. The murmur of the countryside with its creaking activity mingled with the drone of the prayers and made me languorously happy. On still days if I listened hard I could hear the rustle of the fantails in the mill lofts. After church we would walk through the quiet village to the little canal bridge, here to lean over the parapet watching and waiting to see the dragon-flies as they skimmed the dark water. These were the mornings.

The evenings would be different for then the summer night would let fall enchantment over all of us. If my mother was feeling well and able for the walk, the six of us would set out to walk through the lanes and over the fields and across the river to enjoy the quietness of the evening service in the tiny church. On these occasions an instinctive unity joined us closely together. It may have been the peacefulness of the lovely summer evenings that gave us all this sense of well-being, or —and I think this more likely—the influence of my father and mother who with gentle restraint would bring about an atmosphere which unified us all. Their effort may have been an unconscious one as a concession to the spiritual and religious character which marked the setting forth on our simple occasion. Whatever it was, it always gave me uplifting surges and made me purely happy, for in spite of my childish exasperations and rebellious disregard I loved my family in a way I found impossible to explain and was never more consciously happy than when this unexpected wave of unity swept over us. My father would be tolerant and gentle, my mother softly spoken and so infinitely kind and beautiful. Wilfred would be almost demonstratively affectionate towards me. Colin and Mary would be considerate and tender towards us all. As the first hardly heard ring of the church bells floated towards us, we would fall into harmonious silence until, drawing nearer, something in the excited silvery chatter of their tinkling sounds would start us light-heartedly talking again.

The return journeys home were always to me the most beautiful time, especially when darkness was falling. We would file out quietly and solemnly from the tiny church and, after an exchange of simple country benedictions from the vicar, wind our way through the darkening village until we came to the opening at the top of the narrow root-strewn tortuous path leading down to the river, when we would all join hands for mutual safety in our descent to the ferry. The river, as we crossed, would look black and satiny and very deep but gave us assurance of its friendliness in musical clucks and swirling gurgles in answer to the caressing pushings of the ferry's flat square bows. Safely out from the ferry, the long walk through the water meadows commenced, and in the almost and yet not quite darkness of summer this was mysterious and full of delight. In the fields the fragrance of the beast-smells mingled with the crushed buttercups seemed powerful and somehow urgent. The great beasts themselves were dotted about across our path and others could be seen as dark hillocks lying with all four legs neatly tucked under them, the wide white blazes that marked their great heads glowing like ghostly little lamps. On still nights we could hear the rhythm of their grinding ruminations. Now and again we would disturb one. With slow movements of mild reproof it would rise awkwardly and with staggering gait turn towards us and, opening its nostrils, blow out twin winds of scented globuled air that, wafting and misted to whiteness by the chilling air, would roll buoyantly along the top of the layer of mist that lay like cotton-wool just above the dew-drenched grasses, until they mingled and were lost.

On one of these summer-night returns from Uffington church, when we were walking through the last of the meadows before we reached the lane, I had fallen back behind the others as I was sometimes wont to do—I was fond of slowly dragging my feet through the cool wetness of the grass. When I was climbing over the stile leading into the lane I noticed in the half-darkness that my boots looked strange and peering more closely I saw that they were completely covered with buttercup petals; in the darkness they glowed like gold. I was immediately intrigued with this and called out to the others that I had feet of gold, but they were a long way up the lane, the mist was muffling my voice, and they could not hear me properly, so I did not persist and presently I heard Wilfred walking back to see what I was calling to them about. When Wilfred reached me he too was fascinated with the strange luminous effect. While we were still looking at them we heard my father's footsteps turn and come towards us. He was softly calling out as he came to ask if we were all right and I was just about to call back through the darkness when Wilfred gently pressed my arm for silence —hesitated a moment and then called quietly back, 'Harold's boots are blessed with gold'. There was a silence after this, my father did not hear, or if he did, could not make anything of it, but called back telling us to hurry and not dawdle so much . . . we heard the rap of his brisk footsteps as he turned again to rejoin the others . . . Wilfred and I followed on, but with every step my boots lost some of our flush of gold. . . .

Six or seven years later, under what different circumstances, Wilfred was to write the lines in 'Spring Offensive',

> And the far valley behind, where the buttercup
> Had blessed with gold their slow boots coming up.

After the fragrant atmosphere of the summer night that lay so thickly on the fields we had left, the badly lighted, rather sordid streets nearer home seemed hard and dry so that we were glad to be in the house again. Rather tiredly silent now, we would eat our frugal supper and us younger ones would go to bed.

Years afterwards, wearied by the drag of war, I attempted to re-find this curiously religious spirituality that had descended about me during these summer evenings, but although I searched some of the world's cathedrals and many churches I never again recaptured it.

This, then, was the village of Uffington which with its simple power was able—in different ways—to influence all of us during the three or four years just prior to 1914. My mother and father felt it in the unison it created between themselves. Wilfred perhaps found poetry in it: that a fragment clung is certain, how much further he was influenced is uncertain. Mary and Colin found unsophisticated pleasure in the surroundings and joy in being with the rest of us. To me it brought me my painting. Before the middle of 1912 had come, I had painted almost every bit of it and much of the surrounding lanes, cottages, and landscape. More than this, it brought into actual reality for me my profound love for my family and the knowledge that, differ and quarrel as we might, this love between the six of us was indestructible. In the mornings Uffington, tucked securely into the wooded bank of the cool river, had a satisfying freshness for me. In the evenings it had a glory all its own.

The spell of the mysterious beauty of these times, especially our peaceful family meanderings to the little church, remained with me always. Years later, sometimes without warning, the memory of them would flash into my mind—perhaps while I was freezing in the fo'c'sle of a listing tramp steamer labouring in heavy seas somewhere between the Falkland Islands and Cape Horn or perhaps while I was wading through the reeking, stench-filled depths of an emigrant ship's hold somewhere off the West Indies—the memory could always hit me such a violent blow that it became an agony of nostalgic longing.

We were still occupying the same house that we had taken when we first arrived in Shrewsbury. It had always been too small for us, but now as we grew older it was becoming cramped. This in itself did not matter especially except that it made everything more difficult for Wilfred and me, he to keep his books and papers together, and I to find room for my home-made drawing-board and my large sheets of paper. It meant that Wilfred had to work in the bedroom we were sharing and I worked where best I could, but I was adaptable and could usually fit myself into some corner or use one of the other's bedrooms—anyhow I was in my School of Art for three evenings a week. It would I suppose make a nice sentimental scene if I could draw a picture of Wilfred and me working away in the same bedroom, he at his writing and reading and I working at my drawing and painting, but I could never work in the same room as Wilfred nor he with me; we both knew this and never disguised it from each other. We both, I think, demanded our own stages and settings and having built these around ourselves refused to share them. This left our bedroom free for Wilfred in the evenings and with the help of my mother he fitted up the only spare bit of room with an odd table and chair and a cupboard for his books to make a sort of study. He himself always designated this makeshift arrangement thus and in each of our houses this corner of whatever bedroom he was occupying came to be known to all of us as Wilfred's study. This imbued it with sacrosanctity which not one of us even in our most irresponsible moments would have thought of violating. In this way he was much better off than us others until we moved to a larger house.

There was no heating of any sort in the bedrooms; the house was damp and sunless in winter and very hot in summer, so that for most of the year he had to work uncomfortably. Unlike Colin and I who hated wearing thick or bulky clothes, especially in the house, he did not appear to mind this at all and would drape scarves and rugs over and around himself and wear mittens, which my mother had specially knitted for him, in his efforts to keep warm and so keep working. I do think, though, that much of this discomfort was an indirect satisfaction to him, and that the role of a struggling, ill, and striving student was a part which he had cast for himself; and he liked to think of himself playing this part. There was an element of self-infliction and almost a wish to endure bodily suffering in order to emulate the early days of

5. Mother and the four of us
1902–1903

Bushell, Henley-on-Thames

6. The canal, Uffington village. A water-colour I painted in the early summer of 1909

great poets. There is no doubt at all that at this time Wilfred was very much preoccupied with envisaging himself in this somewhat romantic role, so that the prospect of enduring cold and hunger in some dilapidated attic—writing poetry—far from appalling him, had a strong appeal; but he did stipulate that the attic, if it came to this, must be in France. In his day-dreaming he never pictured himself suffering any privation in England; such a thought did appal him. It was something of this that made his freezing bedroom attractive to him, especially the necessity for piling on the clothes and blankets; this and working by candlelight—there was no other lighting—came near in his mind to a right setting for himself. The effect was perhaps a little spoilt by my mother's constant vigilance to see that he was moderately warm and her frequent ministering with hot cocoa drinks, but the swathing rugs and of course the very real cold helped the atmosphere he demanded. This romantic period belonged only to his adolescence, later he was to envisage things very differently indeed.

The house we were in at this time was not unpleasant in a small town villa way. It was, I think, one of six or so in an undivided block which formed the end and joined together two narrow streets that ran up and away from it. It was altogether a curiously mixed locality. Our own little block was humble but considered very respectable. Dotted about here and there were really big stone-built houses with large gardens, walled and well-kept. Before the encroachment of the small houses these had most likely stood alone in rural pleasantness. A few large and very old trees lent corroboration to this. We had in our own narrow strip of garden a beautiful quince tree which was unusual in itself.

The two streets running up from each end of our block had a very different reputation—rightly, too, for they were certainly unsavoury. They had been built as a speculation; all the houses were small, un-separated, and precisely similar, and seemed to us to be inhabited exclusively by women and hundreds of children. Of course this was not so, it was merely that the men and working boys were away at work when we passed through the streets, but the women and children and blowsy young females were always there to pester and venomously attack us with verbal abuse.

In order to gain access to the country it was always necessary for us to walk through one of these streets unless we made a long and tiresome detour. As this added to our uninteresting part of the walk Colin and I, if we were alone, were disinclined to do it. If Wilfred was with us the detour was always insisted upon by him. If either of our parents were with us it did not matter, as this was a signal to the streets calling for non-aggression and studied silence.

Although the traverses through these streets were always embarrassing and the ordeal often hateful, our reaction was always more dislike than dread, for the rough, ill-reared, untrained children who swarmed around them never had the dangerous quality that the ferocious and blood-lusting town boys of Birkenhead had possessed. They were more oafish and for the most part were content to shout insults and jeers, throwing stones and dirt from a safe distance. Occasionally, unavoidable scuffles with an odd blow were exchanged but these usually fizzled out quite harmlessly. I had absorbed some urchin craft in Birkenhead and this stood me in good stead, but although the street did not constitute a real fear in our small existences, it remained for a long time a factor to which we could never become insensitive.

The real trouble was the women who were an idle, blowsy, dirty, and vindictively resentful collection who neither troubled nor cared about seeing that their unwanted children were kept clean either in mind, habits, or bodies, so that the children were not just healthily grubby but visibly unclean, always scabrous and dirty. It was no uncommon thing for us to see tiny toddling children not only soaked with their own urine but smeared about with their own excreta. These women would stand in their doorways and as we passed hurl extraordinarily foul invective and horribly disgusting references to our anatomical parts and what they would do to them if we were their children. It must have been the sight of our well-kept little suits and stockings and clean bodies that exasperated them to such fury and brought forth the streams of senseless abuse. Occasionally, one more infuriated than the rest would lunge out at us with some vague idea of fouling our cleanness, but they were grossly cumbersome and very slow. I was always quick and became clever at avoiding these encounters.

This vendetta continued for several years, but the disagreeableness only took place in the streets themselves and we were not sought out or seriously followed. It was more individual aggressiveness than gang-warfare. It was to end quite suddenly. There was a boy in the street of about my own age. He followed the pattern of the other boys except that he was more noticeably pugnacious and more disgustingly scabby with sores which often ran with suppurating pus. Between us there grew a hatred that had a bitter reality that was unnatural in its intensity, even for small boys.

Our mutual dislike was perhaps just attaining a pitch of unbearability when by chance we met in the street shop. I had opened the shop door to come face to face with him. He was engaged in swearing luridly and rudely at the woman serving behind the table that served as a counter. My entrance caused the woman to turn to me with a whining complaint about the perpetual nuisance of him always begging for white wrapping paper to do his stupid drawings on. At once my interest was caught and I must have flung out a few questions at him. The woman pushed us both out of the shop, fearing perhaps some flare-up. Outside, at first he was sullen and resentful and deeply suspicious of my unaccountable near-friendliness, but I had ignored my past hatred and forgotten my repugnance. I found myself instead using cajolery and consciously being wily and carefully choosing words with which to draw his confidence. I brought all my immature diplomacy to bear to persuade him of my good intentions. I remember being surprised at my success and becoming once again aware of power, a power that could be used—I was dimly realizing—with so much greater effect than force or a pretence of threat. It was curious that in these moments of actual close contact it never occurred to either of us that there was a physical risk that the other might suddenly attack. We were using words and had a common language. Presently he fumbled under his filthy shirt and, bringing out a dirty, much-folded square of flimsy paper, looked carefully up and down the street and unfolded it for me to see. My astounded words of genuinely surprised admiration made him look directly at me and I saw that his eyes were soft and purely childish and glistening with emotional gratitude. In that flashed second our hatred and dislike died for ever.

The drawing was a beautiful one and to my undeveloped judgement seemed to have a maturity that was amazing and a draughtsmanship and sense of design that was superb and made me envious, for I had not even approached such delicacy of craftsmanship. Years afterwards, when being shown a lovely square of hand-made lace, the fine spider-web tracery work in it instantly made the boy's grubby design leap to my visual mind.

In our new-found trust and friendliness he asked me into his kitchen to see some more of his drawings. As we went in through his back door we were roughly seized and immediately ejected by his mother, a profane virago, who with obscene threats told the boy that if he ever brought the bastard stuck-up little toff into her house again she would have the skin off him. To cover up his discomfiture, as soon as we were safely on the pavement again he told me seriously to take no notice as she was only his mother and 'a . . . bloody old bitch, anyhow'.

When I got home I told my mother and father something of what had happened and begged permission to bring him into the house to see my drawings, but quite understandably this was vetoed most emphatically. Indeed, they were shocked at the low contact I had made and with my defence and championing of the boy. I was quite incompetent to explain the magic of understanding that had swept away dirt and skin disease, social strata, differences of speech and the foulest language, so that to me and also to him they did not any longer exist. My eagerness over this boy—I could not get out of my mind the beautiful drawing or the sudden friendliness that had jumped into his eyes— was looked upon at home with much concern as evidence that my tastes were getting dangerously low, and my vehemence, for I did not give in easily, that he should be allowed to come to the house was considered a further indication of my low aspirations. They were, though, quite adamant. With this condemning discouragement from both our homes, our friendship could not develop beyond chance meetings. We did meet in the streets, not only with pleasure and sincerity but with an easy equality that lent dignity to us both. He would always waylay me if—which was quite often—he had a fresh drawing he wanted to show me.

We never had any more bother in the streets either from boys or rude children. Word had gone forth in the street that I was never to be molested. A year or so after this I went to sea, and when I came back he had gone—I never found out where.

When I was older and more able to think, recollections of this boy with the gift for design and drawing would swim across my mind, always with a sense of regret for the loss of so much talent and pleasing personality. I would wish for him that he had been born into some black or brown pagan tribe, and think to myself how, if this happened, his skill of fingers would have been detected at an early age and cherished carefully as a gift from their own gods. A band of nude people, knowing nothing of civilization as we know it but guided only by their instincts and age-old strict tribal morality—how certainly then would the power in his brain and hands have elevated him amongst his fellows and he would have become the chief designer to the tribe, designing all their intricate weapons, later executing in beautiful rhythm and totemic meaning the corrugations and serrations upon human breasts and fore-heads and, in late middle age, carving and creating new images for their gods! Africa had her Epstein long before we did. Thinking this, his predestined lot in Christian England horrified me.

With peace in the streets, the expeditions which Colin and I made into the countryside became something to be looked forward to even more. For although the boycotts of our passage through the streets had never amounted to anything very serious, yet they had been a nagging anxiety, especially on the last lap of the journey home. We were spend-ing longer days out and getting farther afield all the time and before we got home we were generally leg-weary and tired and the thought of having to run the gauntlet had until now rather spoilt our homecoming.

When Colin and I had explored the country within walking distance we became more ambitious and began making train journeys to more distant places. These long days out were great fun for us and mostly happy ones, but there were other days when things went wrong for us. We were both young enough to be fairly easily frightened by strange encounters or unexpected predicaments. Sometimes the weather would turn against us and we would have to trudge home cold and wet and quietly miserable. Other times we would be caught in lonely places in really bad thunderstorms. These made us both frightened and although we pretended not to mind in the least, in spite of our attempted jocu-larity our spirits would sink distressingly. I secretly dreaded the diminu-tion of the daylight more than the noise of the storms. Pheasants, as well, had a horrid habit of whirring up suddenly from under our feet that would set my heart racing madly. Once when we were walking up a narrow overhung lane, apparently deserted, there was a click of a latch and an immediate avalanche of ten or twelve great black dogs bore down upon us with terrible-sounding barkings. We were both knocked off our feet and rolled in the dust and for minutes were the centre of a heaving, black, slavering-tongued mêlée. We both panicked unashamedly and let out squeals of fright. They were called off with a cracking whip and careered away harmlessly enough. They were, of course, teams of shooting Labradors that had been released for their daily run and we had been caught by the impetus of their first madly hysterical rush. We were neither of us in the least hurt, only smothered in dust and slimy saliva, but inwardly we were both rather badly shaken and the rest of the afternoon was spoilt for us.

Wilfred caught something of our enthusiasm for these expeditions, sometimes joining us in them, but he was at this particular age just a little old for us and altogether too inclined to turn them into excuses for instruction—still using his own particular technique of cementing his own knowledge. His interest in botany as a science was well awakened and very active and, while we willingly searched for his wanted specimens, we did not take at all gratefully as he felt we should have done to his slightly hectoring lectures, and although we enjoyed the times he came with us they were not really a great success. Still, when geology became one of his enthusiastic subjects we were able with some pride to lead him to likely quarries and shale-beds, where we would hammer away loyally with our borrowed coal-hammers, splitting rocks for his inspection and always hoping we should find some prize for him. We ourselves got a little bitten with this fever and would load our pockets and eventually our bedrooms with useless lumps of quartz and supposedly metal-bearing stone, some of which when freshly split certainly glittered most alluringly.

Although, as I say, Wilfred did come with Colin and me on some of our journeys into the country, he did so mostly under protest. The protest came from inside himself: outwardly he would want to come very much, but inside him there was always this tormenting fear that by doing so he might be wasting time, a fear which was becoming obsessional and was to remain so always. I am sure that at this early age he dimly realized the possession of a power within himself; he was also aware that this power was tightly locked and that only he himself could force and fashion the key which would unlock it for him. It was both the necessity and the responsibility of doing this which so constantly harassed him. His conviction that scholarship and scholarship alone could bring this release was driving him mercilessly in his application and quest for knowledge. At no time was Wilfred concerned with scholarship for its own sake, but only with the release of power which attaining it might bring about.

All this of course was not at all clear to the rest of us; we just accepted it as a strange sort of wish on his part to excel in every scholastic subject by making this stupendous effort. It was not after all particularly notice-able. In those days many older boys and young men not only read very seriously but studied long and assiduously. What was perhaps noticeable in Wilfred was that whereas these other older boys were working hard, they were doing so with a specific purpose—an already chosen career, or at least a chosen field of definite ambition—but Wilfred, whose ambi-tion was burning him up inside, showed none of it outside, and any inquiry about what he would like or intended to do would be met with a silent but somehow confident stare; or, if an answer was absolutely necessary, then it would be an inaudible vague muttering about poetry and literature. . . . This baffled my father completely, he could not understand where with all this application to his books Wilfred in-tended to go. . . . Poetry and literature in our circumstances could not really be accepted as a serious answer. Another disconcerting thing about it was that he—beyond this mumbling about poetry and litera-ture—showed no desire for specific success; nothing else tempted him or would have done had the doors been open to him, which of course they were not. I only once heard him express with feeling any desire for a particular fulfilment and this was very much in the literary realm. Any other prospect he looked upon as an expediency only . . . it might be used as a prop for his writing—but no matter how glowing, never for anything else. My father found it difficult to understand and Wilfred with his muttering did not help him. The rest of us accepted it as some-thing very much a part of 'Old Wilfred', and later not only saw that he must, but were eager that he should, go his own way. We were pre-pared to let him even if it meant some lessening of our own oppor-tunities.

These were difficult years for Wilfred and to add to his perplexities he was, I think, beginning to worry about this seclusion of his, and perhaps a troubled doubt did arise now and again as to whether he and my mother were actually thinking along the same lines or looking to-wards the same object. My mother's indecisiveness would sometimes propel him in one direction and then, immediately perhaps, she would propound some unformed scheme of her own which Wilfred could not help seeing would lead him on to a different course altogether. This all added to his distraction as to what occupation he might be able to enter and so solve his problem of earning a living. It upset my father as well, for any decision with which he might concur had the immedi-ate effect of further retraction and indecision by my mother. In consequence any ensuing discussion which arose lacked concord, so that if a decision was arrived at it was never clear-cut.

Wilfred was showing signs of overwork and strain, and it may have been something to do with this that caused the holiday in Torquay to be arranged. The idea was for him to go alone, taking me for company. I put it like this because this is exactly how it was arranged, my mother begging me to try to behave well and to make efforts to avoid becoming a trial and nuisance to Wilfred. This was not really necessary for beneath our outer and violent-seeming frictions we both possessed affection for each other; his peremptory manner I looked upon as part of him, I really rather enjoyed it and was not often bothered by it.

We were to stay with a sister of my father's who had a house down there. We set off very gaily, Wilfred quite boyishly excited—what good fun, like my father, he could be when able to throw off pre-occupation and behave naturally. We were both looking forward to the few weeks together in a strange place. We arrived late at night, which was nice, and found our aunt's house without much difficulty. It was somewhere in the centre of the town. It was soon apparent that we were to be very much left to our own devices, for my aunt was wholly occupied with nursing her husband who was seriously and incurably ill.

This worked out very well for us—being left to find our own entertainment I mean—and my aunt was extremely thoughtful and very helpful about trains and buses and in putting up packages of food for our lunch, and most generous with pocket money for coffee or sweets. She told us where we could go for tea, providing us with money to pay for it so that we might stay out until late evening. Wilfred and I made the most of our time and I can't recall being bored or unamused. We would commence our days with swimming in the sea, but only on days when the sun was warm and we felt like bathing. This freedom was in itself a pleasure to us when we remembered the stern and unrelenting pressure father would bring to bear to force us into the water —whether the day was wet or fine—as a rigorous routine during family holidays.

The town itself attracted us very much, more than the beaches, I remember, for once the swimming was over, having most likely made ourselves thoroughly cold and shivery, there seemed little left to do; whereas the town seemed to possess a bustle of activity with an important speediness that was so opposite to the somnolent atmosphere

and slow pedestrian lethargy of our own sleepy Shrewsbury. The profusion of shops with their glittering contents was alluring to us too;
one in particular fascinated me. It was entirely devoted to artists'
materials, and the windows were full of paints and palettes, brushes,
drawing blocks, and canvases—one of the paint-boxes, a professional
water-colour box made by Winsor and Newton, was, to me, a lovely
object glistening with black and white enamel; it had double-banked
rows of brilliant, moist-looking colours all set so neatly in their por-
celain pans, each held so ingeniously in its own place by the clever
arrangement of tensioned sockets. I longed so much to possess it that it
became an obsession, so that I had to see it each day. It inspired in me,
I think, something of the collector's unmoral thinking and disregard of
consequences, and I spent preoccupied hours planning and scheming,
unconcerned with morality, as to how it could be made to pass into my
possession; but fortunately it was well safeguarded by thick plate glass
and the agony of immediate temptation was withheld from me. It was
with something of a startled shock that I realized that it was the sheet
of glass and not my integrity which prevented me from taking it. Ever
since I have felt a sympathetic kinship with any person who can so
desperately covet one special object, for itself only, never for its value,
that scruples and everything, every vestige of training, can be thrown
overboard in order to attain possession. While we were still in Torquay
I tried, in a halting way, to confide in Wilfred my sudden—nearly un-
deniable—urge to possess this paint-box, saying that possession seemed
more important than morality. He answered me very typically. I remember so well his rather level look and his slightly twisted smile as he spoke
four words: 'the young Harold progresses'. We never spoke of it again.

I think we were both eaten up with covetous longings and envies,
for it became a recognized arrangement between us that while I went
off to gaze at my paint-box, Wilfred would walk farther up the hill to
gaze at his newspaper offices. Although we mostly went separately to
our shrines, yet we insisted upon sharing our devotional objects. He
would sometimes come along with me to gaze at the shining beauty of
my paint-box, and I would trot dutifully along, listening to him, to
stare companionably with him, but although I knew it was the newspaper world he was contemplating, I was always hazy about the exact
point of his veneration and was never sure if it was the building itself,
the men and boys who hurried in and out of it, or the immense flaunt-
ing posters.

I was to learn when one morning, as we were walking away from the building, he stopped, turned towards me and, looking straight into my eyes, with terrible bitterness, said, 'You know, Harold, if Mother and Father would only help me, I might be editor of that newspaper—no, no, not that one, a London paper—one day, but I must have help and I just can't get it.' I remember as I looked back into the dark glow of his eyes that this was the first time Wilfred had really spoken to me . . . the mask was off . . . the play-acting was gone: this I knew was the real Wilfred speaking. I felt very proud.

As we walked on up the hot dusty street he looked dejected and I noticed for the first time that the bones in his face were prominent and the skin pale and taut. He walked along beside me with such listless hopelessness that I longed to help him, but I did not know how to do it. Presently I pulled out of my pocket a crumby biscuit that I had been saving up for the evening in case I felt hungry after tea, as I often did. He accepted it without acknowledgement and crunched it up without seeming to know he was doing so. Seeing that he was walking with his neck down and his back all hunched up, I knew the Old Wolf was in one of his brown studies. Walking along beside him I kept silent. We were both soon to be agreeably distracted from our yearnings.

Chapter Nine

TORQUAY

THE next morning we walked out to one of the more secluded little places on the coast, where the bathing was better. After our bathe, Wilfred decided we would stay on and he would put in some geological research while I made some sketches of a rock in mid-bay, the lumpy formation of which had attracted me.

We wandered off along the shore in the direction of a supposedly prehistoric cavern, hoping that this vicinity might provide some good specimens. It was while I was helping Wilfred to collect together pieces of rock and pebble for his classification that we noticed some distance away a young boy, very much intent upon casting large pieces of loose rock and smaller stones upon the cliffside in attempts—noticeably successful—to break them open. His example was being painstakingly followed by two younger girls, possibly about eleven years old. As we passed, a fragment from one of these rebounding rocks narrowly missed our legs. Instantly the boy and the little girls, looking concerned, were profuse with youthful apologies. Interested questions followed and soon our mutual interest in geology became obvious and the boy immediately began showing Wilfred his finds, which were extensive, embracing fossils and crystals. Wilfred was impressed with his evidently more than amateurish knowledge. It soon transpired that the little girls were his sisters and in the same category as myself with regard to geology—very willing but unknowledgeable helpers.

We spent the whole afternoon with each other, for our delightful friendship ripened immediately and spontaneously. After swimming together we shared their tea with them on the sands. Confidences were exchanged all round, and I was entranced to know they were real Americans; this accounted to me for their peculiarity of speech and mannerisms, which I found so pleasing. Wilfred reacted differently to the strangeness of their speech and did in fact, when writing home to tell my mother of our new friends, refer to the pronunciation with some disparagement, but otherwise with admiration for the boy's geological knowledge, although he qualified this later. I cannot recall the little girls very well, except that they were very attractive, friendly, and pretty. Although we had lunch and tea parties together, we really saw much more of the boy and for the remainder of our stay we met every day. This meant a long, hot walk to Meadfoot and back for Wilfred and me, but we did not mind this very much; we enjoyed being with them so much that it was more than worth while.

The boy himself was somewhere in age between Wilfred and me, but much nearer to Wilfred. My recollection is that he was slimly built and wearing rather thick spectacles which gave him a somewhat grave and learned look. I think this misrepresented him, for he was both boyish and possessed of a great charm of manner. Despite our difference in years, he always regarded me as a contemporary, a little to Wilfred's wonderment, and showed a complimentary interest in my drawing. This may have been accounted for by my enthusiastic thirst for everything he could tell me about America. He was genuinely interested in geological matters—but only as a subject and not to the exclusion of other things.

As always happens when very young people meet through their own accidental encounters, as opposed to being introduced by their elders, speech flowed freely and we soon learned that they had been wintering in Europe, that their father was an eminent American geologist who had been connected with Peary and his Polar expedition of 1896 and had later become engaged in some hyperborean exploration. They were staying at a fashionable hotel in Meadfoot, The Osborne I think it was, and later we were to surmise that they were extremely rich.

The weather was so good that every morning the five of us went swimming together, spending whole mornings in and out of the sea. I have no record of the boy's name, but I remember we called him Russell. This of course may have been his Christian name, but I think it possible that in deference to a supposed English custom we used surnames only, although for some reason I have a strong conviction that his surname was Tarr. Anyhow, this boy Russell, as we called him, was a superb swimmer and diver. His small sisters were incredibly good in the water too and delighted me with their fishlike agility.

Russell himself was a constant anxiety to the beach attendant with his daring swims out to sea. He would also dive to astonishing depths from a moored raft, to which we had all swum out, and he would not re-

appear for what seemed to us a dangerously long time. When at last
he came up he was so exhausted and his breathing so difficult that he
was too weak to board the raft. He had trained his sisters very carefully
in a sort of drill, whereby they trod water about where they expected
his reappearance, and as soon as he broke surface they would shoot towards him like little silvery grilse, and with one on either side support
him until he regained his breath and strength; then he would nonchal-
antly display two handfuls of sand and pebbles to prove his prowess.
Neither Wilfred nor I were bad in the water and we both made efforts
to emulate his fantastic skill but never came anywhere near to
success.

Our friendship with Russell became a very warm and happy one;
none of us was content unless the three of us were together. The little
sisters always bathed with us in the mornings, but most afternoons they
would be whisked off by a pleasant but rather severe female, probably
a governess or nanny. Russell did not come under her jurisdiction and
seemed always free to make his own arrangements. It was perhaps this
extreme sophistication that he showed in his manner that appealed so
much to both Wilfred and me. At first I was a bit afraid that Wilfred
and Russell were going to be altogether too erudite for me and that we
might spend all our time bouncing their wretched bits of rock about;
they did have desultory attacks of geology, but while Wilfred did
not seem to tire of it Russell's enthusiasm was liable to wane quite
quickly, which was a relief to me.

Wilfred and I were able to introduce Russell to the town of Torquay
which he did not know at all. We all three of us developed a craze for
tram riding. We would spend whole afternoons travelling about like
this, exploring the main town itself and the surrounding districts; we
would jump on to any tram without bothering at all where it was
going. Russell enjoyed the unexpected fun of this enormously and became quite insatiable. There were only one or two afternoons we did
not spend together: this was when Russell had to go riding with a friend,
some European prince who had a suite in the same hotel. I remember
Wilfred and I were both impressed by his nonchalant treatment of
royalty. In his generous manner he had at first arranged for Wilfred
and me to join them, but as neither of us had suitable clothes for riding
Wilfred very sensibly refused.

It was on one of these afternoons when Russell was riding that Wilfred
confided to me how much he wanted to see the house where a descend-

ant of Coleridge, a Miss Christabel Coleridge, lived. He had heard that it was somewhere in the neighbourhood or, as he put it, a few furlongs away. He had by some means secured the exact address. I remember that he took with him or, again as he put it, 'armed himself' with a volume of Coleridge's poems, so that in the almost impossible event of his entering the house he would have it ready to be enriched by her autograph upon the title page. On the way to the house he commented much upon Coleridge and his work and informed me that Miss Coleridge, he had worked out, must be about eighty years of age, and was relieved about this as being a less frightening proposition than a younger person, should he muster up sufficient courage to call upon her. I was not much in love with the proposition at all, but I was amiably disposed that afternoon and quite cheerfully agreed to lend moral support to him and help to find the house. He made it quite clear to me that should any calling take place it would be wiser, on account of my youth and the extreme uncertainty of what I might say, if I did not come in with him. I was very agreeable to this and willingly fell in with his suggestion that, once having found the house, I should walk on and wait for him well out of sight. Before we arrived there he catechized me unmercifully upon my knowledge of Dickens and demanded that I should supply him with a Dickens episode which would be a parallel to his present predicament and irresolution. The last word —irresolution—he informed me was a clue to the answer. To please him I thought hard to remember an episode which might fit, but failed dismally. But I found Miss Coleridge's house for him, which I thought was more useful, and with injunctions from him to exercise my feeble intellect in seeking the answer to his question, he summarily sent me off to wait for him—out of sight. Twenty minutes later I saw him hurrying towards me. He had, after about fifteen minutes of indecision, at last screwed up sufficient courage to ring the door bell, only to learn that Miss Coleridge was away from home.

He gave me until we got to my aunt's house to satisfy him concerning the Dickens similarity. I knew I did not know the answer and had given up trying to find it, but I pretended to be doing so to mollify him because I was very sorry that he had been disappointed in not meeting Miss Coleridge. I could see his disappointment was great and the irritability he was showing was only nervous reaction from his effort. I could not solve the Dickens question, so he told me that he was trying to make me suggest to him that he was little Doady Copperfield, pacing up and down the road in feverish irresolution outside Dora Spenlow's.

Altogether I thought I liked the afternoons we spent with Russell much better than seeking out the ancient Miss Coleridge and the Dickens interrogation, for he and I had become extremely friendly and I think I became more intimate with him than Wilfred seemed able to do. For one thing Wilfred was inclined to lead him out of his depths in discussions upon literature and other arts, whereas I was content to bombard him with questions about his home in America. My curiosity was not idle for I really wanted to know. His descriptions must have been clever—I remember they were entertaining—for I soon had a picture in my mind, probably quite inaccurate but completely satisfying to me. I could see from his description the long, low, white house with its railed verandas, the green shuttered windows, the main jutting porch, which led to a cool, darkened interior. Outside I could see the hot sunshine, dappling so vividly amongst the winding vines and wistaria that he told me twisted themselves round the lower part of the building. I could almost smell the sun-heated loam of the gardens around the house and see the infinite stretch of blue-grass country that spread to the horizon; I could feel the soft wind as it swept over the prairie-like country. I longed to see it all in actuality and sometimes when riding on the tops of the shabby trams through the streets of Torquay, that seemed so drab in comparison, if he was talking of his home, as he so often was, I would project my mind and get the odd feeling that I was over there and enjoying it all—so real did it become and so intense was my colourful picturing.

Another thing about this boy Russell, which made Wilfred and me think so much, was his, to us, complete disregard for the value of money. It was as if money, or the necessity for it, had no meaning for him at all apart from the convenience of exchanging it for something he wanted. There was no ostentation whatsoever about this, it was just that it was utterly unimportant to him. Wilfred and I would watch— without envy but with profound awe—the way he would pull out from his pockets handfuls of silver and gold to purchase so calmly huge boxes of chocolates for his sisters, books, magazines and other things for himself. His worldly confidence in all his actions, although it astonished us, seemed very nice and important and of this we were a little envious. Wilfred and I would smile intimately at each other, thinking as we did so of how we had trudged the long, hot walk to

Meadfoot, knowing that if we were to spin out our few shillings to make them last over our holiday, with tram rides in the afternoons, we just could not spend our sixpences on this journey.

Quite early in our friendship Russell had suggested—with his inbred and delightful American hospitality—that we should both of us spend the next summer with him in his American home. The idea, as it presented itself to us, was so preposterously impossible that neither of us could really comprehend it, much less entertain the suggestion. It was so much outside the bounds of possibility that the invitation, although it pleased us very much, never became real to either Wilfred or me. I ached with longing for such a visit to come about, but as the project had not, for us, touched the fringes of reality, the disappointment was correspondingly dream-like. Although the whole idea could only be ephemeral, Russell had entertained it with serious expectancy, and on the day when we went to say goodbye he confronted us with pleasurable excitement, armed with a written invitation possessing the necessary parental authority.

We were both of us once again excited and pleased, but of course had to explain how impossible it would be. At first Russell was incredulous and extremely hurt and accused us of not wishing to visit him. Wilfred took pains—I myself chiming in corroboratively from time to time—to try to explain that we had no money and neither had our parents, but this aspect was a difficult one for him to accept. He had himself been travelling all over the world since early infancy, and I am perfectly certain that he never connected the necessity of having wealth with being able to travel. He accepted money as something that everyone had and I am sure it was actually beyond his comprehension that any person in the world could be prevented from moving about as they pleased through lack of it, so insignificant was it to him. Our revelation astounded and perplexed him and he told me with some heat that he would never have told me all about his home if he had thought I did not really want to see it. We convinced him sufficiently to part friends, with promises to write, but he was still sincerely hurt with our refusal and could not quite bring himself to believe that so trivial a thing as money could have anything to do with it. I have often wondered what the effect would have been on us had things been different, and we had been able to spend a summer in America.

Already, in the short time available, the influence of Russell's world-wise travelled assurance was affecting both of us and had opened up

7(*a*). The whole family at Scarborough, on a visit to Cousin May Susan. *About* 1906

7(*b*). On holiday at Kelso

l. to r. An unidentified guest, Walter Forrest, Harold, Bill Bulman, Blanche Bulman, Mrs. Bulman, John Bulman, Colin, Mother, Mary, Father

8(*a*). Father in Bombay as a young man

P. Vuccino & Co., Bombay

8(*b*). Wilfred as a young student

Arcade Studio, Reading

wider spheres and vistas. But there was something about the unfortunate parting from him that attacked us adversely; it perhaps gave both of us a deepening recognition of how much lack of money can circumscribe not only careers but friendships as well. It reminded me, Wilfred too I think, of the stress which was being laid in our home life upon the need for us not to seek the heights but to be content with humble status and not to flinch from the prospect of prolonged poverty . . . blessed are the meek. . . . There did not seem at this period any suggestion from my mother or father that endeavour and concentration could perhaps achieve what circumstances seemed to deny. They were both fond of telling us that hard work would bring its own reward, but did not seem to know in what direction we should apply this vaguely termed work.

Although by now it was an established family tenet, to which we all subscribed, that Wilfred with his studious nature and apparent scholastic promise must somehow be given a real chance, even about this, in these years from 1910 to 1914, there was a blanket of indecision. It could not really be otherwise. My father was still finding it desperately difficult to meet the expenses of running the household, keep up his own appearance which his position demanded, keep up his children's appearances which my mother demanded, and remain out of debt. That he was able to do so on his meagre salary is in itself remarkable. The position of our family at this time left no money over to do any planning with; the very most that could be hoped for was that we, as a family, should somehow be able to manage so that Wilfred at least would not have to become a wage-earner until he was nineteen or twenty. Even to bring this negative plan into being meant, as we were both told, that Colin and I would have to be earning money by the time we were fifteen.

It was not unnatural that our unsatisfactory parting from Russell should leave us both rather flat, with our indefinite longings rather suspended in the air. This was in no way connected with a disappointment over a forgone foreign holiday, for the merest possibility of such a project had not been entertained, even momentarily, by either of us. It was something which our meeting with Russell had epitomized for us in sharp etching, something which we had so far only vaguely felt, a wish for freedom and expansion, a taking part in activities of worlds so remote from the sleepy little county town of Shrewsbury. It reminded me too vividly that soon I should have to face again the dirtiness and crudity of my horrible board school.

To both of us had come a tantalizing glimpse of a wide and exciting world, and in having to say goodbye to Russell we, without realizing it or being able to put it into words, had seen a door half open itself and then tightly close again. Still, our contact with this nice American boy, being able as we were to brush against his sophistication, was undoubtedly extremely valuable to us both; more especially to Wilfred who had reached an age when such mixing was particularly important. I think it was the start of a line of thought that did much to offset the parochial outlook which might otherwise have crept in upon us.

I had noticed during this holiday in Torquay, when we were alone together, that Wilfred was often distrait and given to sudden outbursts of petulance. His vehemence outside the newspaper offices had been unusual for him. He often seemed—although he was actually talking to me —to be really talking at himself, chafing at the restrictions that he felt beset him. He had exaggerated in his own mind the conviction that my father was opposed to him. In muttered asides, he unburdened himself to me about the way he felt father persistently discredited his desire for learning, and how much he knew he despised all mental ability and was concerned only with physical prowess. I was much too young to ably refute or know how to attempt to disperse this mistaken, self-wished feeling, so sponsored and shared by my mother, but I was not too young to be unhappy and miserable (in short spells) about it. I knew that Wilfred was unhappy and hurt by my father's seeming disinterest in him, and worried about his future. I knew now that he was also bitter. His own anxieties, which through working too hard were becoming enlarged, were crowding upon him. This and of course his youth prevented him from understanding my father's anxieties and difficulties. In his overwrought state of mind he was not only inclined to, but did, attribute my father's attitude to Philistinism.

Some of this bitterness shows in a letter he wrote to my mother while we were still in Torquay, referring to Russell. He sent a message to my father—he showed me what he had written with some satisfaction— which read something like this: '. . . this American boy is a splendid swimmer and perhaps he will gain prestige in Father's eyes when I say that he dived from the raft (where the depth is very great) and scraped about upon the bottom bringing up stones, etc. in proof . . .'

The message itself is trivial but the portent is not, and is clearly indicative of Wilfred's supersensitive thinking and his now unshakeable belief that my father not only despised all learning but belittled all those either possessed of it or even of a studious nature. Wilfred became obsessed with this untrue notion and refused all overtures which, by my father's very nature, were not easily given, and he was led into the dangerous practice for so young a boy of considering not only his own mental capacities but his judgement in every sphere sounder than my father's was likely to be. This in itself would have been harmless enough and could have been valuable had it only possessed a suggestion of friendly rivalry and companionability. To offset this, and still further oppose my father, Wilfred was inclined to scoff scornfully at all physical effort and achievement; but the fact that he could feel jealousy of and very often admiration for such efforts proved that he did not really feel like this about it at all. He was not of course really interested in these things for themselves but he did not despise them; he only assumed disdain in order to provoke my father.

Having previously described Russell as intelligent, studious, and a professedly keen geologist, he liked himself to think it necessary to emphasize that he did not expect my father to think much of him on this score alone, and purposely gave his message a bitter sting by the suggestion that, in spite of this, his friend could swim and dive, and for that reason only would he expect esteem for him from my father.

We only had a day or two left in Torquay after Russell had left and they were rather flat for us. I remember extremely well our last evening for Wilfred, with his sense of drama, thought it should be spent fittingly, as a sort of benediction. As well as his wish for dramatic effect, he had in mind a wish to do something that would please me, to make up, I think, for some of his brusqueness to me during our few weeks together. His plan was that we should spend the evening, from about 6 o'clock, on the cliffs overlooking the bay until nearly midnight. We would take our books for the daylight hours, after which, as he put it, when it was dark I could look at my ships—the fleet was in and would be brilliantly lit up—and he would contemplate the horizon and the night sky and ponder the indubitability (his word) of the Universe . . . I did not quite know what all this meant, but an evening on the cliffs sounded fun, especially as we were to be allowed to stay out until midnight. Wilfred added rather wearily that perhaps a few hours of quiet communing with the night might solve some of our problems, adding, with a flashing half smile, if it did it would retrieve in a few hours what the whole holiday as far as he was concerned had completely failed to do. . . .

Wilfred's timing and theatrical sense was absolutely right, the evening was a happy success; the weather was perfect, at first warm with the setting sun, later cool with the friendly darkness of night. While there was daylight we were both content with our reading; when the daylight went we enjoyed each other, talking with desultory laziness. He was relaxed and strangely humble. We spoke of the others at home with warm love, confessing to each other how much we were looking forward to seeing them all again tomorrow. We went over our holiday together and decided that it had been a most awfully good one . . . we spoke of Russell and the little girls and wondered, not very hopefully, if we should ever see them again. Wilfred showed his only sign of discontent when he said how much he would like to see America, but added with characteristic haste, 'not of course until I know France and Italy better than I know England'. Rather timidly he asked me if I would mind if he recited some poetry and was pleased and encouraged by the warmth of my agreement. Later he talked of painting, telling me if I really wished to be a painter I must study all the Old Masters, as he did the poets. As the night advanced we played a game together, pretending that this was not Torquay but some fantastic city in the tropics—this I think was suggested by seeing the palm trees caught in the glare of the town lights. We both played our parts enthusiastically, vying with each other to bring touches of colour to add to the splendour of the scene which we were creating for ourselves. This was not difficult to do, as the whole setting seen from the cliffs had an Arabian Nights effect: the lighted town, the brilliantly lit ships discharging from time to time clusters of brightly coloured rockets, the bay itself dark with gently surging heavy waters. . . .

The evening was memorable for us too because it was then we saw together our first aeroplane. It was one of the pioneers of flying who had decided to fly over the fleet anchored in Tor Bay. Was it Bleriot, Cody, or Graham White? I am hazy about the details—it must I think have been Graham White.

As Wilfred and I sat on the cliffs of Devon on that lovely English summer evening, playing our game of make-believe or talking quietly together of poetry and painting, little did we think that in five or six years' time he would be slogging in the Artists Rifles and I would be flying (mostly abortively) Graham White aeroplanes.

Our holiday was over and the next morning Wilfred was back to his stuffy old self, lethargic and inclined to snappishness. I had great difficulty in getting him to start his packing and it was only by my doing most of it for him and then bullying him to get himself ready, that we were able to catch our train. In the train on the way home he finished his reading of Carlyle's 'Heroes and Hero Worship', which he had set for himself as a sort of holiday task. During the last hour or two of the journey Wilfred held forth elaborately in a discussion upon the work, expressed much disappointment with Carlyle's treatment of the subject, and confessed his difficulty in getting through the book at all.

Our return to our little house in Shrewsbury was a warmly welcoming one, as indeed all returns of members of our family always were. It was a prominent trait amongst us all that, no matter how quarrelsome or opposed we might be, any of us who had been away would be certain of a loving and festive welcome when we returned, the fatted calf was always killed—favourite dishes would be either already cooked or cooking. I find the memory of these times of reunion delightful to look back upon; I feel again through the memory the tenderness of the extreme opposites of severity and kindness, the hardness and the softness, so curiously mixed amongst us.

We were soon back into our old routine again: Wilfred to his Technical, Mary satisfactorily settled in her day school, and Colin quite soundly established in his pleasant private day school, making friends and enjoying himself rather well.

I myself was back in my school and, after my peep into America, detesting it more than ever, but this was not to last very much longer; indeed it could not, for incidents were piling up against me in the school. These happenings were more of a negative than a positive nature and were the direct outcome of my aloof disregard of the school and all it contained, both masters and boys. I had of course—since I had found my School of Art—become genuinely remote, unconcerned, and careless as to what did or did not happen during school hours. For some reason this annoyed both the other boys and the masters, and particularly the Headmaster; my conduct appeared to throw him into frenzied infuriation. It was during one of these states that he accused me of disdain and contempt for the school and all to do with it. My simple but polite wholehearted agreement with him nearly engulfed him in apoplexy and brought upon me threats of instant dismissal and an exchange of notes between himself and my father. This blew over, though I had an unhappy feeling that another crisis was hanging over me. But cunning was entering into me bred by past experience and I made up my mind to forestall more trouble by bringing about a plan I had for some time now had in mind. I would take myself out of this sort of school altogether and get myself installed as a full-time day student in the School of Art. I knew this would not be easy to bring about, but I was quite determined to break away from all day schools. Instead I would go on with my painting, and do nothing else. I had faith in Mr. Weaver's power to arrange things, especially as I was already an unofficial day student during holiday times, for Mr. Weaver had given me permission to use the classrooms during these times so that I could go along and draw away by myself. But I was not always lonely, for quite often Mr. Weaver himself, who spent every day, both term time and holidays, in the building working at his own water-colours, was there as well. He would come along to give me help and instruction, which he mingled entertainingly with encouragement and friendly talk. With all this in mind, I set about laying plans for my attack on the situation.

My age again proved a difficulty, and at first Mr. Weaver was not hopeful of being able to accept me as a whole-time day student. However, my eagerness impressed him very much so that after some deliberation he gaily announced that he would manage it somehow, if I could get agreement from my parents—which he thought extremely unlikely—as, in his view, my ordinary education should take precedence over everything else for the next few years.

I lost no time in putting forward my proposal at home and, after the first surprise, met with less opposition than I had believed possible. In truth, I think it came to them not only as a relieving solution but a heaven-sent one as well. They were genuinely worried about having to keep me in the wretched board school. Another aspect, too, which was causing them concern was the local social discomfiture, especially to my mother and Wilfred, in constantly being aware that I was attending a free board school; and remarks were being passed that something better might be done for me, all of which made for more disagreeable-ness. Considerable argument and changes of mind ensued but in the end, as I was making so little progress where I was and as no alternative means of education seemed available, it was agreed in desperation to let me have my way.

Actually I do not think I would have survived much longer where I was. I was too unsatisfactory and, I suspect, too maddeningly irritating for them to have kept me on. My survival there could only have been a term or two at the most, so I was allowed to leave. My taking myself away caused nothing but happy relief all round. There was, though, one parental proviso attached to this plan, and this was that I should continue some study privately at home with Wilfred as my tutor. This was thought to be a rather brilliant idea for both of us, especially for Wilfred who had now reached matriculation stage. A school-mastering career was being mooted for him if he successfully passed this looming examination. In the vernacular of home it was thought that some tuition of me would be 'good practice' for him. In this way my ordinary education ended, and as it turned out the severance proved final.

This proviso about Wilfred taking me in hand proved—as both he and I knew it would—hopelessly unsatisfactory and wholly unsuccessful. It could hardly be otherwise, for Wilfred had not any real wish to impart information—he was far too busy trying to absorb it himself; added to this, so far as I was concerned he was a dreadfully bad teacher and was convinced, somewhat obsessionally, of the inadequate quality of my receptive powers. His attitude was a mixture of impatience, intolerance, and a biting sarcastic general approach to me. However, he would set me some papers quite regularly with which I would struggle despairingly. When I showed him my efforts, he would take a fiendish delight in verbally tearing them to pieces, putting on all the time a loud hooting laughter quite unnatural to him; but he enjoyed this part of it all very much and he long afterwards told me he always set the exercises for me just too high so that he could enjoy the pleasure of his destructive criticism. It is quite certain he would have made the most shockingly bad schoolmaster.

We kept up the pretence for quite a long time until it became too obviously stupid to us both, after which the lessons declined and gradually lapsed altogether. The tuition did not advance me at all but it served some purpose, if only to lead Wilfred into serious doubt as to his own suitability for a teaching profession in any form, and soon he swung around again and became inclined to favour entry—if this could be arranged—into the Church, much to my mother's delight.

Chapter Ten

ART SCHOOL

M Y final leaving of the board school excited little comment; I
merely ceased to go. Instead I became a full-time student—I
was not yet in long trousers—in the School of Art. Mr. Weaver
had been as good as his word and said he had obtained a special dispen-
sation that could conveniently ignore my age. I suspected later that
clerical 'errors' helped considerably to smooth this over. There were
several meetings between Mr. Weaver and my father, but after some
more indecision in the end it was settled and I made my entry into the
senior school. It was with this entry that my first real and unadulterated
happiness descended upon me. Everything was right. I liked all the other
students. They were of course, as day pupils, a different set to the night-
class boys. The day classes were mixed sexes and most of the students
were nearly adult. I now had the right to use any of the painting rooms
and the run of the whole school, with the exception of the very
occasional Life classes. When these took place I was debarred from
taking part in them, no doubt on account of my age.

It had been suggested that as I was now a day student I should cease
going to the night classes, but I would not hear of this and refused to
give them up, so much did I look forward to and enjoy them. It certainly did make a long day of it; however, there was no instruction
given on one or two days in the week, and never on Saturdays. It was
on these blank days that Wilfred had first tried to give me some lessons
in ordinary subjects. When this attempt was given up altogether I
would go along to the school on the non-teaching days and work alone,
or I would spend long days by myself on sketching expeditions into the
country.

While I was going only to the evening classes I did not come immediately under Mr. Weaver for tuition, except in a supervisory way,
for he did not himself undertake any teaching in the evening. In the
day time I became much more one of his pupils and soon began to feel

the benefit of his astonishing ability to teach. His consistent kindness and interest since I had first called upon him about coming to the night schools had shown itself in many pleasant ways, the nicest and most complimentary of which had been his habit of sometimes waylaying me as I was leaving after the class was over and inviting me into his studio-office for discussion about my own work, and to show me his own current work. I liked immensely the way in which he ignored my juvenility and accorded me respect—as if I were his contemporary. I found the unintentional flattery very pleasant and most refreshing.

He later accorded me the freedom of his sanctum, so that a tap on his door was all that was necessary to give me admittance at any time of the day or evening. He was a genuine worshipper of David Cox and was always seeking arduously to find the secret of his work. This was always a little lost on me for at that time I could not conceive anybody's water-colours as being superior to Mr. Weaver's, so great was my admiration for his work. My own passionate desire was to achieve a similar perfection and paint, as he did, lovely sun-warmed brick-work with delicate greens, tiled roofs with reds and blues, and the warm, almost—it seemed to me—scented depths of his Vandyke-brown shadows. On these visits to his room he never hesitated to initiate me into any fresh tricks of washings and spongings that he had discovered, or to probe deeply into the means by which I might have accidentally brought about some happy effect. He was embarrassingly unstinting with his praise for what he was constantly proclaiming as my capacity for hard work. His enthusiasm would reach such degrees that he would publicly acclaim it to whole classes, and one of his favourite admonitions to any of the more dilettante students who happened to be depressed about their own lack of competence, was always, 'my dear fellow (or girl), do what little Owen and I do, work, work, work and never stop working'. This was never resented and apart from my own burning cheeks it caused no discomfort to anyone. My greatest embarrassment was my guilty knowledge that I could not associate doing what I was enjoying so much with work in any form.

In appearance Mr. Weaver was even more unlike an artist than—as I found out much later—a good artist usually is. This was accounted for by his extraordinary style of dress, for he never appeared in the school building unless attired in a black frock-coat and appropriate trousers and marvellously starched and gleaming linen, with a dark or black tie which gave him a half funeral-mute and half old-fashioned professional appearance. Surmounting this, he wore his dark moustache meticulously waxed into very fine long points, like two pieces of wire springing horizontally from his upper lip—all of which seemed entirely out of keeping and contradictory to his rather youthful and extremely merry countenance. Before I left the school he did bring himself to discard this garb and substitute very dark blue frieze suits and looser neck-wear which, although becoming him much better, still looked quite preposterous as he retained the carefully waxed and finely pointed moustache.

The art mistresses were two sisters, Brenda and Lydia Wheeler, and though they appeared very adult to me they must both have been very young. The elder was a full-time mistress and the younger a pupil-teacher. I never came under the younger one for instruction and only knew her slightly as a fellow pupil. The elder one, however, did take me for some subjects—but only sporadically—and she was extremely helpful and befriended me with much kindness. I do not think either of them was an artist, but their technical skill was amazing and their work in its assured ability often filled me with humble despair. It was rumoured that the elder could rival Mr. Weaver in draughtsmanship. This was quite likely true of drawing, but never in painting or in imagination. Her general austerity, her especial aloofness from creative work, her insistence upon the importance of manual skill and her refusal to be drawn away by any problem except the immediate one presented to her or her pupil at the moment of instruction, made her a sound builder of technique and a first-class teacher. She never approved of my delight in painting cottages and hills and bridges, but did all she could to wean me from it into pure formal design. She would, I think, have made an almost perfect illuminator and should have manipulated vellum and gold leaf with a lasting benefit to England.

The assistant master, the gold-medallist, was always helpful but became rather a disappointment to me, mostly on account of his unbearable facetiousness. He prefixed all his remarks, professional and otherwise, with the exclamation 'Ye gods and little fishes', which never seemed to make much sense to me and in the end became most irritating. His manner of criticism tended to be over-fulsome with praise, so that even my infantile judgement began to reject it. A large amount of gold dust had fallen upon him from his gold medal, which was a flukey one. It had been technically awarded for his submitted work, but he still had to procure a first-class in the annual examination in design before the medal became his property. He had so far, for years now, not been able to obtain better than second-class and not always that, so that the medal had become very 'ginger-bready' indeed.

He let me down very badly in a way I found hard to forgive. I had for a long time wanted to introduce someone from the school into my home, mostly to impress them and gain a little warmth from reflected glory. I had long toyed with the idea of inviting the elder Miss Wheeler, whose quiet dignity I knew would not only come up to my expectations but would be impressive, but I was too diffident and uncertain of myself to get the invitation out. I would have liked it to be Mr. Weaver, but his position, not himself, seemed too august and I felt I could not suitably embark upon it. So to compromise I asked this assistant master. The moment I had done so I knew that I had made a serious mistake and wished I could undo it. The evening turned out very badly for his facetiousness became unbounded to the point of distinct embarrassment to all of us and the whole thing developed into a tired and boring failure. Wilfred was very unhelpful, as indeed he had every right to be, and soon left us to our frightful ordeal of enduring the horrible gaiety. I was sick with anger and disappointment for I had so sincerely hoped for Wilfred's approbation of my School of Art; instead I had substantiated an entirely wrong impression. My father tried to save the evening by singing very beautifully some of his songs, but the man's inane response to them and colossal insensitiveness dried him up completely.

However, it did not dampen my pleasure in the school; for one thing I was more and more under Mr. Weaver's direct control, with great help from Miss Wheeler, and shortly after this Mr. Weaver intervened and decreed that I was no longer to come in any way under this young master's jurisdiction. Although this set up a coolness between us I did not mind in the very least. Anyhow, he soon left altogether but not before, by a clever and calculated move, he had ruined my own rather bright chances of a first-class in design.

These School of Art days were lovely ones for me, for as well as the general atmosphere the school itself with its pleasantly musty smell always had a fresh appeal to me. Both summer and winter held their different attractions. I became particularly fond of mid-winter afternoons and evenings, and although the walk from home to the school would often be wet and bitterly cold, I would battle along against the driving rain or snow cheerfully enough, well knowing that once inside the swing doors I should be enveloped in nice stuffy warmth and would feel the friendliness of the yellow-lighted but rather dim painting rooms and the even darker corridors which led from one room to another. I would often loiter along these looking at the drawings and water-colours—just to enjoy the unruffled friendliness they seemed able to give forth. My favourite room of all was the small painting room to which, as a day student, I now had permanent access, for here we could leave our drawing boards, paint-boxes, and brushes, just as they were when we finished work, knowing they would remain undisturbed and be waiting for us in their familiar places when we continued again.

I think 'cosy' is the only word which adequately describes the feeling this small room always gave me on those winter evenings. I always enjoyed my arrival in it after the cold walk from home, and rushed eagerly to see my work again—even if I had only left it two hours ago—with the thought of two or three hours of tranquil but intense activity with pencil and paper or cloth and oil paint, for I was much engrossed at this time with repeating designs cunningly intertwined. To do this, I would cut out stencil plates from strong paper and after carefully varnishing them would be able to repeat different plates to make a co-ordinated whole. Dark velvets were my favourite cloths, and I experimented very much with black and gold and midnight blue and silver. There were many many failures and complete disappointments and often manual slips in the final stages which, while not really mattering, ruined the final perfection and spoilt it all for me, but just sometimes everything would go right, when dexterity seemed not only possible but undexterity utterly impossible and the design would go well, the colours be just how I wanted them, and for hours in my childish way I would be intimate with bliss.

A fragment of one of these—a velvet one—survived in the family for thirty years. Wilfred had fallen in love with it at first sight and begged it from me, which was why it was never destroyed for it remained amongst his possessions. When I saw it again for a few fleeting seconds —for the moths had done their deadly work—I was filled with envy of myself as a small boy and a deep mourning for my lost skill.

I was becoming sensitive to my materials and developed a passionate love for them. I could gloat over a chosen piece of Whatman paper and feast my mind with how I would stretch it with such care on the drawing board, giving it the exact amount of wetting necessary, so that when a marginal dry inch all around was glued to the board the sponged centre part would have the right amount of shrinkage left in it to dry itself back taut and unshrinkable, and not too much to make it split. My mind was always envisaging tubes of gorgeously coloured paint and red sable brushes that could only be properly drawn to a beautiful point with lips and saliva—I saved all my weekly pennies to purchase some of these things, always insufficient, but the thrill of anticipated purchase remained powerful. On the extremely rare occasions when some visiting relative would give me a tip, perhaps one shilling, and once or twice—marvellous days—a whole half-crown, then I would spend delicious hours budgeting how I could divide the money to gain my best purchasing advantage for paper, paints and brushes, often with the added titillation of trying to recall if half pans of cobalt cost three-pence halfpenny or fourpence halfpenny, and the ensuing advantageous rearrangement if the luck was in and it was after all only threepence halfpenny.

The work, materials, and the building itself, of this Art School all invested me with a happy sense of fulfilment and worthwhileness that has never been easy to recapture.

It was to bring me a minor family triumph and a tribute from Wilfred. The family triumph pleased me in a natural and ordinary way, if only because it brought some enlightenment to them all at home about the seriousness of my work in the school. The tribute from Wilfred moved me profoundly. Perhaps it was the surprise of Wilfred's unreserved commendation, so unusual in itself, that took me off balance; whatever it was it caused an extraordinary upsurge of emotional feeling in me so that for days I went about feeling quite lightheaded over this unexpected recognition. I was not used to encouragement, much less recognition, and coming from Wilfred with his guard down I felt quite overcome with happy elation.

It appeared that Mr. Weaver, finding out that I had an elder brother in the other department of the school, had sought Wilfred out and in his impetuous way had at once started talking enthusiastically about me and my insatiable greed for drawing and painting. This quite unintentional penetration of Mr. Weaver's into Wilfred's citadel of thought about me really broke through his bastions and left him genuinely astonished. Mr. Weaver's eulogies had thrown a light upon me which was completely fresh to him. He must have come to me after this interview with Mr. Weaver. I recall very clearly his calling out through the house to find out where I was and discovering me in Mary's bedroom

where I was working on a large drawing of Virginia creeper. Closing
the door he came over and looked over my shoulder at what I was
doing. For quite a long time he did not say anything until he started
muttering and mumbling something about having been talking to Mr.
Weaver. I pricked up my ears at this but went on drawing with a continued pretence of boredom, for I was a little uneasy about what might
be coming; I could see that the Old Wolf in his quiet way was quite
worked up about something. Suddenly stopping his inarticulate muttering he shot out in a clear strong voice, 'Mr. Weaver thinks that you will
be a great painter one day.' I was so surprised that I leapt out of my chair
to face Wilfred, knocking over my water jar as I did so. He was already
at the door, but he gave me a twisted smile as he said, 'That surprised
you, didn't it?' and after a moment—not wanting to let his wolfish
manner quite go—'but not nearly as much as it surprised me, I am not
sure I believe it', and went out of the door. Then he pushed his head
inside again—I think to make up for his parting sting—to say 'I should
mop up that water if I were you before it drips through the ceiling on
to Father and starts him bull-roaring.'

Wilfred was genuinely surprised over Mr. Weaver's praise of me and
deeply impressed, the more so perhaps because this aspect of me was
so novel to him that it really did strike him as extraordinary that merit
of any sort should be found in me and proclaimed so vehemently. As
he told me later, he was very much shaken up and perturbed, so much
so that he recounted the conversation with all its extravagance to the
rest of the family and my prestige ballooned up accordingly, which was
very nice for me while it lasted; but I still had a most unhappy knack of
bursting my own balloon, especially in Wilfred's eyes, so wisely I did
not set too much store by it but made the most of the speculative
glances and looks that I noticed he bent with serious intent upon me
from time to time. These appraisements—which I feigned not to
notice—afforded me a great deal of secret joy, for I noticed that any
ascendancy of my reputation, no matter how illusory, had a ruffling
effect upon him and made him grind all the harder at his own work.

The summer terms were different, although the routine of the school
remained just the same. Outdoor sketching or landscape painting was
not at any time a part of the curriculum, but Mr. Weaver's own private
water-colours, especially the ones with drawings of old water-mills or
farm buildings or wagons half in sunlight and arched doorways deep
in shadow, fired me to do the same. Mr. Weaver encouraged me in

this, promising me special help and arranging for me to bring all my work to show him. This mostly took place after the evening classes when I would stop behind. His criticism, which never took many minutes, was more concerned with what he did like rather than anything he did not like about my bits of drawings. On the whole he rather obviously preferred me to teach myself and the time was more often than not taken up entirely with the getting out and contemplation of his own work. I was undoubtedly his most appreciative viewer and my naïve and quite uncritical acceptance of his work's perfection—for I looked upon it with wondering awe, at that time it certainly symbolized for me the highest mastery—I think he found satisfying and pleasing. So, in the summer terms, instead of going to the empty school to draw, I would set off into the country, my mother packing me some food and a bottle of water. Sometimes I would walk, as in the case of my Uffington village, at others I would use my father's cheap railway facilities and travel this way my ten or twelve miles into new country. As I grew a little older I ventured farther, often over the border into Wales.

At first, though, I found plenty to satisfy me in and around my village of Uffington. I discovered many rutted lanes and old farm buildings or cottages that I felt I could put on paper to make pictures. Having found something that pleased me, I would squat down, get out my box of water-colours and my piece of board with the paper all ready stretched tautly on to it, and commence washing in my sky, always enjoying the trick of breaking the wash to leave the clouds, and running in the lamp-black or sepia to get the greys to give body to them. While this was drying I would pencil in my trees and buildings and work away at it all day, and on sunny days when drying was speedy use the sponge freely to get quality into the paper. All my days were not by any means successful. So often drawing or colour or both would go wrong and I could not get a semblance of what I wanted and the day would seem flat and pointless and I would feel dispirited, but I was usually able to comfort myself by thinking of how much I was improving the texture of my paper by scrubbing out, and managed to cheer myself with the thought of a fresh start on another day.

As if to make up for this, some days would be red-letter ones when everything went well. One of these I remember particularly. I had set off very early to get in a good day's painting of the mellowed red brick hump-backed little bridge that spanned the canal outside Uffington.

I had previously found a position from which I could bring in the bridge, a wooded blue distant hill behind it, the canal itself, and its neighbouring broken-tiled cottages, all of which it seemed to me would compose itself—with a little justified manipulation—into a most pleasing picture. I became certain of this when, arriving at my selected spot, I found moored on my side of the bridge a fine long, low canal boat, all newly painted in reds, blues, and yellows, the blue of its hull and the red of its ribbing reflecting beautifully in the still greeny water. This was a good day, and my pencil and brush seemed possessed by a flukey aptness, so that the picture finished itself almost without help and by four o'clock I felt if I worked any more on it I would only spoil it. As I was collecting my things together to go home, the bargeman and his wife who, I had noticed, had been watching me off and on all day, but always from a mannerly distance, hurried up to me and asked if I had been painting their boat and, if so, might they see what I had done. They were greatly taken with it, and after admiring it for a long time walked away a little distance and conferred together, after which they came back and asked if they could buy the picture from me. When I told them 'no'—for I felt it was the best thing I had yet done, and I could not bear the thought of parting with it so soon—they were greatly disappointed and after a little more persuasion to make sure I meant it, their good manners preventing them from further insistence, they asked me instead to come aboard their narrow boat and have some tea. I was very pleased and went eagerly, for I had been wanting to see the barge at close quarters all day.

I wished very much that I could bring myself to give them the drawing and began to feel uncomfortable about it. It was while they were plying me with strong tea and delicious thick bread and butter and jam, that the idea occurred to me that I might quite well be able to do another one straight away for them. I hurried away without saying to them what I was thinking, and setting up my spare board, started another drawing. My enthusiasm, this time with my idea, now carried me along and in two hours or so I had a fair replica. I knew it was not as good as my first one but, sensing their real interest, I had been careful with the boat and stressed some extra details—which when I again boarded the narrow boat to present it to them they were delightfully quick to notice. There followed some embarrassed fumbling with silver by the man, but I had thought of this and decided that to take any money for it now would somehow spoil my idea. It seemed altogether out of place and displeasing to do so, especially after the splendid tea and the kindness they had shown me in spite of their first disappointment. I was able to refuse payment without any offence and instead they showed me the place of honour where it would hang after they got a frame for it, which they meant to do in Gloucester. It was getting very late for me now, so I took my leave, during which they both shook hands with me very solemnly and grown-uply.

The memory of them, and the day, has been an extraordinarily pleasant one for me ever since. I so often think that this immature water-colour probably gave more real pleasure, and received more approbation and honour, and was liked by more people, than later major works of mine ever did. During my summer sketching outings I was to sell many small water-colours and be involved in varied transactions—some of them awkward, but most of them pleasant; none, however, equalled the grace and charm of the narrow boat encounter.

My first real sale brought me in ninepence. I had been sketching a brick and timber cottage. The working-woman occupier came out to see what I was doing and just as I was finishing it off she came out again to look at it, went back to the cottage, then came back once more, this time with nine pennies in her hand, saying to me that she would give them to me if I would give her the picture. I thought quickly that nine-pence meant two large sheets of Whatman paper and one indiarubber, and very promptly handed it over, which pleased us both. Before I had packed up to go, the woman from the adjoining cottage came running out and told me to come back next day and do her cottage and if I would do a bigger one she would give me not ninepence but a shilling, which seemed to show how good jealousy was for business.

At one time and another I made many shillings like this, the price ranging from fourpence—never less—to elevenpence or a shilling—never more, except once when a vicar, becoming intrigued with a sketch I was doing of the interior of his church, offered me ten shillings for the finished painting. I was highly delighted and felt sure success was knocking at my door with no uncertain raps. But the vicar ratted on me, and when I presented the painting for payment, without look-ing at it he told me he could only give me seven shillings and sixpence. I was so incensed that I walked out of his church without speaking. He came after me for a few steps calling out something about full payment but I refused to notice him. I was very sorry about the ten shillings, for I had already mentally spent it and intended laying out most of it on paints and brushes, especially a very large red sable brush I had wanted for a long time. When I got home, I told Wilfred I hoped he would make a better clergyman than the one I had just met—if he could not, I told him to try being a bargeman. As he was not fully aware of my financial transactions, this mystified him considerably.

Otherwise these small dealings were very pleasing and made a useful impression at home, so that I began to realize how very much success depended not on good work but upon turning poorer efforts into money. But my good work—or, rather, what I thought was good—I could not bear to part with and would never sell, preferring to keep to swell my collection.

Only one other business performance went awry during this time. This happened when a farm labourer's wife bought a picture I had done of the lane leading up to her cottage. She offered me a shilling, which I took. Upon looking back I can see how uniform all these methods of purchase were, for there was never any bargaining; I expect my childish age and dress precluded this. In nearly every case it was a woman who bought and they always came armed with the exact sum they were prepared to give, and the odd amounts such as fivepences and elevenpences made me suspect they came from a vase on the mantelpiece and must have been hoardings from housekeeping money. This particular woman had paid at lunch time with a silver shilling, but I had stayed on to paint another view I liked. At about five o'clock the husband must have returned, for a terribly angry man came running up to me demanding his money back. He was furious, cursing and swearing in a frightening and most threatening manner. I couldn't return it as I had already spent twopence in the village shop on ginger beer and acid drops. I explained this as best I could whereupon he demanded the tenpence back, but I was recovering from my first shock of his violence and would only agree if he would give me back my drawing. I suppose thinking tenpence better than nothing, he hurried back to the cottage to get it and with mutual distrust the exchange was made.

I was really rather frightened by the man's harshness, but I felt a little better on my way home when in a puzzled way I worked out that although I had lost tenpence, I had really made tuppence. But this meagre comfort did not last long, for when I recounted the incident to them at home I was ordered to take back the woman another tuppence the very next morning. Not to be outdone, but mostly because I did

not care for it myself, I went the next day with my tuppence, taking
the picture as well, thinking it would be nice to give it to the woman.
Her pleased relief at getting the tuppence back seemed unduly great,
but her adamant refusal to have the picture even in sight showed even
greater fear of her husband. She went on to explain to me, with stark
details wholly unsuited to my years, just exactly what he would do to
her if he ever saw the thing again. Very shocked at her near-indecency
and having no wish whatsoever to risk meeting the man again, I hastily
withdrew.

When I went alone on these trips into the country I always painted
seriously. On Saturdays, however, and other days during ordinary
school holidays when Colin was free I would always take him with me.
On these occasions I would sometimes take paints and sketching block
and while Colin went off bird-nesting or rabbit chasing with his terrier,
I would for an hour or two draw some tree or building that I liked;
but I was not so serious about these days, so if I heard excited yelpings
in the distance I would usually leave my drawing to join in the fun.

Colin had unofficially and rather cleverly acquired this little dog
through devious means: although it was known to be his it was not
really recognized by my mother or father, and while not actually
secreted, it had to be secluded at the far end of our small strip of garden.
My mother was genuinely frightened of all dogs and even in later years
when surrounded with familiar and friendly ones never lost her instinctive fear. She had been badly savaged when a very young child
and this may have had something to do with it. My father remained
neutral but with a ready bias towards disapproval if the dog caused any
trouble. However, he enjoyed him as much as Colin did when they
were all out in the fields and would become just as enthusiastic as
Colin himself in upholding the little animal's ability nearly (but only
once, quite) to catch rabbits and equalled him in his clever excuses for
the little dog's perpetual failures to do so.

The little terrier was and always remained Colin's special property,
which was recognized by us elder ones as right and fair. Mary and I
had passed through unsuccessful phases of pleading for different animals
but never succeeded in being allowed any. Colin had adopted insinu-
ating tactics, first getting the puppy lent to him and gradually winning
ground, keeping it for a start at the bottom end of the garden, then
gradually working it closer to the house to accustom the family to it,
until permanent acceptance was assured. In this way, Spot—for this was

his unimaginative name—was able to share in outdoor pursuits, but not the indoor family life, and the keeping of him always seemed to have an uncomfortable sort of dependence upon his good behaviour. Colin really became very clever at shielding him from the over-hanging threat and skilful in covering up his misdeeds. He remained the little dog's devoted champion and spent much energy in emphasizing to us all its extreme usefulness to us as a rat killer and mouse frightener. We had neither rats nor mice. Our attention, as well, would constantly be drawn to its great courage as a watch-dog and its extreme value to all of us in so loyally guarding our several properties.

Wilfred reacted towards Spot with a disinterested aloofness—as he did to all animals. I cannot recall him ever putting his hand on the dog and he always spurned any responsibility for him. The real merit he found in Spot was the second-hand one of providing his adored little Colin with pleasure and amusement. It was unthought of at the time and is inconceivable to me now to imagine Wilfred in control of a dog or any small animal, so temperamentally unsuited was he, and such an idea has to me a ludicrous aspect which I find difficult even to imagine. When I do succeed in visualizing anything so unlikely, I find it very difficult not to laugh.

I myself had no very strong feeling for animals and never felt possessively about Spot or even wished for part ownership. Like Wilfred I had other interests which obscured from me the rather special appeal. Unlike Wilfred, I was more companionable with Colin and for his sake I was always willing, although never eager, to share responsibility and uphold the small animal's gilded reputation.

During the period which foreran my going to sea a remarkable companionship did exist between Colin and myself—so much so that we shared not only our time but our every possession; our mental interests remained different without affecting our enjoyment of each other, and dove-tailed without actually joining, quite astonishingly, so that we were able to follow our own pursuits in company with one another. We were never antagonistic in spirit; the slight superficial hostility which, unbidden, seemed to creep between Wilfred and me never came between us; on the contrary we each wished only to further the other's ideas and plans. Apart from phases, natural to our ages, we did not disagree; instead we would both go to great lengths to try to please each other, which often involved considerable—but very happy—argument. We were not critical about one another but always wishfully, if not practically, helpful; we were inclined to 'bolster' each other, and both of us were indefatigable in 'covering' our misdemeanours. This in itself is unimportant except to throw into relief the really too mature unsociability and lack of co-operation which was so evident in Wilfred at that time, so that in spite of his very deep love for the small Colin and his affection for me, companionship from him—in its more recognized form—was unknown to us, and during the occasions when we did all three go out together while enjoying each other's company, we never even remotely made a trio. In many ways it was as if he was a third parent and, like a parent, unpredictable. Some days he would join in with our high spirits, sometimes overreaching us in gaiety, but mostly he would ignore our frivolity and disapprove of any natural levity. But we were both terribly fond of the Old Wolf and gladly put up with his tooth-baring and show of hackles if we could persuade him to join us now and again.

This self-enjoined isolation prevented an early intimacy developing between the three of us and left Colin and me very much to our own devices, which were mostly these days of exploration into the country-side—he with his dog and I with my paint box. As I have said, I was not too serious on these occasions and was easily diverted by any fun Colin might call out to me about. I would leap up at once if I was excitedly hailed to watch Spot's incredible turn of speed when chasing a rabbit, and would become vehement in praises and ever-ready with excuses to explain away poor Spot's final defeat, and quick with comforting assurances of the absolute certainty of his getting his next rabbit. In return Colin would exclaim appreciatively about my skill in drawing and proclaim the exactitude of my reproduction—quite often with reference to the wrong object, but this never mattered in the least, so good were we at explaining away such trivial details as this.

Colin's passion in life at this age was horses and dogs and farm animals, and we would follow for miles assisting drovers with their herds along the roads or stand for hours watching milkings and other agricultural activities. Horses, though, were his real mania and in a stable of any kind he was blissfully happy and quite fearless. This last was a trait which, try as I might, I never succeeded in emulating. I always remained uncertain with horses and could never rid myself of dark and suspicious doubts about their good intentions. In later years I was forced to have many dealings with these much applauded creatures and made sporadic efforts to convince myself that I liked them, but in reality I was never able to alter my opinion that they are quite the most unintelligent animals I have ever tried to communicate with. I have no doubt whatsoever that they feel the same about me, and they seem to take every possible and even unlikely opportunity dangerously to impress the fact upon me—which perhaps refutes my unkind suggestion about their stupidity.

But for Colin's sake I would 'gallantly try to hide my misgivings and help him round up some half-wild ponies belonging to a friendly horse-coper who had given us permission to ride any we could catch. Unfortunately, we always managed to secure one or two, and Colin with enviable aplomb and agility would leap on to its back and gallop madly round the hundred acres where they were running out to grass, after which he would head it straight for me in a most alarming manner which I found difficult to dodge and, dismounting, would demand a similar performance from me. Unfortunately, I never had the moral courage to refuse. However, my seat was so insecure that my discomfort was never very prolonged and I always welcomed the hard bump on the grass which signified my ordeal was over. Honour being satisfied, I would become uncommonly unselfish and insist upon Colin having my share of the riding. At first we used to catch the horses by the forelock and ride them by holding on to their manes. Later we got hold of an old rope halter, but even with this we had little control over direction, we just let them go where they liked and the fun was in trying to keep on them as long as possible. Eventually Colin was able to borrow some old saddles and bridles which enabled us to ride exciting races, which was fun.

Strangely enough, this rough-riding appealed very strongly to Wilfred; he would tear himself away from his books and reading to join us if we could promise him a mount. He showed the same fearlessness and almost as much aptitude as Colin but he was never quite so good. In the end they could both ride these wild creatures with a grace and instinctive assurance that I found bewildering after my clumsy fumblings and ill-balanced efforts to remain on the wretched things at all. This natural affinity with the horse which they both seemed to possess forged another bond between them which was very pleasant to feel; they would talk and nod knowingly to one another in the best possible manner, slashing away at their non-existing riding boots in the most horsy way, and hissing like muted steam engines when rubbing the beasts down with bunches of carefully selected dry grass, conspiring together with all the horse lore they could lay their tongues on. It was only when we could manage to secure three horses that we would ride races. The two of them would streak off to a good start, with me trundling along—more off than on—if I was lucky somewhere in the rear; if I was unlucky I would be right off the course and heading in the opposite direction.

Had I been a little more interested I should most likely have been jealous of the other two. As it was my sagging helplessness when on a horse was so obvious that it placed me outside any competitive sphere and left me free to admire and, through them, enjoy their triumphant breakneck gallopings. It was indeed an intriguing sight to see the dark and neatly built youth, with the thin and fragile-looking hands, and the very little boy tearing about on their rough sweating horses with such recklessness and abandonment.

Colin's zest for horses and riding was more deeply seated in him than it ever was in Wilfred. In different circumstances and surroundings Colin might have achieved his never wholly quenched longing to spend his life among horses. He would have liked to become, in his spare time of course, a gentleman rider. A ride in the Grand National would have meant as much to him as an acclaimed epic poem would have done to Wilfred or recognition of a painting to me.

For Colin and me there was always the rough fishing in the Severn— my beloved Uffington even provided some in its canal. This was not good, nor really was the river fishing, but my father encouraged us, though we did not need much of this for we were both extraordinarily keen. We would set off full of hope and with a certainty that this would be the day when one of us would get into a really big one. Most of our days we did not catch very much, for our knowledge was often faulty and our fishing gear improvised; still, a half-pound roach or perch or a big chub would come to one of us and if we both got such a one then our day was considered perfect. We took great pains with our rickety rods and were for ever strengthening weak places with bindings and whippings of coloured silk. We would varnish these with great care, after which they would look nice and glisten beautifully.

The evenings before these days became ritualistic in the devotion with which we damped our casts and checked our knots, gravely discussing all the time the merits of various thicknesses and colours of lines, hooks, or gut. Any new idea or extra bit of gear always filled us with renewed hope; we became certain that we had the answer at last and were sure that tomorrow's catch would prove it. We would dream of returning home next evening loaded down with fish. We spent exasperating hours manufacturing long lines of horse-hair, for we had been told that this had far superior deceptive powers and could be guaranteed to lure the largest and cleverest roach into imagining the bait to be unattached.

If spectacular success did not come our way, we always had lunch to look forward to and would spend the morning in anxious speculation as to what it might prove to be; for it was an agreed law that we should never be told what had been put up for us, preferring to wait until the glorious moment arrived when we could undo our packages and enjoy the surprise of finding out for ourselves. These lunches were always, to us, splendid ones, and although they were simplicity itself, my mother always took great trouble over them and would see to it that not only was there over-abundance but a surprise packet of some sort as well. It might be a favourite sort of tart, a halfpenny bar of chocolate, or a screw of sweets. One of our specially favourite lunches was an unopened tin of sardines and an unbroken loaf of bread. The sardines were considered a little extravagant so it could not happen very often. We would fish seriously enough in the mornings but if by afternoon we had no encouraging excitement, we would lose concentration and either fish carelessly, splashing at the water—both to assuage our boredom and have our revenge on the stupid fish—or we would cache our things and wander away, seeking some new interest to beguile away the remaining hours.

Those were good days full of warm summery charm. I did not know then that I had only a few more of these burning summers to spend in carefree fishing or exploratory wanderings through the lovely countryside with Colin, or that I had only two or three more to devote to my solitary jaunts to paint my landscapes and cottages, my barns and buildings, my water-mills and canal boats, or my ambitious panoramic efforts in pencil and wash. Nearly all these last efforts I did from the top of a high hill from which I could look across several counties. I liked the patterning the fields made, enclosed by their dark hedges into irregular squares of golden wheat or silvery oats; and the green of the pasture lands that, turning to blue with distance, caught in with the summer haze until the superb design mingled and lost itself among the shadows of the wooded foothills of the Black Mountains of Wales.

I did not know that for me upheaval was soon to set in, that indecision was to torment me and baffled disappointment to wrack me. I did not know that in the vortex which was to engulf me I would have to make a decision—a decision which would too quickly destroy my childhood and thrust manhood with bludgeoning starkness too early upon me. I did not know that I was soon to be caught up and swept away on the flood of a seafaring career. However, before all this was to come about, I had still in front of me some more of these childhood days, days that looking back seemed filled with blue and white skies, air that was charged with humming vibration and golden with the gently burning heat of English summer.

It was on one of these hot, blood-warming days that my first urgent intimation of masculinity had floated through me. I had already, in an undefined way, been aware of sex, but so far I was undisturbed by it, I had not in any way found any connection between it and myself. In my always ungentle and mostly coarse and rough journeyings through the schools and streets of Birkenhead and Shrewsbury, I had become half aware that there were mysteries and knowledge that had not yet unfolded themselves to me. The deceitful cloaking and conspiracies of the other boys in their efforts to impart unmannerly intimacies—for this is how they appeared to me—had only made me instinctively apprehensive, so that I shied away from such things with violent disinterest. It was because of this that, while possessing an indistinct awareness, I had little or no detailed conception. Obscenities and lewdness had washed over me with as little effect as the sea over pebbles, but with something of the same infinitesimal frictional action.

On this special day I had made an early start to walk to the other side of my village of Uffington so that I could paint an old barn that I had seen. It was a beautiful old structure, complete with upper-floor granary from which projected winding derricks for hoisting up the sacks of corn. What had excited me most was the open doorway, large enough for waggons to be driven through. Looking in, I had seen that much of the elm boarding had rotted away from the stout oak framework and the effect inside as the sun streamed through was as if the building was fitted with gigantic Venetian blinds. In the patches of darkness the uprights and crossbeams had a dark bony look; I thought this in conjunction with the slatted sunlight would be intriguing to try and paint.

I worked all the morning but I was restless and ill at ease, my tranquil pleasure in drawing had deserted me and with it my skill; I felt clumsy and ineffectual. I found myself wandering about rather aimlessly, kicking at growths of tufty grass or pulling leaves from the twigs in the hedges. From time to time I would return to my drawing but my zest had gone. In its place had come an uncomfortable urge to be doing something else, the nature of which I could not understand, and conjecturing about this set me fidgeting. I tried hard to discover what was agitating me so much. I felt inside me a pent-up force that was struggling with impelling demands for escape. There was an urgency about this unconscious bidding from within that demanded obedience, but I could not know in which direction this illusive goading was trying to send me. I was being urged to do something but I did not know what, which increased my unhappiness. I felt tired and fretted, I could not eat my lunch, but I was thirsty so I drank all the water instead.

In the afternoon I gave up trying to draw and wandered into a hot field of sun-scorched stubble where farm workers were loading waggons with cut corn. After I had talked with the men a little, I made myself a bed of corn sheaves and lay down to watch them. The horse teams were steamy with sweat and about each tossing head a dark circle of flies gyrated with maddening rhythm. Presently the heat of the sun, the pleasant dry creaking of the groaning waggons, the sweet musical tinkle of the horse-brasses, and the melodious summery sound of the men's drawling unimpassioned voices drifted around and about me, at first close and clear, but as sleep commenced sweetly to caress my eyes, in ever-widening circles. . . .

In my fitful sleep I was haunted again by the intangibility of my need and desire; in my dreaming I became obsessed in my searchings to find the answer which would assuage this unknown yearning for release, release from what I did not yet know, I only knew that somewhere inside me urgent instinct was at work, which with persistent thrustings demanded acknowledgement. In my sleep—in one instantaneous flash of revealing light—the truth was vouchsafed to me, but in the immediate startled awakening which followed, it fled from me and I lost it. After a few minutes I slept again, this time dreamlessly. When I awoke the sun was lowering for it was late afternoon. The men and waggons had gone with their last load of the day, leaving me undisturbed in my couch of sheaves.

After I had collected myself and my things, I started on the walk home. It was a perfect and glorious evening. Something of the loveliness seemed to spread all around and into me, so that it seemed I was walking without effort and with an unaccountable ecstatic excitement mounting in me, constricting my chest and detaching—it felt—my feet from the ground, which gave me a feeling of feathery lightness that had something of blessedness in its quality of ethereality. It was while I was crossing a field of stooked corn that the full beauty of the golden light poured into me, flooding me with an awareness of the coppery warmth of the lowering sun. All around me a warm moist smell was rising from the ripening wheat; subconsciously I could feel the rich breath of the dying corn as it eddied in faint vapours to lie like wreaths suspended on the still evening air. The corn plants themselves were dead, but the air about them was charged with promise from the seed lying in them—the fruit of their exhausted fertility—that, still swelling in their constricting sheaths, emanated moist potency, to make the atmosphere heady with fecundity.

My restless day had made me sensitively aware of the hot richness of the fields and the vitality for reproduction that came from them in wafts of strong scented exhalations that tantalized me afresh with unknown desire. Hot tremors rippled over me and with them came a renewal of the eagerness that had assailed me so tiringly all day, but now a chill evening wind had suddenly sprung up which set me shivering slightly with delicious refreshment. This and the curious sensation I was feeling—that I had now returned from a mysterious journey from some unknown territory into which the restless agitations of the day had led me—brought me back to childhood again.

With a further jolt, this time a childish one, I was perturbed to notice now late it was getting, so that I started to hurry along towards home, my thoughts now only occupied with whether by being so late I should miss something really good for supper. I was comforted by the thought that my mother would see to it, as she always did, that something nice was kept for me. I started to run, meaning to run all the way home, hoping all the time that there would not be too much crossness over my lateness. Mingling with these thoughts, as I hurried along, was some wonderment about my strange feelings during the day and I found some difficulty in really associating them with myself, for my return to childhood was complete and absolute, except that I was now half aware of, but not awake to, the possession of masculinity; but I had no knowledge, so I was left happily content and without inquisitiveness—only with a vague and hazy acceptance of something still awaiting me. I had not yet realized femininity so the necessity for a female counterpart did not occur to me, and although masculinity had lightly laid its demanding fingers upon me I could not as yet suspect completion, for I had no knowledge of consummation and felt no curiosity about it.

My arrival home, with my mother's tender anxiety about my flushed appearance—for she feared I was sickening for something—and the nice feeling of importance this gave me, finally put out of my mind this strangely perturbing day. I destroyed both my mother's anxiety and my own feeling of importance as a prospective patient by the inroads I made upon the supper table—not having eaten any lunch I was by now very hungry.

For all these years up to this time we children were encouraged to find and improvise our own entertainment. Except for sporadic treats and very occasional 'surprises', not much in this way was arranged for us apart of course from our fishings, days in the country together, and my father's early morning expeditions. In this way none of us ever played any organized games, though Colin was to do so later in his pleasant day school, but for the rest we had to rely on our own self-sought and self-organized pursuits.

My father tried to teach us some cricket at one time, but here again there were no facilities of either ground or equipment, and of course there were not enough of us to make sides so it could do no more than provide amusement for us and then only while we were very young. We soon grew out of it. Wilfred showed the most promise and, for him, seemed to enjoy the trivial games rather unusually. I was the least adept and applied myself with a light-hearted disinterestedness and lack of seriousness which visibly annoyed my father, so that he would become savagely cross and upset with me, showering scorn and invective upon me for my stupidly unskilful displays. These attempts nearly always ended in hysterical fiasco, my father seething with disappointed rage that out of three boys he could not produce one cricketer. With different conditions, and had the understanding between my father and Wilfred not been so tangled up by both of them expecting prejudice where none was contemplated, my father might have got his cricketer in him, for Wilfred had a nice free swing with a bat and occasionally really seemed to enjoy playing with us.

It was as well that in these early years we were so able to make our own amusements, for to find or form friendships was difficult enough for Wilfred, Mary, and Colin, and for me quite impossible. My ordinary schools had been so disastrous that I had never been able to make pleasant contacts. At the School of Art the other students were too old for me, and my first social effort, by inviting the assistant master, had been unfortunate and disappointing. My father, I think, would have liked—had he not been so peculiarly unable to do so—to have widened our sphere, but my mother always showed the greatest reluctance. It was as if she must always jealously guard her family from outside influence, and certainly from outside associations of our own choice or contact, so that she was, I think, always fearful that we might find for ourselves interests and people which might distract and weaken our allegiance to herself and our home. For this reason she would quite unconsciously depreciate and present to us in a poor light a child, or other person, or pursuit, that she felt might be competitive to her own influence, and was full of fear that our loyalty to her and our home life might be lessened. Working in with this feeling of insecurity concerning our devotion to her was her inherent and dangerously potent Calvinistic intolerance and the accompanying puritanical fear and horror that some unfortunate outside influence might contaminate us or in some way endanger our souls. Combined with this was the curious simplicity which allowed her so calmly—having first placed me in the care of God—to leave me in my tender years to run the gauntlet of the board schools.

However, some children of our own age were encouraged to the house, but as these were of her choosing—usually clergymen's or other religiously active persons' offspring, often spotty and always dull—we did not like them very much. Their appearance was always preceded by panegyrics on their excellence, and their desirability as models for our patterning—so that we, including Wilfred, hated them before we saw them and were intolerant of them for ever after, and any subsequent contacts with them only caused us to form an even stronger family union to oppose their infliction upon us. Here, again, the extraordinary acceptance by my mother of outward and visible facts made her serenely convinced that, because they were children of people pertaining to the Church or openly practising religion, they must be nice children and therefore it would be good for us to see a lot of them. None of us could ever share this view.

I was the least able to dissemble, and my mother would scold me for being uncouth and rude. Actually I was neither, but was only exercising my right as a child to discard emphatically what I could not tolerate. Always on these occasions Wilfred would back me up in our technique of discouraging these unwanted visitors and would defend me over my actions if recriminations followed, which was a great help. We both of us became pretty adept in keeping these spotty faces at bay and at these times Wilfred and I would be perfect conspirators, our secret smiles to one another full of communicated understanding.

We did all make friends with one family who lived in a large barracky sort of house not far away from our own small one—it was a relic of the days before the smaller houses had been built up around it. They were an enormous family of mother and father and certainly eleven children, and I believe these eventually totalled thirteen. Wilfred formed a sporadic friendship with the eldest son, who was somewhat older than himself. They found several common interests, one of which was a mutual attraction towards antiques, and another the search for and classification of Roman remains. For us other three children there were children of all ages and of both sexes to fit. We would all of us from time to time spend many hours playing with them in their huge, gaunt house. They were an interesting family, for apart from the attractive size (which lent itself to such infinite choice of companionship for ourselves) they possessed an unusual disregard for parochial conventions, which in those days in so small a town was quite remarkable. They must have been people of very considerable means for all the children were educated at public schools or for the professions. I believe at one time four of the boys were together at once as boarders at Shrewsbury. The father was a director, I believe, of one of the big tobacco firms. He was away from home a great deal, so we saw very little of him. The mother was a woman of great driving force and strong personality. Not only did she produce and rear this enormous family without aid from nannies or nurses, but ran her own household without a standing staff of servants.

They lived in this unconventional way not from any lack of means but merely to substantiate the strong convictions of the mother, Edith Webb, on how a family of babies and children should be reared and trained, for she maintained that a family should be brought up as an integral unit with only the minimum outside help. As a consequence the household often appeared chaotic, but never out of control. Mrs.

Webb was a strict disciplinarian; she was a very kind person, but her matriarchal severity cast a chilliness around her and this, combined with her strict handling of the family, sometimes gave the impression that they lived in a state of rigid austerity. This was true, but outsiders often looked upon the running of the régime as akin to hardship, which was not true. We were all a little in awe of her except my mother, whose admiration and approval of Edith Webb was very great. She and my mother became close and permanent friends. They had, I think, something very much in common with one another.

I became very fond of the numerous little girls and boys, and Mary, Colin, and I would very often go over to play with them. No invitation was required, but hospitality in this house was strictly taboo, both for adults and children—as well it might be with so large a family and no staff; so that except on very rare occasions we never shared their meals but would go home for our own, returning later if we wished. When Wilfred and Stanley, the eldest one, wanted to visit each other, they would do so alone and not in company with us younger ones as we were considered too juvenile. They would often come to our home and mostly for a simple meal of some sort. Our small house and uninteresting strip of garden did not lend themselves to any wider form of entertainment but the lavish meals made up for this.

I particularly remember my mother and father's extreme kindness towards one of these Webb children and their absolute insistence that our own behaviour to this boy should at all times be considerate and gentle. He was one of the older ones and since birth had suffered from a serious impediment of speech. My mother was kind to this boy in a very beautiful way. He was sensitive about his disability and enjoyed coming to us as a change from his own understanding but busy family, and he would spend many happy hours in our house. We set ourselves out to bring to him pleasure and consolation. I cannot recall any other person over whom my mother and father were so much in accord between themselves as they were over this boy. The memory of their concerted and unselfish efforts in the extremely difficult task of entertaining him is a very precious one to me.

Strangely enough Wilfred was the least tolerant and compassionate and rarely showed any disposition or willingness to help to amuse our uneasy guest. However, his outward indifference and self-absorption were so inherent and of such permanency that his attitude was accepted by us and, by its very consistency, passed unnoticed by others. Just the same his attitude was indicative of him at this period, and proof of his tendency to disassociate himself from any commitment which might rob him of his own time. It was perhaps the first indication that although he was sensitive to compassion, he would yet instinctively withhold any personal or practical expression of it. Even then I think he was aware that his role was more to expose the need for pity and tenderness, and himself to remain the vehicle for doing so, than be the administrator of practical action. This trait of always being the vehicle and never the actor was to remain a marked characteristic throughout his life.

Of Mrs. Webb herself we did not see a great deal, which was not unnatural as she must have been perpetually nursing infants, and her standards of infant feeding were exacting. When we did see her, we found her serious severity a little awe-inspiring and cold. My mother had great admiration for her obvious parental qualities and held her in much esteem for her austere disciplinary powers. She was indeed a most remarkable person, for as well as the innumerable domestic and household burdens which she so easily took upon herself, she was the leader and organizer of the local Emancipation for Women Movement and addressed meetings with immense dignity and acumen. She also took part in active and militant demonstrations and headed protest marches. She was in fairly frequent contact with Mrs. Pankhurst. Edith Webb, however, did not believe in the use of violence, preferring clever and convincing argument to forward her passionate views upon Women's Suffrage. I do not think she was ever arrested and she certainly never suffered the indignity of imprisonment. I believe, however, that some of her caustic invective in her public speeches brought angry warnings from exasperated authorities.

When, first of all, I left home, and then Wilfred went away and the Webb children started to disperse, our two families saw less of each other. The outbreak of war in 1914 broke more of our childish ties, but out friendship—now more casual—remained. Wilfred and Stanley wrote to each other intermittently until Stanley was killed in France. The war took its grim toll of this nice family; one of the other boys was very badly wounded. All the eldest ones were caught up in some way or other in it. One or two of the girls went nursing. My mother and Edith Webb continued their friendship and after we had all left Shrewsbury still went on writing to each other pretty regularly up to the time of Mrs. Webb's death.

Our last contact with the family was when one of the boys, Arthur, called to see my mother and father when they were living in Caversham. In our early days he was looked upon as something of a comic and therefore destined for the stage. He had seriously embraced the theatre at an early age, but I rather gathered that he had found it all uphill work and a severe struggle. He was touring at the time, combining stage management with occasional parts.

Although the war was in itself such a ready solvent for acquaintanceships and half-formed friendships, nevertheless I know that it was not wholly responsible for something which we either lacked as a family or which our peculiar social situation brought about. This is something which I find hard to describe about ourselves and our environment, for it had existed in us as long as we had been a family and became most evident several years before the 1914 war broke out. The conditions under which we had lived in Birkenhead had allowed it to remain unnoticed, but now that we were settled in a smaller town and living in a localized circle of people it was becoming more obvious.

It was, I feel, an inability to stabilize ourselves socially as a family, or, more correctly, it was that owing to our lack of means, we found difficulty in achieving this social stability. A result was this unpredictability about us and what our real position was, exactly, in the social scale. This led to awkwardness and difficulties in fostering embryonic friendships, and sometimes destroyed them altogether.

All this would be unimportant had Wilfred remained quite an ordinary young man, just one of many thousands of others who were killed in the war. It becomes important only through the later recognition of him as a major poet.

Chapter Eleven

KELSO

W E were to have one more holiday together, probably our last as a complete family unit, before our childhood came to an early end and family dispersal began.

As well as Wilfred's rather worrying appearance and general air of being off colour, I think the rest of us were looking pinched and run-down, for the small house in which we lived was hot and airless in summer and cold and damp in winter. My mother was far from well and her congenital anxiety over Wilfred did not help matters, so that for her there were recurrent spells of having to take things easily and periods when the general difficulties of the household seemed somehow to overwhelm her. At these times the tiny Mary stepped into the breach, and, in spite of her tender years and really frail physique, ran the house with a mature confidence which, when looked back upon, seems remarkable but at the time we all took it very much for granted.

My father was restless and disliking his work more intensely than ever, and the responsibilities of it were weighing on him more heavily than they should have done. His executive control ranged over a wide area, and as both his immediate senior and immediate junior had been laid up with long illnesses, he had more than his share of sudden emerg-ency night calls—to take control of breakdowns and accidents—so that beneath his healthy and, for his age, youthful appearance, he was very nervy and overwrought.

Since leaving her own home my mother had kept up a correspond-ence with her girlhood friends and connections, one of whom was Nellie Roderick, later to be known to us all as Aunt Nellie. She had first become a friend of the Shaw family when my mother was only three years old. She had remained an intimate friend of my grand-parents until their deaths. During my mother's childhood and up to the time of Nellie Roderick's marriage, in spite of the difference in age, she and my mother were very close friends. After both of them had married they did not see one another for a great many years, but they continued the letter-writing with unbroken regularity. Although my mother kept up this exchange of letters, she had not, I think, dwelt at all on her own circumstances, sketching lightly over them and only emphasizing her own happiness and delight in her children.

Nellie Roderick had married a Scotsman, Andrew Bulman, and gone with him to live in Scotland. They had a family of two sons and one daughter. Nellie Bulman was widowed rather early in life. She was, however, well provided for with sufficient means to remain untroubled by financial considerations. When the younger son was old enough to leave his preparatory school he was sent to Shrewsbury and it may have been something in connection with this which caused her to pay an unannounced visit to us in our small house outside the town. She was, I think, a little perturbed to find her Susie in such different and pretty obviously difficult circumstances.

It was during a subsequent visit from Aunt Nellie that she perhaps noticed that my mother was less well then usual and that my father was showing these signs of overwork. It must have been evident to her as well that both of them were worried about Wilfred, not only about what his future was to be but how best to deal with his present insistence upon over-driving himself with his studies. I think too that as a family we appeared to have a general air of non-wellbeing, giving the disguised but somehow indelible impression that always there was just not quite enough money to go round.

Aunt Nellie's devotion to my mother had increased through their reunion, she admired and liked my father immensely, and without hesitation instantly took all four of us children to her heart with unreserved liking which we all returned with real affection. It was perhaps with something of this in mind that she pressed us so hard to spend a few weeks with her and her nearly grown up family in Scotland.

Aunt Nellie's ready acceptance of us, with all our oddities, had cheered us all up. It was not only her unqualified acceptance of us for what we were as a family, but her expressed affection individually that did us so much good. Forty years later her daughter was to repeat this enthusiasm for Colin's own young family on a voyage they all made together to Africa. . . .

At first, my father was a little dubious about the invitation and reluctant to impose upon the Bulmans his whole family, so he suggested that instead of this my mother, Wilfred, and Mary should go. However, the invitation became so pressing and obviously so sincere, and the idea seemed to fill my mother with such pleasure, that he finally agreed. They had a pleasant house in Scotland with plenty of room and well staffed, and we all began to look forward to the stay with pleasure and excitement.

The holiday was arranged, my mother somehow got round to getting our things together, and the packing—which in our family was always such an exaggerated and temper-fraying undertaking—finished. Out of the astonishing chaos of getting ourselves off, we, with some surprise I think, found ourselves all in the train for Scotland—at least not all of us for there was some complication over Wilfred. Either it was end of term, or he had some appointment, possibly with London University—whatever it was it was arranged for him to travel up by himself four or five days later. It may even have been some private thing Wilfred wished to do, for I remember my mother was rather sad that he was not with us and my father somewhat unreasonably annoyed about it, and until the rest of us were safely relaxed in the train he had kept wondering aloud to himself, 'Why must the boy always be so awkward, couldn't he for once be like everybody else.'

Our arrival was an extraordinarily happy one, the warmth of welcome quite unmistakable, with the whole family present, including the two old family retainers, Katie and Phemie, to receive us. We had already met Blanche the daughter, for she had arranged to meet us in Carlisle in order to make the last part of our journey as comfortable as possible by escorting us to their house in Kelso. It was obvious from the very start that they were all of them determined to make this holiday a tremendous success. Bicycles had been hired for us children, fishing arrangements made, and, perhaps best of all, Blanche—or Blanchie as we were soon to call her—and her two brothers, John and Bill, had unselfishly cut all their own engagements so that they could be free to amuse us. These two young men were indeed exceptional in their disregard for their own pursuits, setting out with the one idea of giving us all a splendid holiday. I should say three young men, for immediately we were joined by Walter Forrest, Blanche Bulman's fiancé, another young man similar to the two Bulman boys and just as enthusiastic in preparing delights for us young ones.

Blanchie with her fresh good looks was a very pretty girl of about twenty, with beautiful auburn hair and a rose and milk complexion, and she soon captured us all with her gay charm of manner and infectious laughter.

John, the eldest, I seem to remember, was darker in looks than the other two; at the time of our holiday he was down from one of the Scottish universities where he was reading medicine. He too was full of high spirits and loved enjoying himself. I remember so well how he would regale us with amusing stories—suitably adapted for our tender ears—of the wild parties and rags in which he became embroiled as a senior medical student. He was, I think, brilliant enough not to have to apply himself unduly to his studies, which suited him very well.

Bill, the youngest, was perhaps a little quieter in manner than the others, immensely strong and built for what he was, a magnificent rugger player. Like so many powerful men he was very gentle, and possessed, as I can see now, of a great sensitivity that enabled him to enter into a small boy's mind. My devotion to him was instantaneous. His nature was innately chivalrous and his thoughtful attention to see that the small Mary was never left out in the cold, as she might have been during all our masculine talk, was indicative of his courtly presence.

Walter, too, was exceptionally understanding with small boys, and when he produced countless sporting guns and rifles, fishing rods and flies, all of which he placed at our disposal, the guns of course under strict supervision, our excited pleasure knew no bounds. Later, when he demonstrated his remarkable prowess with them all, his popularity with us rocketed. He, too, was a rugby player—was 'capped' several times, and considered one of the finest full backs that ever played for Scotland.

Aunt Nellie, whose companionship was a joy to my mother, pervaded the whole household with the sweetness of her character. She was adored by the four older young people, and affectionately revered by us four younger ones.

It was with this delightful family that we spent these unexpected and pleasant weeks. For Colin and myself the holiday was an enormous success, that is after the first four or five days. On the morning after our arrival I had woken up with one of my awful sore throats and the unwell sensation which always accompanied them, and the feeling that the holiday was already doomed. I knew that any disclosure of my state to my mother would not only be awkward but would also probably deprive me of liberty, so on the whole I thought it better to say nothing, but when violent toothache assailed me I was forced by pain to disclose this in desperate hopes of some relief. However, as I feared, this too proved to be difficult and nothing was done about it—except to hope that it would subside without causing a lot of bother. I was very miserable for some days, until I woke up one morning to find both the sore throat and the toothache gone. After this everything was all right, and Colin and I particularly began to enjoy every moment. Wilfred, when he joined us a few days after our own arrival, looked so strained and dispirited that he worried everybody.

Blanche herself had already taken charge of my father, seeing to it that he never had a moment's dullness; if he was not occupied with us and our rifle shooting or fishing, she would whisk him off to give him golf lessons. When Wilfred arrived, she at once took charge of him as well. This was extremely good for Wilfred for he did not really quite fit in with our more sporting activities. Aunt Nellie was adept with him, too, and she and Blanche between them arranged many excursions and visits to places of historical interest or famous birth-places, perhaps connected with his current reading. These pilgrimages gave Wilfred more external pleasure than any other physical activity; even when fully adult he could never resist making them.

There was one memorable day connected with these journeys. Blanche, knowing his anxiety to make a long visit to one of the battle-fields (it must I think have been Flodden), had arranged to take him there. The two of them set off, intending to spend the day together, perhaps taking in other points of interest as well. They had arranged to get back well in time for dinner. When the time for their return came round and there was no sign of Blanche and Wilfred, we all started to wonder a little what had happened to them—it was so unlike Blanche to be late—and as an hour or so went by, conjecture turned to a faint anxiety. It was when anxiety in its turn had changed to alarm that they came back, footsore and completely tired out.

It appeared that when they arrived at the site Wilfred had become greatly excited over actually standing on the battlefield, had insisted upon exploring every acre and establishing the perimeters and, not content with this, had persuaded Blanche to represent the opposing forces (this entailed much walking). He had then proceeded to recon-struct and carry out the supposed manœuvres until in his mind he had the battle alive and taking place. He himself all the time walked about rapidly without seemingly tiring as he adjusted the imaginary armies. When his interest was really aroused Wilfred could be, and was, inexhaustible. It transpired that they had spent the whole time at Flodden, Wilfred indulging in alternate spells of rushing from place to place to decide some positional detail; while he was doing this he would be very voluble, explaining to Blanche his theories, exhorting her to follow his reasoning or perhaps asking her to take up a position at some distant point the better to illustrate his argument. For other spells he would sit or stand, quite silent, enriching his mental picture of the conflict as his gaze ranged over the field. When it was time for them to start back, Wilfred did not want to leave and, as Blanche said later, he seemed so wrapped up in the history of the place that she had not the heart to insist until it became imperative that they must go, then she had to drag him away. It was probably at this point that somebody, thinking how boring this must have been for Blanche, asked her what she did—apart from running about—to pass the time while he fought through these battles for himself. Quite cheerfully she answered, 'Oh, I just went on fighting his battles with him.'

On the days when he did not go on any of these special expeditions he was content to sit reading, which really baffled and nonplussed the other three young men—the youngest of whom was his contemporary —for they were not used to such serious concentration and I think found Colin and me, who were so much younger, easier to be companionable with. Indeed we were not difficult, for they arrayed before us this small boy's paradise, so that the whole atmosphere seemed shot through with fishing rods, flies, and guns and rifles. They taught us to throw a cast of flies and gave us long hours of fishing in the lonely streams that ran through the enchanting countryside, and saw to it— under their guidance—that we filled our baskets with the smallish trout that abounded in them. We were, of course, already fairly adept rough fishermen, and our fierce enthusiasm made us apt pupils with the dry fly. It was, I expect, this serious enthusiasm and not our adroitness— which could not have been great—that fascinated them so much, so that we both became their protégés and any failure on our part became as keen a disappointment to them, or so they made it seem to us, as it was to ourselves. They had as well a heart-warming way of excusing and glossing over our failures and dwelling upon and enhancing our successes so that our keenness and ambition was always high-pitched to increase our skill with rod and gun. They had fixed up a rifle range and butt in the grounds especially for us and so cleverly handicapped us according to age and efficiency that the results of the competitions, which were constantly in progress, remained always close and exciting.

Wilfred never joined us in the fishing, but would sometimes take part in the shooting matches, when he would surprise us all with his accuracy and more especially with his exhibition of boyish pride in a well-shot target; but even over this he could not resist some scientific investigation and would dig out the bullets from the two-inch planking and backing sand of the butt, take measurements, and from these calculate velocity and penetration.

Blanche was especially kind and thoughtful with Wilfred, not only to taking him about to these places of interest but in a general understanding way. She felt a compunction for his obviously self-imposed loneliness and isolation, so much in contrast to her own brothers' light-hearted gaiety. Indeed, there was something in the atmosphere of this house party that threw him into pronounced relief and made him appear—even for him—almost pathetic and in need of consolation and distraction. He was going through one of his moods of abstraction and self-condemnatory introspection, which emphasized his lonely aloofness and created a barrier which prevented him from losing himself and taking his part with us. Blanche was quick to realize this and, when not engaged in teaching my father his golf, would with a blithe happiness take Wilfred in hand and, by showing sympathy with his interests, in some way manage to imbue them with an infectious gaiety which helped to disperse his sombre reveries.

In spite of my own undisguised juvenile zeal in the pursuit of sport and high shooting scores, I was still drawn to my paints and would go off when I found opportunity and work on a water-colour. There was a nearby bridge over a stretch of river which had caught my imagination. My adult approach to this business of painting and my professional air of setting up my home-made easel out in the countryside—and all alone—intrigued and in some curious manner seemed to enchant the three young men, so that they became my devotees and insisted upon scrutinizing my work at every stage. Their extreme interest often made them persuade me to go on painting, so intrigued were they, which nearly endangered our fishing. Bill was very anxious to have a painting of Kelso Bridge to hang in his study. John commissioned me to do another, this time a moorland scene, similarly to display in his rooms in the medical school. They each gave me half a sovereign for my drawings; these were not disguised tips—their generosity over these had to be heavily curtailed by my father—but a genuine business arrangement. They were pleased and I was delighted, and my father was impressed which was I thought helpful and a good omen for the scheme I had in mind for my future. I have often, especially in the lean and hungry times to follow, looked back on my juvenile days with bemused envy at the ready market my childish unframed drawings seemed to create for themselves—a market which ceased in 1915 and has never since willingly re-opened its doors to me.

We spent part of this holiday in a small cottage which Aunt Nellie either owned or leased. It was from here that we did most of our fishing. It was in a lovely little village surrounded by moorland. The cottage itself was minute and the improvisation which had to be resorted to, not only to fit us into the tiny place but to arrange meals for so many of us, was huge fun for us children—I seem to remember some of us had to overspill into a neighbouring cottage. Here, in the early mornings, Bill would rouse us out of our bunk-like built-in beds, and we would bicycle off to a lonely stream and without bothering with bathing costumes or towels frisk about in the icy water.

My father, although so passionately devoted to swimming, would never come with us on these early morning swims. Running through his strange composition he had a lone, almost out of place streak of puritanism, in no sense akin to my mother's restricted vision which was often so heavily reinforced with prudishness. This puritanical vein in my father came out in a strong dislike of nudity. It made little difference that we could not possibly be overlooked, he just could not approve of it and would never permit it for us boys, except during this holiday, when to have stood out over it would he thought be bad manners—if nudity was unpleasant to him, as it was, ill-manners were abhorrent. He compromised by excusing himself from coming with us.

We were, at least Colin and I were, experienced cyclists, for although we did not yet own a bicycle we had learnt to ride on the Webbs' bicycles, for being such a huge family they had sizes to fit all ages. Actually we were something of trick riders, and could make bicycles do the maddest evolutions. Wilfred had been riding for a long time, sharing my father's machine; he was much more prosaic about it and looked upon it only as a quicker and easier means of getting about than walking, and not as Colin and I did as an end in itself for thrilling pleasure. However, this over-confidence of mine when riding a bicycle was to lead me into further depths of knowledge, this time to an awareness that it was possible that I myself could cease to live. I had so far accepted death in others as something normal, but I could not in any way believe the idea that I myself could be extinguished.

It was almost at the end of our time in Scotland that we were invited by some people we had met to go over and spend the afternoon with them. We had met them by chance when out fishing. They, too, were from the south and had taken for a few weeks a large, lovely old house, part of which was still being used as a farmhouse. This was some little distance away, so my father engaged a horse-carriage to take us there. To leave more room in the carriage and for the sake of the horse, for it was hilly country, it was decided that Wilfred and I should bicycle there.

Wilfred was in a cantankerous mood, because he did not really want to come with us at all but had been prevailed upon to do so. Because of this the start of our long bicycle ride was not a good one. Under the best of circumstances, mostly because of our difference in age, we did not make a satisfactory cycling pair, our ideas upon the proper use of a bicycle being so hopelessly opposite. I was inclined to sudden dashes at the fullest possible speed I could obtain, and to abrupt brakings to bring about skids which made the road surface fly, sometimes into Wilfred's face. This he considered brainless and unedifying, as indeed it was. When my wild cavorting which took place so irritatingly close to him resulted in a collision—as it sometimes did—his furious crossness would burst upon me. He would demand my attention and, dismounting, discourse with wholly ridiculously long words and absurdly erudite phrases upon my silly behaviour, with appeals to be more circumspect. Sometimes during these tirades there would be a mischievous gleam in his eyes, and he would end them with a sudden mounting of his bike and a quick chase of me and a complete turning of the tables. I enjoyed these flashes of fun immensely; much of my baiting I only did to bring them about. When they could be prized out of him, he would match any of us in fun and senseless hilarity and when this happened our high spirits would roar and soar to heights of exuberant, irresponsible happiness. If the gleam wasn't in his eyes, but only the dark sombreness of his introverted thoughts burning gloweringly, it was better to leave him alone. On this special afternoon I could see little signs of a gleam and our first collision brought forth a vituperative harangue, the theme of which was his misfortune in being forced into the company of such a moron as myself—a newly discovered and pet word of his at this time which he liked to air at every opportunity. We gave him many of these. . . .

Seeing there was no hope of fun with him but only a certainty of continued provocation, I rode ahead as fast as I could so that I should be out of sight to do my acrobatic prancing alone, and also to try and think out just exactly what a 'moron' was. I finally decided it was a deep sea monster and wondered what it would be like to be living on the bottom of the sea. I had been cogitating amiably with myself like this, riding with my arms above my head or folded across my chest—a trick which particularly infuriated Wilfred, partly because he could not master it himself and partly through anxiety about the risk to me—when, swinging round a bend, I saw stretching down in front of me a gloriously long and steep hill, which promised at least a mile of high-speed free-wheeling. I had for a long time been wanting to test out my skill by riding down just such a hill without touching the handle-bars. My pique with Wilfred's scathing belittlement of me was mounting. It was this as much as anything which propelled me into my extreme foolishness. In a few seconds I was hurtling down the hill, my hands held away from the bars, and in no time I was rapidly developing a dangerous swinging wobble. By now my balance was so uncertain that I felt unable to regain my handle-bars, as I knew that to relax my intense effort of balancing would throw me off. A stone in the road settled this for me by swerving my front wheel so badly that instinctively I clutched the handles. After frantic seconds of uncontrolled rushes, which brought my heart like a live thing up into my throat, I found myself again with some control of balance, but the bicycle was bucking so badly, the front wheel lifting so violently at every unevenness in the roadway, that this small control became nightmarish and developed into a fantastic see-saw between powerless loss of control and convulsive regain.

So swift had my acceleration become that I was now incapable of checking it in any way. This realization must have steadied me, for although the road hedges and telegraph poles appeared only as streaming grey ribbons which I seemed to be dividing into a lane-like tunnel as they streaked away from me on either side, I felt that they too, like the road, were solid walls. I was rushing through a grey tunnel with only enough room for me and my bicycle. Every moment my speed was increasing. It was now I think that an exhilarating sensation of irresponsibility came upon me, born out of the instinctive awareness that beyond retaining my seat I was not only helpless to do anything else but blessedly not required to make any other decision. The certainty of this in its very absoluteness was curiously comforting. I was, in later years, to experience this same feeling of isolated disassociation from actuality, when sitting in aeroplanes I was piloting, and about to crash.

It must have been when I was commencing to lose speed, and the bicycle began to rock and leap about once more, that fear in its stark horror again swept through me, so that I knew with appalling certainty that to fall now would be to cease to live and, with this, came a terrifying appreciation that to hit the road would break and smash my body. It was my first revelation of death and its possible connection with myself. It presented itself to me as a simple realization of my own vulnerability.

It was the opposing hill which finally slowed me down and another loose stone which tumbled me and the bicycle in a heap on the grass verge of the roadside. I scrambled up and felt I was trembling, not from fear or the tumble but from an ecstatic experiencing of triumph over danger. I felt sore and ached everywhere—I expect from the taut rigidity with which I had been steering. In spite of my reaction, I felt most of all an overwhelming sense of elation and a feeling of surprised relief at my escape from calamity, and with this feeling came another that in these exciting moments I had been lifted out of vague ignorance and put down inside the fringe of serious knowledge.

I was feeling lonely now and had an overpowering wish to talk to somebody about what had happened to me. Thinking of the Old Wolf trundling along behind so morosely, I set off back to meet him and tell him all about it. When I came up with him he sprang off his bicycle in great concern, for my appearance seemed to alarm him, and commenced to clean up my face with his handkerchief. Unknown to myself, I must have scratched my cheek in the brambles when tumbling off. Satisfied that my hurts were harmless, he at once accused me of falling off and continued a censorious gloating over his prediction coming true. A few moments later, my agitation and his intuition told him that something more than an ordinary fall had happened and he dropped his hectoring manner and tried, with gentleness, to draw me out, but it was too late now. My childish unreasonable expectation of immediate sympathy had fallen flat; in my disappointment I became silent, and when I did speak it was with bravado and airy dismissal. But Wilfred was smitten with compunction and was humbly placating to me. A warmth of unspoken understanding crept up between us and made us talk of other things with pleasure and happiness, so that we ceased provoking one another and the journey that had commenced with so much friction ended in unusually affectionate vein as we both pedalled away in the brilliantly hot afternoon sunshine; I, now, with great circumspection and enormous care not to swerve too near Wilfred or in any way jeopardize his even and rather stately progress; he, on his part, being solicitous as to my continued bodily well-being, with grave exhortations to inform him immediately if strange pains or sensations attacked me.

Dismounting from our bikes at a discreet distance from the farmhouse, we sat in the shade of a tree—silent, now, and contented over our recent misunderstandings—to await the coming of the carriage with the others, so that we might all go up to the house together. Sitting there in the cool and peaceful shade of the tree with the golden heat running up to the edge of its pool of darkness gave me the not unpleasant feeling of being imprisoned in a patch of coolness. All around us the golden heat built itself into walls of shimmering brilliance that secluded Wilfred and me in a cage of blue shadows. A peculiar mood of restless expectancy came upon me so that I felt tuned to a receptive pitch, which made me sensitive to, and aware of, an indefinable suspended enlightenment that I felt was hovering around me.

My recent experience of taut and quivering tenseness, as well as giving me my first chill glimpse of death, had keyed me up to an awareness, the electric quality of which I found troubling, and I was filled with an unsatisfied seeking for some revelation I felt was about to be vouchsafed to me. In a restless and agitated way I was conscious that if this would only happen, it would bring me relief from this unknown uncertainty and that the revelation itself would offset and in some way balance the cold and deadly certainty that had struck into me while rushing so helplessly down the dangerous hill. I remember feeling remote and somehow suspended. My experience of extreme physical danger had tautened me into a state of extreme receptivity. It was mostly, I expect, because of this, that illumination, when it came to me on that afternoon, came not only swiftly but with such penetration that in a fleeting moment of time the veiling mists of femininity were to be lifted for me, and knowledge come to me.

Wilfred shook me out of my remoteness by telling me he could see the carriage coming. In a few moments everything was stir and bustle again as we all made our way down to the farmhouse. As soon as we passed through the garden gates I knew that I was going to enjoy this party. There was a warmness about everything, our gay welcome, the collection of young people who rushed to cluster around us in friendly interest; even the flagstones of the path were warm, I could feel them through my thin plimsolls with tingling pleasantness.

The garden, which seemed beautiful to me, was massed with colour and wandered about in an entrancing way in and out of the farm buildings, cowsheds, and barns so that the farm and garden inter-mingled with alluring unexpectedness. The heavily sweet beast smells from the byres and hayricks floated about, mixing with the headier and sharper scent of the flowers. The summery sounds of farm and garden,— the distant rattle of a chain, the champing and shuffling of a horse, and the clank of a pail—blended with the drone and gentle buzzing of the garden and were interwoven with the tinkle of young laughter and the hum of clear and happy voices. All the chill and fear of my frightening ride down the hill was melted away, leaving only my perception and vivid awareness of living, over-heightened to a pitch of stimulation that made me feel airy and without weight. Among all this medley of scents and smells, sounds and warmth, laughter and mingled voices, a long trestle-table had been set for tea, the dappling gleam of its white-ness flirting with the shadows of its overhanging boughs.

When looking back, the extraordinarily English air of it all smites me very hard with a longing to recapture its magic; so great sometimes has the wish become that I have worked and searched to find it, but I have never done so. It was I think something—almost an aroma—that belonged to the years just before 1914. Whatever it was, August 1914 extinguished the subtlety of it all for me for ever. On this summer after-noon, so peculiarly pre-1914 in its untorn clothing of warm winds, its jewelled beauty of sun-glutted flowers and gardens, and the promise of sustenance in its breastlike founts of farm and husbandry fertile with green mounds of swelling earth, no hint or fear of the disaster of war came near us as the brightly coloured afternoon whiled itself gently away.

There was in this gathering on this afternoon a young girl just out of childhood. I did not know who she was and have never known. At the time I only knew that she was a visitor from another country, probably from Norway or Sweden. Quite early in the afternoon she had attached herself to me, and shown me much attention and affectionate kindness together with a complete disregard of any grown-up condescension, which made me feel warm and happy. Her ingenuous and unreserved showing of her liking for me drew me strongly towards her. She took possession of me, sometimes holding me tightly by the hand, at others throwing her hot bare arm around my neck; I liked the friendliness of this although it made me tingle rather unaccountably. We explored the farm and animals and when we came to an open space we would with unspoken agreement release one another and, making a race of it, tear madly across the paddocks. To recover our breath and still our panting bodies we would seek the cool dark interiors of the great brick barns and, throwing ourselves down side by side on the hay, breathe ourselves back to ease and speech. Her English was good but not complete, and our amusement over it was gay and full of fun.

It was perhaps our perfect unreserve with one another which added mystery to delight; with her I found I had lost most of my shyness, and all my embarrassment. While close to her I had the extraordinary sensation that whatever I did or said was said or done with all the privacy of being alone, and somehow this gave me a strange feeling of affinity. So curiously strong was it that I had the sensation that I could say anything or do anything without the usual commitment that a second person would bring about. It gave me a lovely safe feeling and made me strangely sure of myself. We heard the tea bell ringing. Hungry and thirsty now, hand in hand and strangely happy, we wandered slowly back to the house.

It was while we were having tea that an unveiling came about in my mind, which half disclosed to me the mystery and purpose of my own body and wholly disclosed to me the beauty and loveliness that lurked in its complementary oppositeness—femininity. Knowledge began to float through me but now it did not impact itself upon me, as it had done during that restless painting day when physical urge had surged up in me to manifest stark masculinity. This time perception, when it came to me, although so linked seemed only to be intimately concerned with this sensitiveness to femininity. It did not affect me physically, it only illuminated my perceptions with image-like reflective awareness. I was expectant of comprehension but I could not yet comprehend—between my instinct and a complete knowledge there still remained a screen which left me vaguely incomplete, without awareness of the necessity for linkage between mental imagery and physical action. My body remained undisturbed.

I had, though, had a glimpse of them both. On the hot evening when I was walking home through the corn-fields into the setting sun I had encountered the surprise of physical promise; now this hour or so with this enchanting girl had enlightened my sense to the psychological beauty of the contact of male and female. Before the afternoon was over I was to experience the loveliness of visual appreciation of sensual beauty, but in spite of the intensity of emotional recognition which was to sweep over me, this day did not bring to me completion; the physical and the abstract were still separate in me—fusion of the two was not to come to me yet; indeed much of both was to be withdrawn from me again—both experiences were but passing portents. Each experience was only a presage of the drawing back of a curtain.

We were late in arriving in the garden for tea, but the two end seats had been left for us, so that when we took our places we faced each other across the narrow trestle. I remember so well how the late after-noon sun was pouring slanting rays of golden mote-charged loveliness over everything; even the starchily white tablecloth was palely yellow. Shimmering pools of lovely colour danced around the dishes of jam, deep yellow from the apricot, rich ruby from the raspberry, and pale purple from the blackcurrant; over it all hung the indefinable sharp smoky scent made from boiling water being poured over china tea, and the fragrance which only comes when out of doors in a garden full of sun-warmed flowers with hot sunshine blazing down.

It was when she jumped up and leaned over the table to ply me with jam that some of the mysteriously charged meaning of the afternoon came upon me, and with it a fulfilment of intensely awaited revelation. As I lifted my head to thank her I beheld her small body and knew that in seeing her thus I had for the first time become vividly conscious of an oppositeness to myself. Intuitional knowledge, difficult to formu-late, eddied around my senses; with a glorious sensation of startled surprise, I realized the significance of the counterpart to masculinity . . . I became instantly and exquisitely aware of femininity. I was entranced with the perfection of promise the revelation unfolded for me. Un-knowingly absorbed, my eyes accepted the hard closeness and golden warmth of the small bosom. I did not immediately look away—indeed, I could not and did not want to. Instead, I absorbed delight and slow awakening from what I beheld, for I felt no consciousness of guilt or wrong-doing, nor yet any sense of trespass towards her. This enthralled fraction of time held for me only freshly exposed knowledge and inviting beauty, which my wondering spellbound gaze could not refuse.

The cheerful clatter of the spoon hitting my plate to shake off the jam made me look up to meet her eyes, which I saw were gently smiling into mine; she did not withdraw immediately but quivering slightly slowly drew away. Laughing and chattering together once more, we finished tea and springing up left the table. We both realized the existence between us of immature need and fragrant understanding, strangely we recognized in our crossed paths a completion which we must not disturb, silently we parted to lose each other; in the commotion and hubbub of dispersing guests and children this was not difficult: it left us the fragrance of our spiritual and bodily journey towards sexual emotion fresh and sparkling. We never saw each other again.

I felt invigorated and intensely happy, with a quickening knowledge that told me of splendid and lovely emotional experiences that, although yet dormant in me, would later become exquisitely alive. Femininity, with all its creative swelling promise, had brushed me softly and beautifully with the light gentleness of a falling petal.

On the way back Wilfred expressed his pleased astonishment at what he called my successful social début, for although it had passed unremarked by others, Wilfred had noticed the pleasant preoccupation of the young girl and myself and was eager to know what conversation I had found—out of my imbecility—to interest her so much. But I refused to speak of it or even answer, always a good defence of mine when he became persistent. So he huffed-up and revenged himself by telling me that she must obviously be the kind sort of person who went out of their way to be nice to little boys of low intellect. His question started me thinking, and I suddenly realized how little the young girl and I had said to one another and how much we had depended upon a language which had no need of words. Wilfred remained huffy and glum. I was glad, for I was tired and enjoying the aftermath of my summer afternoon thoughts; I never even thought to bump his back wheel but lagged as far behind him as I could without bringing his reproof down upon me.

Although I was tired I was not weary, and bicycling along the mountain road, through the eddying currents of clear evening air that alternated with the stored up warmth rising from the road, I found delicious. My thoughts, too, sent a surging prickle of sensation all over my body that was tantalizing without being irritant. The unknown promise it seemed to foretell I found uplifting, and curiously heady and vaguely portentous.

These penetrating flashes of experience, whilst brilliantly illuminating for me during these isolated fractions of time, were transitory, so that eclipse took place before complete recognition could bite deeply into me, and in this way knowledge did not become immediate but rather only maintained the fugitive brilliance of diamond fire. My wonder was aroused but not my curiosity, and this left me contented and with an instinctive certainty that somehow complete understanding would come to me and the more absolutely if I refrained from probing into these strange physical feelings and emotions. My childhood was to remain intact for some time yet; indeed before Wilfred and I got back that evening my thoughts had already slipped forward to the next day, because Bill had promised to take Colin and me to a special fishing place where the fish ran big. I was already visualizing in my mind the enormous basket of trout that might come to me tomorrow and gloating over the picture I conjured up of the gleaming monster that would surpass in weight and magnificence anything that even Bill himself had ever caught and so bring me undying fame and glory. Before we dismounted I found it hard to believe that I had not actually caught the fish, for my heart was pounding away at my visionary picture of myself hauling it out of the river.

When Wilfred and I reached the house the evening was darkening and cooling and I suddenly felt tired and cold; it had been a long bicycle ride and the excitements of the day were taking their toll. On the last mile I had drawn abreast of Wilfred again when he started good-naturedly to try and draw me out about the girl at the party. I surprised him—and myself—with the vehemence of my demand that he should 'shut up' and with the fury of my threats of what I would do if he said anything about it in front of the others. We were dismounted now on the last hill. Leaning across his handle-bars he peered closely at me in the gathering darkness and said 'The young water-colourist indeed grows up.' We pushed on the rest of the way in silence. It was when we were putting out bicycles away in the dark shed that, squeezing my shoulder, he said 'All right, Harold, I won't say anything in front of the others, but remember, if I don't, it puts you one up on me, and I shall expect the same from you; if your perspicacious [his word] advancement continues at this dangerous speed, I may demand a return of equal discretion.' I gave him a friendly thump on the chest to which he retaliated by pushing me in fun but quite violently out of the shed, after which he linked his arm into mine as we walked up to the house.

This holiday was an altogether different one from all of our other ones, I suppose because we were guests and not on our own. The last day was taken up with fierce arguments between my father and John, Bill, and Walter, who knowing our keenness for shooting were mad to give Colin and me a rifle each; but my father would not allow us to accept such lavish gifts. It was a fearful disappointment to us but he was adamant. I think their own disappointment equalled Colin's and mine. They tried to get around it by tipping us so heavily that we could buy our own guns later on but again my father would not hear of it, and insisted that the tips were reduced to normal ones.

The 1914–1918 war, when it came a few years later, killed both Bill and Walter. Bill was killed fighting against the Turkish armies at Gallipoli in July 1915, Walter in Palestine—Gaza— in April 1917. They had been gazetted to the same regiment—the King's Own Scottish Borderers. John of course served as a young army doctor and survived. After the war he returned to civilian medicine, settled in Hereford and remained in practice there until shortly before he died on 17 February, 1960.   Aunt Nellie undertook enormous amounts of war work for which she was awarded the M.B.E. As her lieutenant, Blanche undertook similar work. Aunt Nellie lived to be over ninety and in her later years she and Blanche—who had not married—took to worldwide travelling. After her mother's death Blanche kept on the house in Kelso, and except when she is visiting some remote part of the world, which she frequently is doing, still lives there.

Chapter Twelve

WILFRED

OUR return to our little house in Shrewsbury was welcomed, as any return home always was, with happy excitement by all of us in our different ways: my father because he liked being in his own home again and the freedom it gave him to rise in the mornings as early as he liked and, taking one of us with him, refresh himself in the fields or with a swim in the river before going to his hated office; Wilfred because he could maroon himself once more in his eave-sloped bedroom-study and brood undisturbed, or nearly so, amongst his tiny library of cherished volumes, or discount himself with melancholy introspection and brood dismally and rather hopelessly upon his future, or perhaps after all dream of brilliant self-satisfying achievement; Colin because he could get back to his beloved Spot, and continue his concocting of doses—mostly areca nut—for the supposed good of the little dog's health; Mary because she could again see her small aviary of breeding canaries. She was becoming adept in the care of them, and especially skilful in feeding the minute chicks which appeared so unaccountably from time to time; but mostly perhaps she was glad because she could give undivided and—more important—unrebuked attention to my mother, for the remonstrance from our hosts about her unselfish devotion had been constant and disturbing to her during our holiday.

My mother was glad to be home partly because the time away had not been a complete success for her. Her wretched colitis had been attacking with even more than usual vigour, so that she had not been really well all the time we were away. There had been, too, more than usual disagreement between herself and my father about Wilfred, and all the old arguments about the correct treatment for his attacks of morose depression had redoubled in intensity—as they always did when we were away from home, my mother rallying to his defence and discouraging my father in his attempts to draw Wilfred out of himself.

Wilfred

I, with the others, was pleased to be home again, and immediately we got into the house I would not wait for anything else but rushed upstairs to get my paintings and designs, and—with my eyes averted—laid them all out on the bed. Then I let myself feel the first few seconds of trembling excitement while my gaze devoured and my mind assessed the work I had not seen for these few weeks. All my life, this intense looking forward to seeing again any work of my own hands, after separation from it, has always retained the power to stimulate me to high excitement and realization of the purest joy of living. I was looking forward as well to the autumn term, and once again being absorbed into the dear musty 'museumy' smell of the Art School; to drawing again from the chalk-white plaster casts with their Corinthian intricacies of fat, beautifully sweeping leaves; to rubbing in the black shadows against the matt white of the high lights, and enjoying the lively feeling this gave me that the drawing was jumping out at me from the paper. I was crowded too with ideas for designs which I wanted to work out whose ambitious size prevented me from working on them at home.

I had also—as I thought—a specially marvellous idea for a balanced but in no way repeated design. This was to be at least four feet by three, and I intended to make dozens of small drawings from Virginia creeper, each one carefully drawn from different sprays and following with exactitude the different stages of growth, with special emphasis on the way the leaf stalk locked itself so strongly on the main stem; after which each drawing would be traced on to the meticulously joined sheets of Whatman's hot-pressed paper and each drawing experimented with in different positions to complete the whole design. Then I wanted to redraw the pattern as a whole and colour it with water-colours, sponging it down time after time until I had the right quality and delicacy of scarlets, pale greens, withered browns, and warm russets. I would then outline with a sable-brush every leaf, stem, and tendril in a uniform colour to give the design slenderness of character. I was so enthralled with this idea that I was in a fever in case one of the other students should think of it first, and so bring my joyous expectation to ruin. However, this did not happen and soon after commencing the new term I had established my right to what I thought of as my inspiration too firmly for any of the others to purloin it from me. It turned out well and its unorthodoxy caused some comment.

The study of plant form was rather strong in this school, but so far it had only been applied to a design in a tight and stylized manner, and always with one half of the pattern exactly similar to the other half: my introduction of a free design with no part ever repeated was looked upon as interesting and led to experiments amongst the other students —with such startling results that a halt had to be called and a return to orthodoxy encouraged amongst us all. The thought of all this and the joy of execution helped to fade from my mind the strange and lovely experience that had folded me and the Norse girl so closely together during the farm-house tea party, and the episode slid smoothly into the background of my thinking—always there and ready to emerge, but not obtruding at all.

This winter which followed our visit to Scotland found us as a family much more settled, and in many ways more placid. The special fact was that it was now accepted without question between my father and mother and the rest of us that it must somehow be arranged for Wilfred to continue with his studying and in some way be helped towards a literary or at least a sholastic career. Gone was the immediate necessity for expedient settlement of him in any job, no matter what, which would bring in wages or salary, and it was perhaps this now final agreement on this point between my father and mother which brought peace and so much more understanding to us all. Gone was the wearying conflict which had see-sawed so violently between them, and in its place had grown a mutual determination that somehow he was to be given a chance to wrench for himself a career which would lead him to something beyond the humdrum and ordinary future to which our lack of means and influence, at that time, so clearly pointed. Gone was my father's insistence upon immediate safety and the wish to see Wilfred launched into some bank or office.

It was a big sacrifice and a generous gesture on my father's side, for his fear for us all was still haunting him and his instinctive distrust of his own ability to help any of us materially bowed him down with a heavy load of responsibility. His dearest wish was to see us all started in some money-earning capacity at the earliest possible moment: first of all for our own security and the consequent easing of his own anxiety and responsibility; and secondly because above all things my father was very human and in his youthful and romantic way felt still young enough to get something for himself out of his own life, and so recompense himself for the years of dull, unrewarding monotony spent in the work he hated so much. His very openness of character did not allow him to make any secret of this, and from my earliest recollection I can remember his bitterly avowed determination that as soon as we were all safe and settled he would take himself out of this dull and dreary England and go back to the Far East or voyage around the world.

There was in all this no lack of love or affection for ourselves, and his thoughts would probably not have needed to find escape like this had he been receiving an adequate salary, which would have relieved him of financial worry and the everlasting economizing over petty but necessary trifles. For all his sacrifices of his natural desires in order to keep this so-called safe job, all he received in return was a pittance instead of a salary—and no security whatsoever, and well he knew it. A bit of bad luck, misjudgement, or even a show of his natural fiery temper could throw him out and leave him resourceless, without counting the ever-present fear of physical accident or disability.

How my mother was to fit into anything like this, or even where she could fit, we never really gathered. I do not think his own projection of thought went as far as this. He was content to surmount his first obstacle—us children—before attacking the second. That she did fit in somehow is quite certain, but even my father must have baulked at the impossible idea of transporting her to India, Tahiti, or Peru. In any case, perhaps at the bottom of his heart he knew that his dreams would never materialize and he used them mostly as a lure held in front of him to lighten a little the plod of reality. As the years rolled away and he grew more tired, his ideas reduced themselves until retirement on pension at sixty became his only focal point. When retiring age came and went, the point reduced itself to a wish just to visit India again, if only for a few weeks. This last flickering hope he never relinquished. Even when the deadly fingers of angina began their horrible groping, he would have still set off with grim courage had a chance offered itself.

My mother was always peculiarly unsympathetic towards this side of my father. She was so much more parochial in thought and outlook that this was to be expected; what was unexpected was her attitude of airy and slightly superior dismissal of it all as childish nonsense, and her refusal ever to discuss seriously such ridiculous ideas. She encouraged us children to view them in the same frivolous light, which was a little unfair and hard on my father, so that for a period we came to share with her an inclination to treat any suggestion, serious or trivial, that he made as something not to be dwelt upon with consideration but rather to be dismissed with slight ridicule. This unusual hardness in my mother was most likely engendered by fear that if my father's fervour to break with England and routine life were not laughed away, upheaval might come about with consequent danger to us all. She was right in thinking that with the slightest encouragement and co-operation from her, he would have attempted some such upheaval. He argued, sensibly enough, that short of his being workless it was difficult to see how we could be less secure than we already were—to say nothing of the wretched misery of having to think a dozen times before spending pence on necessities, never mind the impossibility of hundreds of pounds on education. She was wholly wrong, though, in even fearing that my father by any action of his would place us in jeopardy. This he was incapable of doing at any time. Nevertheless, with genuine enthusiasm on the part of my mother he could, I think, have arranged for a change of country with, at least, equal insecurity—for security was not ours to have or to hold. My mother was never able to give this word which would certainly have upheaved us and could possibly have set our family fortunes going more favourably.

By nature and inclination my mother was disinclined for change, and possessed a complacence which allowed her to accept these circumstances for herself, and, at times I am sure, held it to be wrong even to wish for betterment, sincerely thinking it wicked to attempt to alter and, as she thought of it, improve upon the 'Divine Plan'. Her indifferent health and the tiring years were also bringing her to submissive acceptance of her lot as decreed.

The supine atmosphere this created in the home would have been more seriously retrogressive had not my father's irritated intolerance of it livened things up a bit, for although his thwarted dreams of change did not lead him far, at least they kept him railing loudly and often—sometimes very bad-temperedly in a healthy way; and if in these attacks he often upset my mother and us children, at least they helped to prevent submersion and ward off threatening apathy. This was just as well, for my mother at this period was converging towards a state where minor upheavals and discordances were over-exaggerated and assumed the look of near disasters. The major issues, such as the future of her family—apart of course from Wilfred—she would only face with a sublime and contented refusal to take any notice of them. Her unsatisfactory health and lack of stamina accounted for something of this and aggravated the feeling of accepted invalidism which was growing upon her and was to develop into a drawing-back from conscious effort.

Although it was now settled beyond further dispute that Wilfred was to pursue his studies, irrespective of immediate earning capacity, the ways and means were difficult to see and find. He still persisted in flogging his flagging energies and forcing himself to work far into every night, so much so that blue patches of overstrain were blotching alarmingly beneath his tired eyes. The pallor and weariness and its attendant unreasonable intolerance and irritability were causing desperate anxiety to my mother and father. My father still chose to disguise his own concern with disapproval of Wilfred's habit of refusing to take enough exercise or get out in the open air. My mother showed hers with constant applications of food and exhortations to rest, and with devoted ministrations to his wants and efforts to ensure his comfort. With it all she maintained a saintly refusal to be perturbed or ruffled by his often petulant dismissals.

It was an especially critical and trying time for Wilfred. The Shrewsbury Technical School, having brought him to matriculation point, would not be able to take him beyond it and, as far as this school was concerned, he was virtually finished with it, dependent of course upon the result of the examination which was not yet known. He had sat for his matriculation at London University and had returned from the examination bitterly disappointed, for the papers had not suited him but had with the malign mischance of these things laid to waste long months of organized and careful preparation. He told us all rather dejectedly that he might as well have enjoyed himself these last months following pleasanter pursuits, for all the good his months of application in preparation for the exam had proved to be. He was apprehensive about the result. His actual receiving of the news imprinted itself very vividly on my mind. I think my mother must have been away from home, otherwise it could not have fallen to my lot to deliver the fateful letter to him. As it was, I rushed up to his bedroom with the embossed and sealed letter—to find him, as usual, buried deep under the blankets, only the fringe of his dark hair showing from the top of his head and stupefied with over-tired sleep.

My excited shout about the news I bore stabbed him awake. He sprang up in bed and snatched the thick creamy envelope from my hand and then commenced—again to use his own words—an ecstasy of fumbling, for he was trembling and shivering violently and his hands were all mixed up with the bedclothes and the envelope was obstinate and refused to open. At last he had the letter out and I shall always remember the few seconds of stillness, and then the long dragged out sigh of disappointment, despairing in its melancholy, and his inert slumping back on to the bed and the burrowing under the blankets. I asked him to tell me but he would not answer or speak, so I left his room and went down to my father who was impatiently waiting for the news before going to his office. I was sent up again to make sure he had failed and, drawing away the sheets and blankets covering his head, gave him my father's message. Glaring fiercely at me he growled, 'Tell him I have passed if he must know. He's not interested and doesn't care, and you go away. Go away—and leave me alone—only leave me alone, I tell you.' He would not speak to us all day, and refused to get up until just before my father was expected home at six o'clock.

Later we learned that it was a good pass but not a brilliant one. His morose subsiding on the bed was caused through overwhelming disappointment that was pathetic in its intensity and miserable to feel and live with. He had dreamed and hoped so long for first-class honours and absolute triumph that his moderate pass seemed to him to be failure. It was a long time before he became reconciled. It was in France years later that his phrase 'ecstasy of fumbling' was born out of the horror of adjusting gas masks to try and cheat the sleeping death that lay in the yellowish vapour clouds which rolled along so insidiously towards himself and his men. Anxiety was no greater in those moments than it was in the few seconds he spent trying to open his stubborn envelope, in the safety of his bed in the dark dingy little room in Shrewsbury.

In retrospect, these small happenings seem unimportant and trivial, but at the time the whole episode of the examination had developed into an urgent anxiety, shared by all six of us, and was very much a significant family affair. We were all proud and delighted that he should have attained even the chance to sit for it and we were desperately keen that he should pass and, as we thought of it in our simple family way, bring honour to us all. In each one of us there had lived for so long a foreboding of failure for the cross-tempered Old Wolf and tenderness for him at the hurt we knew that this would bring. There had, too, been the uncertainty of whether he would stand the prior strain or perhaps go down with one of his awful chest colds or bouts of incapacitating headaches, all of which had brought about a tenseness which was disconcerting in its exaggeration of the event and not the best preparation for Wilfred. Just the same, our undivided loyalty and longing for his success struck deeply into his heart. To hide it he heaped raillery and scorn though his eyes belied it. But towards my father, it seemed, he could not soften.

This was tragic, for my father felt more deeply about it than any of us, and his pride in Wilfred's eventual pass was astounding in its sincerity. In making one of his speeches to Wilfred about it, he dwelt on the pass and its significance and tried to comfort him by pouring scorn upon such silly details as honours, especially first-class ones. This—un-unexpected to Wilfred—and vehement championing did much to bring him around to a more rational view of the result and to think that perhaps after all he had not done so badly. My father, in his generous way, threw off all past rebuffs and misunderstandings, unreservedly withdrew all active opposition, and allied himself whole-heartedly with any scheme the two of them, Wilfred and my mother, might hatch up between them to further his scholastic career. This set up a pleasant respite and my mother got to work amongst her canons and other church dignitaries to see just what could be done about getting him the chance of a scholarship, if any were available, or some other means of getting him up to Oxford and eventually, as she still hoped, into Holy Orders.

Wilfred himself was toying with several ideas in a desultory and somewhat awkward sort of way and was a little lost because at this time no career in itself made any definite appeal to him; for even at this age he was vaguely aware that all he really wanted was independence so that he could continue his reading and lever out of himself the creative poetic force which, uncertainly as yet, he knew to be in him. All that he could and did say was that he wanted independence from wage-earning for another five years, which would have brought him into his early twenties. Knowing this to be impossible, he could only look upon any suggested occupation as a means to an end, and never as an end in itself, and was only interested in a choice insofar as that choice would help him to decide the means which would be least adverse to his own determined goal of poetry and literature.

Teaching, of course, was thought of. Later he was to show some aptitude for tutoring, but then only if the pupil was really liked by him as a person; as a teacher in the accepted sense he was quite unfitted and as a junior elementary schoolmaster he would have been hopeless. A junior mastership in a single subject, languages, English, or science was thought of, and even sought for, and the idea of obtaining a post as a French master in some obscure private school appealed to him as a stop-gap—he was almost bilingual in his proficiency here. But it seemed that the most humble of these posts demanded some knowledge of games and the organizing of them, for which of course he had not the slightest ability and still less interest. Some arrangement for him had to be thought of and worked out. Direct financial expenditure was so utterly out of the question that it never arose in my father's mind. He knew too well that the utmost he could manage was the negative help of enabling Wilfred to remain at home as a non-wage earner, thus allowing him to continue his reading for a degree and hoping—without perceiving how it could happen—that some sort of opportunity would present itself. In the end it was the canons and clergy with whom my mother had previously been in so much contact who brought forth a suggestion which it seemed might bring about a preliminary solution.

It so happened that news came to my mother of a clergyman who held the living of a very small village in Oxfordshire. The village was tiny but the parish itself was a large and outlying one. The vicar himself was a man of middle age, and specialized in the preparation of young men destined for the Church. Having this in view, he was in the practice of receiving into his vicarage as residents two or three of these novitiates, usually graduates from the universities. There were, I suspect, varying financial arrangements, as his object was more the seeking of talent and practical assistance with his parish work than augmentation of income. Apart from this the scheme had, until he met Wilfred, remained much the same for all of them. In return for tutoring and post-graduate guidance, the students were expected to do some parish visiting and other work, partly as experience; the amount of work expected beyond this varying somewhat according to mutual adjustment.

Introductions were effected, letters exchanged between the various people concerned and my mother, and finally between Mr. Herbert Wigan, my mother, and Wilfred, and a week-end visit arranged so that he should meet the Wigans, see the vicarage and, of course, be interviewed. The week-end was a success. Mr. Wigan was a quiet man and a great lover of seclusion, and something about Wilfred—perhaps his quiet gentleness and dark shyness—appealed to him; indeed the unaffected modesty that suffused Wilfred's bearing when first meeting people was hard to resist, and the totally unassumed poise gave an impression of maturity far beyond his years. Besides taking an immediate liking to him the vicar, like so many men of a retiring nature, was a man of keen astuteness and I think realized when meeting Wilfred that here was a very young man indeed but, in spite of his boy's years, already very adult. He perceived as well, I think, the conscientious integrity that was inherent in him.

Mr. Wigan beyond everything else was a sound and—more rare—utterly sincere churchman, and I think at once saw in Wilfred the makings of a priest of great promise, who later might prove to be an acquisition to his Mother Church—his first thought—and, in the meantime, would be a valuable assistant to himself in his arduous parish work. Before the few days' visit was over he had offered Wilfred a post in his household more or less as a full-time lay parish worker, which really amounted to the suggestion of an unofficial curacy. At the same time he promised that if Wilfred would, after consideration, accept the position, time would be fitted in for reading, tuition, and preparation. If this arrangement was acceptable there should be no fees or living expenses and, to put the position completely in order, he would pay Wilfred a token salary of five shillings a week.

At first glance, this did seem to Wilfred to be the answer to his problem, but in thinking it over he realized uncomfortably the real implication inherent in the proposal, for, as well as this very satisfactory arrangement, the vicar had without any specific commitment promised him that, should everything work out under the plan as they hoped it would, he would do all in his power—except of course financial aid, which was neither within his means nor desired by Wilfred—to help him, by exerting his not inconsiderable influence, to enter a university or by some means obtain his M.A. degree. This last, however, it must be understood, would be contingent upon Wilfred's implied willingness to enter the Church.

Very early in the discussions Wilfred had in his tentative and shy muttering way tried to make it clear to Mr. Wigan that he felt no distinct vocational urge for the Church and was uncertain of himself in this direction. These assertions had not been received seriously and were treated more as hesitancy due to youth than as considered thought, and were dismissed accordingly. My mother's eagerness and possible emphasizing of his inclination towards Christianity and the Church, in earlier correspondence, had I think given the vicar the impression that

Wilfred would not be difficult to persuade and would be malleable to suggestion. Wilfred's apparent gentleness and seeming ready acquiescence could be, as many people discovered later, disconcertingly misleading. Somewhere beyond midway in these negotiations he had again felt impelled to disclose and emphasize his own doubts as to his suitability or even his wish to seek ordination, this time with a vehemence which gained in force from his feeling of being tempted not to complicate everything by hesitancy now, but to seize this chance for his first objective—a university degree—and salve his conscience later. Wilfred's fine integrity never had its foundations in any lack of realization of self-advantage, but sprang rather from brilliant awareness of his ability for deception and the obvious danger to uprightness that this could hold. This would have surprised my mother to shocked unbelief had she even remotely apprehended it. This renunciation, as it so often was to do in later years, led him too far into altruism and inclined him to place himself sometimes at an unreasonable disadvantage.

With halting persistence he made the vicar accept his view that any agreement must not morally bind him to embrace the Church or in any way impede his freedom of choice of a career, but allow him at any time, and for no given reason, to change his mind. Warming up, he went on to discourse lengthily upon the extreme likelihood of this happening, giving as his reasons his grave doubts as to the authenticity or even desirability of orthodox religion, and his almost certain conviction that he had other aspirations which would preoccupy him to the exclusion of interest in a church appointment. He was shy, as ever, of putting into actual words the truth—that he was writing poetry and only longed to be able to go on doing so. Instead he preferred to wrap around his ambition a cloak of vague and uncertain obscurity. This sometimes caused him to give a false impression of unsureness—almost vacillation—which, again, was extremely deceptive. However, there was now nothing undecided about his determination to make Mr. Wigan see and understand clearly his resolution not to be implicated in any scheme—no matter how enticing—that might in the future make it difficult or embarrassing for him to follow his own instinctive course. The vicar was quite unprepared for this, and possibly was not a little shocked and surprised by Wilfred's forthrightness and his sudden revelation of unsuspected firmness, which his first impression had so belied. It proved something of a setback, and the vicar decided he must have more time for further consideration and conferring with

God. Had he known it, this last bit did more to alienate Wilfred from the idea of the Church than anything that had gone before.

After considerable pondering and, I suppose, a conference or two with God, during which he must have misinterpreted God's answers, he came to the wrong conclusion that Wilfred could be won for the Church. He then laid another proposal before him—that he should come to him at the next vacancy in the vicarage and commence his parochial duties. This might help Wilfred to make up his mind. A limit of two years was to be set for him to decide for or against the Church. With many expressions of hope that this decision would be on the right side, he renewed his promises of help towards a degree and eventual ordination if Wilfred decided on this course. It was with this understanding—which did not differ in any way from the original, except that now Wilfred's moral and actual freedom of choice remained open—that they were both satisfied. With this finally settled Wilfred returned to us, if not very excited about the prospect, at least happy that he was not committed seriously in any way except to take up the post in due course, which at any rate made him more or less independent of the family and at the same time promised tutoring and time to read. The rebound caused him to force himself seriously to read theology, but this wore off and the will disappeared before the time came for him to commence his pseudo-curacy; the pleasant hiatus was filled mostly with his poets, the tutoring of myself, and his own grave writing of poetry.

With him settled for the next year or so, attention was focused a little more on me and the shocked discovery made that while I was advancing rapidly with my drawing and design—and this was now freely admitted—I was in serious arrears with ordinary school subjects, so as Wilfred was going to be at home for some time yet it was thought a good idea for him to resume his attempts to tutor me.

The dear Old Wolf—how much he hated it! However, although his powers of teaching were no stronger, the results were a little more encouraging for both of us for, truth to tell, I was a little concerned and anxious about the matter myself. Uneasy conversations and vague plans for my future were floating about the house, and my father's constant reiteration that it would be necessary for me to earn my own living before I was fifteen made me apprehensive and troubled, especially when my father told me straight out that if I failed to pass the ordinary elementary examinations required by the humblest office or business house, I should have to be put to something more menial still. This in itself did not alarm me so much as the troubled feeling that my father and mother were veering away from my own certain plan for myself to continue at the School of Art until I qualified as an art master. I was quite fixed and unwavering about this and had no other plans— not having imagined I should need any, so confident was I that I could qualify early. I had taken the first steps and had already passed one examination and taken a first; but this constant deviation by the family from my plan really began to frighten me and I came to think that if I was not to be able to continue my art career I had better be prepared in case I was faced with having to pass some frightening entrance examination. I was also genuinely beginning to wish for more knowledge about general subjects. My passage through the School of Art, while only dealing with drawing and painting, had envisaged for me the fascination of accumulated learning and the exciting possibilities of power that such knowledge could endow. This was only a dim realization but it was sufficient to make my attitude to Wilfred's teaching more tractable and very nearly eager.

He approached the discouraging task with no whit more liking for it but with an increased sense of duty, due to his feeling that he himself was anyhow temporarily established and at the moment only indefinitely occupied. His opinions of my receptive powers and his profound incredulity at my expressed eagerness to acquire knowledge remained as blanketing and disheartening as before, but the combination of his sense of duty and my eagerness—born of fright—must have achieved something, if only factual knowledge. It must have been enough, anyway, to construct a tiny nucleus around which I was, later on, able to build for myself some sort of semblance to normal schooling. My father, as well, joined in the general panic and brought home with him railway clerks' entrance examination papers, and coached and crammed me—with patent bad temper and annoyance—in the evenings. It must have been their joint efforts—and my own, for out of this fear that I might be made an errand boy, I worked like mad—which provided me with some essential proficiency, for on looking back I can see no possibility of any scholastic training having come from elsewhere. Neither of them, though, was able to nurture my awakening desire for further knowledge and learning, my father failing through his tired irritability and Wilfred through his nonchalant intolerance, so my eagerness and feeling of enjoyment wilted. This did not die though, and a few years later the refreshing rains of independence and some success as a junior sea-going officer revived it.

The arrangement which had come about for Wilfred made my mother pleased and happy and relieved her from the anxious fear that he might be forced into some unsuitable post for the sake of employment, although she was devastated by the thought that the flight of her first-born was now near. Even this was offset, when the time came round, by the generous holidays the arrangements allowed for. They must, I think, have coincided with the university vacations; anyhow, he seemed to be at home quite a lot during that time. It was indeed entirely due to my mother's determined efforts and practical wisdom in getting the right introductions that this valuable arrangement for Wilfred had come about at all. This unusual concentration and will to surmount difficulties and gain for Wilfred what she so much wanted, sprang from and was strengthened and buttressed by her passionate and unalterable love for him.

It seems now that this burning flame of loving devotion imbued her with a strength and an ability which were alien to her and enabled her to grapple with difficulties and details with a precision and decisiveness that in all her other projects was for ever denied to her. There is no question that had she not bestirred herself so well, the two years in the vicarage would never have come to Wilfred. Instead he would have been avalanched into some crippling job. That the two years there held something of disappointment for them both, in their different ways, could not detract from the respite they provided for Wilfred at least from the need to earn a wage. It was to her that he owed these valuable formative years, though the value lay not so much in the actual tuition that he received, for in this he was disappointed. He was put out, too, by the grindingly hard parish work and often uncongenial duties that he was expected to carry out, but all this did not—as so easily could have happened in other more ordinary employment—retard his poetic vigour or prevent the actual writing of poetry. They did, on the contrary, add to his range of reading, and between duties and during his generous holidays allowed him time for self-searching and meditation.

My mother's and Wilfred's disappointments came from different reasons but arose from the same cause. The cause was his widening swerve away from the thought of a clerical calling, and if, before Dunsden, he had out of his youngness, felt some attraction (perhaps through the careful fostering of my mother) for such a life, the period in Oxfordshire served only progressively to wear away any slight urge there might have been.

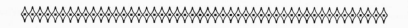

Chapter Thirteen

SUMMER 1911

MR. WIGAN, the vicar, was a man of great erudition and fine culture, and of a distinguished and gentle bearing. His foremost concern was theology and the advancement of the religion of the church which he served so truly. This theological bias, his innate desire for seclusion, his liking for philosophical discussion and a desire to be sedulously followed by his students to the conclusion of his theses—these traits, while serving so well with the other novitiates, made him a difficult man for Wilfred to read under, harassed as he was by his strengthening conviction of his lack of sympathy for orthodox religion—uncertain even of his own desire for any personal religious conduct—and his growing awareness of his unsuitability for religious work (both most secretly and carefully hidden from my mother).

Mutual liking and esteem remained between them and there was some sporadic tutoring, but sympathy in thought grew ever more divergent and, not unnaturally, with this and the vicar's unwilling realization that Wilfred was not going to be won for the Church, there came a lessening of tuition and guidance and a consequent increase in rather dreary parish work for Wilfred, and he became more and more disappointed. A pleasant enough sitting-room was provided for the two or three young men but Wilfred, while getting on well enough with the others, did not mix awfully well. He found it quite impossible to work in the common-room and consequently had to have recourse yet again to his bedroom. This was fireless and ill-lit, so once more he was back to working in discomfort and brought to bear his technique of working in overcoat and gloves and blankets taken from his bed. Mr. Wigan did not like this solitary working very much, but by now Wilfred was so useful to him in the parish that he did not raise an issue about it—neither, though, did he provide a fire.

Wilfred remained at Dunsden vicarage for two years, but long before this time was up, although he carried out his religious and parochial duties over-conscientiously, thereby enabling the vicar to spend more time in seclusion and the pursuit of his own thinking, Wilfred himself became more and more certain that an ecclesiastical vocation was not for him. He found no disappointment over this but he did become despondent when he found himself thrown back, for his reading, on his own resources, and disappointed that Mr. Wigan had not continued his promised role of mentor. He became frustrated, too, as he realized that all the church work he was expected to do was eating too heavily into his own reading time; it irritated him to have to admit that he was really just a full-time curate, and the knowledge that he was not even being paid for it irked him.

So Wilfred had very largely to revert to his old habit of selecting for himself his own post-school reading, at the same time secretly continuing with the writing of his by now maturing poetry. He was certainly over-working during these two years in Dunsden, and sitting in his cold bedroom did not help to check the chesty colds he was so constantly plagued with. What was really depressing him now was the growing certainty that there was no longer any avenue left open to him through which he could go up to a university. His chance for his coveted degree had disappeared for ever through his renunciation of the Church. To remain any longer in Oxfordshire he knew would be futile. He must look elsewhere for something which would advance him towards his intended writing. His looking eventually led him—as an English instructor—to the Berlitz School of Languages in Bordeaux. If he could not have his university at least he could live in his beloved France.

So it was for all of us during these quiet years in Shrewsbury that preceded 1914 a time for hopes and speculations, difficulties, disappointments and anxieties; but these we did not dramatize and, indeed, we were able to cast them off, so that often fun and gaiety visited us, for outwardly we accepted our rubs and bruises as commonplace and were not given to bemoaning our lot.

Strangely enough, in retrospect, there seems to have been left suspended over these few difficult years a charming quietude of family life which I cannot remember either in the years before or the years after. It may have been that my mother's health was better, my father's roving longings more subdued, Wilfred unsettled but all the same fixed in his determination for literary achievement; because Mary too was stronger and more able to devote herself to service to the rest of us, because

Colin now had plenty of riding (having made friends with a farming family who could muster saddle-horses) and now had some—as he called them—racing pigeons. These were beautiful creatures but of course, to the rest of us who knew, just very homely homing birds. But to him they were racers, and there was not one of us who would not have preferred to cut out his tongue rather than disparage the pigeons' racing qualities—what they raced was always a mystery—or in any way detract from his vast pride in them. On the contrary we bolstered up his sublime belief that nowhere in the whole world were there such fast and nimble fliers, and if some of them failed to return when they should have done, how quick and loud we were to explain that cruel vandals would often lie in wait to shoot down unsuspecting valuable racing pigeons. This comforted him in his losses, invested the survivors with heroism, and increased his pride in them. I myself was absorbed in my drawing and my School of Art. Possibly it was none of these things but only the natural culmination of family life, which had been built with care and craftsmanship and now, coming to fullness, was about to spill over and send us out into our different and separate streams.

Or is it only a nation-wide nostalgia that attacks our generation and spins a web of gold over these pre-1914 years? I think there must be something true in this, and my reading confirms it, for there seems present in every narrator of that period a wish to embellish those years with a glamour which must surely be overdrawn—perhaps not, I don't know. Even the very seasons are invested—the spring-times with untold verdure, the summer with hot sunshine and lazy ease and bursting granaries; autumn clothed in her gown of russet and gold, veiled about with mists and jewel-like, lamplit windows; even winter himself during those years seems to take on the air of a kindly old curmudgeon whose severity is unnoticed through contemplation of the beauty of his white hair.

What I do know is that those actual years which seem now to glow with so much friendliness, were not only difficult but harassing ones for all of us, and for me were full of misunderstandings and sometimes acute anxieties. I had got myself out of the board schools and made this life for myself in the School of Art. I was not only happy about it but felt satisfied that the plan I had prescribed for myself would very well take care of my future—anyway save me from the railway or some office; I was absolutely confident that I could in a few years obtain my Art

Master's certificate. With this once gained I felt my living would be assured and from then on I could paint seriously or teach, as I saw fit, just as I pleased. My age—these plans of mine were all being formed between my twelfth and fifteenth years—precluded me, unlike Wilfred, from visions of an epic future. I remember at that time I was only concerned to keep myself out of some meaningless occupation which I would not like. As this was constantly being forecast for me by the rest of the family I felt the danger to be very real. To avoid this was in those years my only immediate problem; I could not look further but could only hope that I might somehow follow Mr. Weaver's footsteps and start my career in some nice friendly-smelling School of Art.

My fears were not unfounded. The uneasy conversations which had begun to float about in the family talk increased, which disturbed and troubled me. In an increasingly general way they took to not treating my plans for continuing my art work at all seriously; instead they emphasized the feeling that it was a useful way of filling an interim period brought about through the failure to find a decent elementary school for me to attend or one of any other sort which could hold me. I found a growing trend—this alarmed me—to treat my work as a nice hobby which should be cultivated but not thought of at all as a career, which gave me a horrid feeling of insecurity and this it was that made me keep on working so madly to catch up with ordinary school subjects. For it became clear to me that what had seemed at first friendly discouragement was developing into an inimical firmness of opinion that I must discard this plan of mine and, it was hoped, cheerfully accept my lot and like the countless other young boys around us find some ordinary, perhaps menial, work to do for a livelihood.

It was repeatedly being pointed out to me that what this work would be depended so much upon my ability, apart from drawing and painting, to fit myself for something else, and it was later brought more into the open and left cruelly undisguised that unless I increased my efforts only a most menial job—even were I able to procure that—would be available to me. Life took on a frantic sort of feeling of responsibility for myself and menace encircled the frightening age of fourteen or fifteen which was the mark set for me to become independent. And although I had a year or two to go yet, there were times when I became oppressed and bewildered by its closeness, for I had little confidence in my ability to pass these vague entrance examinations which seemed so necessary. I saw horrid pictures of myself as a grocer's boy, or worse a butcher's boy, or still worse, a farmer's boy, all of which were laid before me as extreme and (if it had to be) even desirable probabilities. The prospect seemed overshadowing to me and, although I meant to fight tooth and nail for my drawing and painting, instinct warned me to try and keep my other slight resources in some sort of working order. To the surprise and disappointment of Wilfred I went on trying to follow his instruction, working out fractions and decimals with furious enthusiasm, and became greedy for geography and history.

Wilfred, as I have said, was purposely awkward in his teaching and designed it all so as to expose my ignorance rather than to extend my knowledge. This exposure was a never failing delight to him at this time, and he was ardent in his repeated assertions that I must content myself with humble ambitions for I was fitted for no others, which maddened me to rudeness and often into violent abuse, so that we spent more time quarrelling than working. He threw sarcasm upon my idea of qualifying as an art master and made me boil in infuriated argument when he refused to see that if I did not succeed in holding on to this idea I should find myself an errand boy; and he would leave me white and inarticulate with rage when he promptly told me if such a thing did happen he would disown me for ever. At these moments we hated one another, but somehow the hating never lasted long and after it had spent itself we would grin again, yet remaining on the alert, eyeing one another, much as boxers do in the ring. Nevertheless, out of all this some bits of learning must, I suppose, have stuck to me. Apart from this accidental sticking, the Old Wolf was no help to me whatsoever and in family discussions and the more frequent private discussions between him and my mother, was always inclined to weight the scales against me.

In later years when the bandages had been removed from both our eyes and we could see one another clearly, he freely admitted his early limitations of vision and in poignant moments would be bitter in condemnation of his own blind intolerance.

I like to think that neither my father nor my mother could have known what the effect their own blighting proposals and forecasts had upon me, their small son, or just how deeply their rather careless and seemingly callous talk which drifted across and around me bit into me. The talk all seemed so horribly impersonal and made me feel rather like a parcel of goods, the value of which was dubious but the destination of which must in some way be settled.

These constant reiterations of the necessity for early decision and the placing of me in some occupation, the occupation itself not appearing to be of much importance, left me with a feeling of meaningless emptiness. This was bad enough, but the sensation that some fateful turn in my life was always drawing closer with the nearing of the dreaded age of fourteen–fifteen—when even this fumbling guidance from home would be finally withdrawn, leaving me alone in my responsibility for my own safety—made me desperate to get something arranged for myself. It is little wonder that I began to scheme for this and make efforts to win to my side that clever arranger, Mr. Weaver, to help in the struggle I saw looming ahead in my fight to continue my painting. At the same time I worked like mad to increase my stock of ordinary ammunition in the hope that it might prove sufficient to cut my way through the barriers of entrance examinations, if my own plan for an art career collapsed, and so save me from an utterly menial job, which I now knew would be the alternative. In the end an entirely different solution offered itself, but I was to have no inkling of this just yet.

Although they were not conscious of the consternation their unguarded talk was producing in me, perhaps it was not entirely their fault for, unlike Wilfred, I could in those early days be poker-faced when under emotion and unlike him was not given to verbal vehemence or shows of violent feeling in order to establish a case. Oppositely, I possessed, I think, a stronger feeling of individuality and secretly felt that in the end it would be myself who would have the last say in everything. I was able to comfort myself with this nice thought and the sense that I was a person in my own right—small and puzzled certainly, but not to be wafted about just the same. Feeling this, I was content to remain silent and let the froth of turmoil wash over me. I had, I think, considerable confidence in my ability for final decisions.

Wilfred, like my mother, was less confident of himself and felt the need always for the perpetual strengthening of whatever position he meant to take up. He had a fear that to relax or remain silent would weaken his position, which in turn led to vehemence and constant hammering to secure what he wanted. I think he always felt that circumstances and especially family influence might at any time be too strong for him, and for this reason was inclined to suspect opposition or undermining when none existed.

Just the same, even if my mother and father were not quite alive to what was going on in me, they had nevertheless made up their minds that ambition or even choice of a career could not be allowed to stand in the way of immediate expediency, and it was this more than anything which made them discuss my future so openly in order to make their meaning quite clear. I think the long triangular misunderstanding and struggle over Wilfred had exhausted them both, lassitude was creeping upon them and possibly a general acceptance by them both that, having decided at last that Wilfred should be helped to the extent of being a non-wage earner—as it looked now—until he was twenty or more, we two other boys must be dealt with quickly, more drastically, and much more practically.

My mother, having won the battle over Wilfred, seemed to have no ambition left for the rest of us and remained acquiescent and rather hopeless about us. My father—not unnaturally, I fear—felt that having launched one son into the Arts, it was impracticable as well as impossible to allow another one to slip into these troublous and precarious waters. My mother, whose practical sense—except where Wilfred was concerned—could at times be stronger than my father's, agreed and put up no further struggle. I was the next on the list.

However, this time was not to come yet and I was able to go on advancing well with my drawing and as it were building up my case for continuance, which I fully realized had got to be a good one to have any hope of success. I had in front of me the autumn of 1911, and I meant to make the most of it, for, although the discomforting conversations floated about so freely, there was hardly as yet a distinct or definite threat, and I was still happy in the thought of the pleasant life I was arranging for myself. I had actually worked this out, without much detail certainly, but with a sureness of main arrangement which I found satisfying. I would qualify and obtain a post as junior art master which would support me until such time as I could live by my painting alone. The strong desire for success was with me, but I believe the real appeal came from the pleasantness I found in the work itself, its trappings and the long days it gave me for painting cottages and barns, fields and lanes, and the rutted cart tracks that spilled over with white dust on roasting summer days, or filled with glittering rainwater on winter ones when they would flash brilliantly and with so much blueness. At this age, these solitary days of painting in the open air represented for me quite the nicest form of existence and the excitement which came with increasing skill made each day different and better than the last. It must have been this facility which made me want so much to scheme for its continuance, for I was, as yet, too young for it to have been sure ambition or any defined wish for recognition other than by Mr. Weaver and the small coterie in my painting school.

My father must at this time have been unconsciously holding his hand. I say unconsciously, for I shall always think he was altogether too guileless and lacking in craft to have premeditated his actions or attitude to a purposeful design. However this may have been, while he held forth so much about the need for me to seek independence, yet the suggestion —which had been so much to the fore in our dockland days—of sending me to sea had not again been brought up. He could not at any time resist the inclination to build up in me the desire for ships and the sea, which had been and still was so dear to his own heart, but the actual proposition was withheld and, instead, the undesirability of all sedentary jobs of any sort as a career for me was strongly underscored. My mother, who had been so obsessed with aversion during Wilfred's infancy to my father's thoughts of the sea for him, or for any other sons yet to come, had later not been able to disguise her dislike of his own passion for ships and docks and sailors, nor his persistence in taking me with him on his dockland adventures. This had either made my father wary or dispirited; whatever it was, he recognized that my mother's dislike of all to do with ships and the sea had not lessened with the years.

I think, too, my father's natural affection for me and his realization of my love for drawing (which curiously enough impressed him as much more valid than Wilfred's literary aspirations, with all the seclusion and antagonistic withdrawal these brought about) made him genuinely loath to disrupt my own scheme if it could be proved workable. Altogether, he was content to wait, without showing either too much antagonism about the art-mastering or making any attempt to resurrect the sea. I expect, though, that he had navigation in mind when insisting upon the importance of my arithmetic—for my efforts here were so elementary that we could not even pretend to call it mathematics. He had become very friendly with Mr. Weaver and was impressed by the glowing enthusiasm he received from him concerning my aptitude, which made him proud and pleased, but he was still very sceptical about there being a proper livelihood to be gained in anything to do with the Arts.

Unfortunately, Mr. Weaver did nothing to dispel this feeling of my father's, and the talks which they had concerning my prospects were for the most part at cross-purposes. For one thing Mr. Weaver himself was a little bitter and disgruntled by the meagre and wholly inadequate salary he was receiving as headmaster; for another thing he assessed my father's means completely wrongly and was convinced that he was a man of considerable substance. My father's general bearing, his good clothes, and his position in the town as a high-ranking railway official, combined with my own well-turned-out young boy's appearance (for I had an eye to my clothes), confirmed Mr. Weaver in his belief in my father's astuteness and sound financial position, and it was from this point of view that he talked to my father, feeling bound in honesty to disclose the poor remunerative prospects in store for any boy going in for the profession of art. All of which did little to forward my own plan and brought about the strange situation whereby he preached to my father the unsatisfactory financial outlook of my following his own career as an art master, when in reality, fixed financially as my father was, it was in every way a golden opportunity, for on my family's own showing the alternative was some humble obscure clerkship, if not an actual errand boy. However, Mr. Weaver retrieved himself by staking everything on my ability to qualify—and this very quickly. Anyway, I was nearly half way through already. In this direction my position remained not only unshaken but was consolidated and my father was convinced through Mr. Weaver's confidence in me that I could succeed.

My father was no fool and, while not disillusioning Mr. Weaver about his supposed financial soundness, did not altogether fail to see that what I was planning for myself held opportunities which he could not hope to better—at any rate with any alternative he was prepared to disclose at the moment—and he became, if not enthusiastic, worriedly unsettled about it all; and if not quite optimistic, anyway not wholly discouraging, although still worried with his doubts as to how soon I should be able to earn some money. Here the matter was allowed to rest.

From now on my father was more kindly disposed towards my painting and designing and would come more frequently to the school to meet me after the evening classes, arriving early and chatting with Mr. Weaver until I was ready, when we would walk home together. I always loved these walks home with him. He would more often ask to see my work, especially my country studies, and I noticed at these times that a warm suffusing would drive away the ice from his eyes, as he looked first at the immature work and then to his small son, and a lovely glow of pride would wash over me—that I had been able to melt his icy glance. He was diffident and would ever disclaim, sometimes bitterly, any knowledge of such things.

To our eternal misfortune as a family we would agree with this wrong assessment of himself, but I was always eager for his opinion and always disappointed when it did not come. A rare flash of praise from him would live in me for a long time—far longer than any that came from the others. If, as small boys will, I often sided with the majority in easily dismissing his opinions, and joined in the family trend of thinking of his views upon the Arts as valueless, I paid dearly for my young arrogance. There were times even then when a look would pass over my father's face and I would feel a little what Judas Iscariot must have felt. Still, the soundness of our family life absorbed these small poisons healthily enough and ejected them easily.

My mother was always accorded the right to sit in final judgement upon all matters of intellect and art, for had she not taken painting lessons as a girl and did not her still-life studies of cut and juicy melons, dripping with ropes of seeds, and her Highlandic shooting scenes of pointing pointers and rigid setting setters even now adorn our sitting-room walls? My father, in his deep humility, never sought to usurp this untrue intellectual superiority but rather, out of his profound loyalty, built it up to secure her eminence. His hidden pride in me and my seeming achievements in draughtsmanship were so much at variance with his own desires for my future that they were the cause of much of his worried uncertainty about me. He was being pulled in two ways and found it difficult to be decisive. On the one hand, he had his life-long desire to see a son of his commanding a ship; on the other hand, my rather surprising bent and enthusiasm for a painting career had awakened again in him an intellectual hunger and a desire to see expressed through his blood the innate but so long suppressed urge—so strong in himself—for creation and the fostering of fine thought. How strongly his Welsh ancestors were plaguing him here.

Although in Wilfred he had sought for and found—and forever lost —something of this indefinable spiritual chord for which he longed so ardently, the everyday battle for existence and above all the usurpation by my mother of Wilfred had done too much to destroy his touch on the finely tuned strings, so that they refused him sweetness, offering only vibration and discord. My own childish seeking for beauty and awareness of mystery and loveliness awakened in him again the far off clamour of voices from his ancestors, and he became torn with the desire to assuage his thirst through me and my painting, or rid himself for ever of his heritage which had so bitterly disappointed him through Wilfred, and smother for all time the gnawing hunger of this mysticism in himself and discourage it in me his son. He did not know which to do.

However, I still had this autumn and winter of 1911 in front of me, and, sensitive now to uncertainty and rather over-full of foreboding as to what was lying in store, I became more determined than ever to make the most of my time.

Had I needed any weighting to determine my inclinations, it would have come to me from my meeting with a water-colour painter from London. It so happened that one morning I had made my way to Uffington to finish off a sketch I was doing, a wooded landscape this time, with plenty of posts and rails running away from the foreground in pleasant perspective. I had settled down and was enjoying the warm smells that my Vandyke brown and Cobalt blue washes brought out as with a loaded brush I slid them over the sun-heated paper, when I noticed a man walking across the fields towards me, carrying what seemed to me to be a sketching easel. When he was within some hundred yards or so of me he put down his painting materials and wandered about studying the landscape. Having decided on a spot, he put down his handkerchief to mark it, walked over for his things and, after erecting them to his satisfaction, was soon steadily drawing. He had placed himself well to the right hand but a little in front of me, so that I was able to observe him quietly and without any show of rudeness. I was very intrigued, for it was the first time in all my excursions that I had encountered a professional, or any other artist, and as he was obviously working on the same scene as myself I became possessed with a great curiosity to see his work and to compare it with my own. I resisted the many tempting schemes which occurred to me whereby I might gain a look at what he was doing: they were all too obvious and I decided that if any meeting was to come about it must be left to him to make the first move. He was obviously a middle-aged man and his expensive-looking paraphernalia made me feel that he was someone pretty important.

Lunch time came and I lay face down on the grass and commenced to eat my lunch and drink my liquorice-water, to which I was much addicted. Very soon after, I saw him delve about, produce some paper packets and do likewise—except, of course, that he did not lie flat and face down as I was doing, nor yet drink liquorice-water. This peculiar habit of mine, when eating out of doors, of lying face down to eat was always discouraged by my family, who thought it most odd, but when alone I always looked forward to doing this and never failed to indulge myself. In spite of small difficulties about swallowing and the extreme awkwardness and immense neck-strain involved when drinking, especially from a bottle, I always enjoyed this recumbent position more than any other, perhaps because I was able to swing my legs up and down and drum my toes on the turf. In this position I could gently grip my wrist with my teeth; I found this restful and conducive to thought about my painting. After finishing my meal, I strolled in as casual and undesigned away as I could towards the hedge that seemed to offer convenient cover for my purpose. As I was returning, I found my unknown painting companion walking towards me from the opposite direction, no doubt having been on the same quest. As we approached one another he gave me a friendly wave but much as I wanted to I did not treat this as an invitation and merely uncovered my head ceremoniously in acknowledgement and reaching my own spot took up my painting again.

After about an hour of this, my co-worker rose up and walked slowly towards me. When about fifteen yards from me, he stopped and asked permission to come and see what I was doing. Jumping up and again taking off my round grey felt hat, I managed somehow to show my pleasure. His unusually courteous approach made me more than ever glad that I had resisted making any overture myself. He carefully scrutinized my effort, commenting most pleasantly, seemingly unaware of our vast difference in age (he must have been quite thirty years older than I was), and we were soon conversing most agreeably as one painter to another. Having exhausted my own work, he asked me to go over and look at what he was doing. I was greatly pleased and, when I saw his work, tremendously impressed with the beautiful colour drawing he had almost completed. I studied it eagerly in the hope that I might find in it some trick of technique, some new colour, or any fresh aspect or means of manipulation that would help me in my own striving after perfection.

I must have been—and still am—quite unmoral, and would always search work that I knew to be better than my own in the hope that some trick or solution as yet unknown to myself would jump out at me, to be seized and in some way applied to the betterment of my own work. I was not only eager but voracious to learn, and would mentally probe and dissect any work that I had the good fortune to see, to try and wring some advantage from it, so that I could apply it to my own painting—once having acknowledged superiority in any work, I became instinct with greed to gain from it. It may have been for this reason that always while looking at drawings or paintings that so obviously were in every way superior to my own—including those of contemporaries—they did not so much depress me as fill me with a strange exhilarating excitement and, while full of envy, I was also full of this fierce acquisitiveness and an almost exalted sensation that this might be the instant when revelation would burst upon me and that at any moment some extra magic secret might become mine. Tingling to the finger tips, instead of being depressed about my poverty of achievement, I would be frantically impatient to try out fresh work, applying to it some idea or trick which I thought I had gleaned from what I had seen.

Some of this enthusiasm may have bubbled over in me. Anyway, this nice man soon began to expound, and answer my feverish technical questions. He was soon drawing me out and I found myself telling him of my own plans for my future. This I did not find difficult as he seemed to epitomize so much of what I wanted for myself, and his way of treating me as a grown-up person and a serious artist swept away my usual diffidence. His appearance of cleanly well-being and seeming affluence and the fine quality of his clothes impressed me more than ever with the wish to pursue for myself such a pleasing career. With this in mind, I put to him many questions about the possibilities of earning a living from painting. Probably amused by my naïve but sincere curiosity, he told me much about his own manner of living— of how his painting rewarded him reasonably well but without real riches. It also, he told me, enabled him not only to travel over England but the whole of the Continent as well in search of subjects, and he was able to sell all he could paint and was free at all times from actual financial embarrassment. He concluded by telling me that there was no reason whatsoever why I should not follow suit and begged me without hesitation to do so. He was the first and I believe the only person I can remember who recommended without any reserve or qualification of any kind the material reward painting could bring—which after the sorry stories of hardship and struggle and discouragement of outlook for painting as a livelihood, I found most refreshing and buoyant in its certainty.

While we had been talking, the early afternoon had passed away. Taking out his watch, he told me that he must return to the village as he had to pack and catch a train to London that evening, suggesting at the same time that if I liked to walk back with him to the inn where he was putting up he would show me his portfolio of the sketches he had done in the district. Immensely pleased, I hurriedly gathered my things together and we set off over the fields to his inn. He took tremendous pains and trouble to display his drawings in the indifferent light of the dark little room, so that I could get the best advantage from them for myself. He sought my opinion upon them and made me comment, no doubt valuing—as I was to do myself years later—the unspoilt reactions of a young person's untrained vision. When taking my leave of him, he made me promise to write to him and tell him of my progress. This I pledged myself faithfully to do. Giving me his card and telling me that letters to the address of the London club on it would always be forwarded to him, he walked a little way through the village with me, shook hands, and waved me out of sight.

Altogether elated, I trudged my way home, going over in my mind how I would apply all the added knowledge I felt I had gained from him to my next painting, with the certainty that it would transcend anything I had yet done. This as always made me feel breathless and gave me an unaccountable prickly feeling behind my eyes. When I got home, while we were all having supper together, I tried to tell them of the important artist I had met and how much kindness he had shown me. However, my account did not seem to evoke any enthusiasm and was passed over casually as an everyday sort of occurrence and I was bidden to get on with my supper and talk less. Worse and most maddening of all, though, I saw dawning in Wilfred's eyes—he had been listening more intently than the others—the well-known look of slight disbelief, which I knew unless I could substantiate myself would turn to downright unbelief. Rather menacingly he asked me for the man's name. Confronted with this, I suddenly remembered that I did not know it, for when the card had been handed to me I had been too shy to look at it and had stuffed it into one of my pockets and, being occupied with thoughts of the man himself and visions of pictures to come, had not since thought to look at it. Delighted with the thought that I could produce the evidence, I put my hand in my pocket, meaning to take it out slowly and with all the nonchalance I could muster hand it to Wilfred. The effect of this was first spoilt by my failure to find the card at once, and later ruined by my failure to find it at all. A triumph that had promised so well ended in an undignified scrabbling search of my overladen pockets—but to no avail, nowhere could I find the small card. Wilfred, sardonically amused now, told me not to worry —the loss was not great for it was quite certain that no famous or even important artist would have taken so much trouble over such an unimportant boy as myself.

The next day, with the excuse of finishing my drawing, I retraced my steps in hope of finding the small pasteboard, but search as I did I could not find it and to this day I do not know to whom I owe that gracious and charming encounter.

I was upset at the time, as I wished to be able later to keep my promise to write. This was perhaps the first of many opportunities from personal meetings that I was to let slip, although the remainder were not always lost accidentally. Years later when I was very much older I realized the preciousness of these chance and undesigned encounters and how very much the jewel-like quality of them could be blurred or even marred by pursuance, and I would purposely refrain. Wilfred had his triumph over the episode and I my consequent discomfiture, but boy-like I soon forgot it and the disquietening feeling that my painter friend would think me ungrateful and churlish, although it worried me very much at the time, gradually lost itself amongst the difficulties of decisions and the disappointments which were before very long to beset me.

It could not have been very long after this episode that the first wavelets of threatening change began to approach me and, gathering power in their unseen and insidious way, flooded about me and eventually washed me away not only from Uffington and Shropshire but out of England itself, to bear me, bobbing like a cork, and wash me up the Hugli River into the furnace of the docks of Calcutta, where death himself disguised in glittering, brain-melting heat held out his burning invitation and so nearly collected me, only just failing to drag me into his stoke-hold. Before he reluctantly let me go, he had seared the flesh from my bones.